T0151963

MAY WE SUGGEST

MAY WE SUGGEST

Restaurant Menus
and the Art of Persuasion

ALISON PEARLMAN

SURREY
BOOKS

AN **AGATE** IMPRINT

CHICAGO

Copyright 2018 © by Alison Pearlman

All rights reserved. No part of this book may be reproduced or transmitted in any form or by any means, electronic or mechanical, including photocopying, recording, or by any information storage and retrieval system, without express written permission from the publisher.

Printed in the United States of America

Library of Congress Cataloging-in-Publication Data

Names: Pearlman, Alison, author.
Title: May we suggest : restaurant menus and the art of persuasion / Alison Pearlman.
Description: Chicago : Surrey Books, an Agate Imprint, [2018] | Includes bibliographical references and index.
Identifiers: LCCN 2018021593 (print) | LCCN 2018024199 (ebook) | ISBN 9781572848221 (e-book) | ISBN 1572848227 (e-book) | ISBN 9781572842601 (pbk.) | ISBN 9781572848221 (eISBN)
Subjects: LCSH: Gastronomy. | Cooking. | Menus. | Restaurants.
Classification: LCC TX633 (ebook) | LCC TX633 .P32 2018 (print) | DDC 641.5--dc23
LC record available at https://lccn.loc.gov/2018021593

First Printing: October 2018

10 9 8 7 6 5 4 3 2 1   18 19 20 21 22

Surrey Books is an imprint of Agate Publishing. Agate books are available in bulk at discount prices. For more information, visit agatepublishing.com.

In memory of my dear father,
Daniel David Pearlman
(1935–2013)

This is the first book of mine he wasn't able to read drafts of, or offer, as he always did, with gentleness and patience, his incisive suggestions for editing. I only hope that I was able to learn enough from his example that I could apply something of his eye to these pages, and that I may one day, in exercising what he taught me since the time I looked up at him as a giant in the house, achieve a fraction of his wit and mastery of structure, qualities he so emphatically displayed in his genre-bending and often side-splittingly funny works of fiction, novels such as *Black Flames* (1997) and *Memini* (2003); the 2011 novella, *Brain & Breakfast* (one of my favorites!); and treasure troves of short stories, including *The Final Dream & Other Fictions* (1995), *The Best Known Man in the World & Other Misfits* (2001), and *A Giant in the House & Other Excesses* (2011)—all ideal introductions to his impressive range. The many short stories he contributed to anthologies are also well worth your while to track down.

CONTENTS

INTRODUCTION

"I'M WRITING A BOOK ABOUT RESTAURANT MENUS. COULD I ASK YOU some questions about the design of your menus?" I blurted, seizing the chance after dinner on the way out to meet Sarintip Singsanong, a.k.a "Jazz," then co-owner and front-of-the-house maestro of Jitlada. Cheerfully checking on guests in the two small, but full, dining rooms, the practiced host had not stopped moving.

I knew I wouldn't throw her. Jazz was used to inquiring writers. Jitlada's accolades for best Thai in Los Angeles, blessings by critic Jonathan Gold, and more articles about the place were hard to miss under the glass tops of the dining-room tables and in the otherwise modest front window. Part of a Colman Andrews feature in *Gourmet* was the "About" text for the restaurant on its website.

Jazz beamed and immediately steered me outside to meet her (now late) brother (also co-owner at the time) Suthiporn Sungkamee, or "Chef Tui." It was 11:00 p.m., just after the dinner rush, and Chef Tui sat in a chair looking out over the strip-mall parking lot on a Thai Town slice of Sunset Boulevard. He was still aproned but taking a well-earned respite. Jazz insisted, "He's the man to speak to about the menu."

Did the chef design the menu pages? I wondered, not sure Jazz understood. I traced a rectangle in the air with my fingers to specify what I called "the design of the *physical* menu." No matter. They both began speaking with passion about Jitlada's food.

Who could blame them for thinking that, by *menu*, I meant food? The word *menu* is ambiguous, after all. It can refer to the dishes on a bill of fare, not the artifact itself. What's more, Jazz and Chef Tui were justifiably proud of their cuisine, honed by the chef's more than fifty years of experience. Finally, judging by their media coverage, Jazz and Chef Tui weren't used to fielding questions about the art of menu design.

And yet, their nine-page document—which overflowed, by the way, onto a glow-in-the-dark board with another list of handwritten specials—was part of what made Jitlada exceptional. The menu was notoriously long. That night I counted 252 items just on the main menu. I've seen longer lists in Chinese restaurants, but Jitlada's was a contender even among those. It was long enough to have inspired—indirectly, at least—a feature in the *Los Angeles Times*. In 2011, food blogger Jo Stougaard made news by challenging herself to eat every dish on the list.

Furthermore, the menu looked—if not graphically hip or crafted by professional menu consultants—methodical. The prices, for example, were all expressed as "X.95," whether a dish was $5.95 or $64.95. The listing for Crying Tiger, a dish so-named because your choice of beef or pork would be eye-watering if you poured on too much of the accompanying chili sauce, mentioned that the dish was featured on Food Network's *Best Thing I Ever Ate* show. Also, the listings were selectively redundant. Several dishes from the main menu repeated on a list that stood on the table in a clear plastic stand—a table tent, in industry parlance. It didn't seem random, either, that the word *spicy* in the phrase *spicy smoothie*s was the only one in bright red. Collectively, these features showed at least a little thought and definitely a conviction that how a menu communicates matters.

A few days later, I clarified what I was after and Jazz generously answered questions about the physical menu. But she and Chef Tui would not be the only restaurateurs with whom I had the same miscommunication at first.

Without meaning to, restaurant critics make such misunderstandings more likely. How often have you read a review that seriously discussed the artistry of the menu? Readers want to learn about the food, the service, the setting, and the overall dining experience, so they can decide if they want to patronize a place. Reviewers seldom have the space to elaborate, as I shall in this book, how the menu, like an operating manual, is the thing that coordinates them all.

I didn't always analyze menus. For decades as a restaurant diner, I related to them mainly on emotional and personal terms.

On a rare trip with my mother and stepfather to Europe as a teen in 1985, I began collecting menus from restaurants that stirred my imagination. My mother's clippings from *Gourmet* ensured us a succession of impressive restaurant outings, and the permanence of menus compensated in part for those fleeting meals.

I already had a fondness for restaurants. My mother and stepfather's habit of trying new places with me in tow in San Francisco, where I lived most of the year, gave dining out an air of aesthetic adventure. So did the exposure my stepmother and father gave me in the summer to diners, roadhouses, Sun Valley surf and turf, and old New England taverns and chowder institutions over the years they lived in Idaho and Rhode Island. Establishments they brought me to on sojourns to Manhattan after their move east also amazed me. My stepmother planned our escapades in culinary culture high, low, and ethnically eye-opening. We'd go from the bohemian El Faro in Greenwich Village (now closed), where dusky murals of flamenco dancers had held on to memories of smoke-filled nights since 1927, to the dapper (and also no more) Le Train Bleu, the signature restaurant in Bloomingdale's designed to look like a first-class railroad dining car.

Throughout my teens and early twenties, I saved restaurant menus diaristically and sporadically. But early in my professional life, my perspective on menus and habits of collecting them changed. After earning my doctorate in art history and landing a job as assistant curator at the Museum of Contemporary Art in Chicago, I earned just enough to patronize some modish spots. I started keeping tabs on restaurant trends as much as art-world fads. Art history trained me to see aesthetics as conduits of cultural values and social relations, so I saw restaurant style increasingly through that lens. Because the menus I encountered encapsulated the aesthetics of their restaurants, collecting them allowed me to chronicle restaurant fashions I found significant. Most of my Chicago specimens epitomize late-nineties penchants for multicultural "fusion" and creative takes on comfort foods.

Not until the first decade of the 2000s did I make restaurant design, including the artistry of menus, the focus of my professional work. Then, I was back in academia and one of the few art historians writing about restaurant aesthetics. As a result, my menu-collecting habits changed again. To do research for my first book on restaurants, *Smart Casual: The Transformation of Gourmet Restaurant Style in America,* I didn't visit a single restaurant in my new hometown of LA, or in Washington, DC; New York City; Chicago; Napa Valley; or the San Francisco Bay Area without asking for a menu. My recordkeeping got equally systematic. I took pictures of all the dishes I ordered and made digital files that cross-referenced menu descriptions. In a passage of my book, I wrote about menus for the first time.

For *Smart Casual,* I considered menu design as evidence of social history: shifts in menu style signaled the changing values of restaurant producers and consumers. My entire collection of menus to that point, even what I'd saved before my art-historical consciousness, now served as more than a dining-out diary. It testified to my book's conclusions about American culture.

A discussion of menus as sales tools didn't belong in *Smart Casual,* but my research on restaurants, during and after its production, taught me more and more about this aspect of menus. From reading about the industry and conversations I had with restaurateurs, I realized the profound contribution a menu makes to a restaurant's success—or failure. The menu impacts everything from operations and profits to diner experience and behavior. Behind the scenes, the contents, size, and scope of a menu determine a restaurant's needs for and uses of space, equipment, and labor. The alignment between menu and resources decides a restaurant's fate. For example, if a menu lists mostly grilled items, yet the kitchen devotes minimal space and staff to the grill while maintaining a relatively large dining room, reducing the number of grilled items on the menu could avert financial disaster. Meanwhile, a menu also determines a lot of public relations. Because it does most of the work of communicating what a place sells, business success depends mightily on the menu's ability to make those offerings attractive.

This recognition of a menu's vital role changed how I thought about restaurants. But it wasn't the only thing that drove me to write a book about menus. The final catalyst was the cognitive dissonance I felt knowing that menu design is crucial for restaurant success while also thinking that, beyond the occasional enticing picture or noticeably sensuous dish description, I had never sensed that my consumer choices were swayed by a menu's design. For most of my encounters with a bill of fare, I felt as if I had determined my craving for a particular dish on the list, I had decided whether or not to start with an appetizer, and so on.

The question hounded me: Was I truly unmoved by menus' efforts to sell me, or was I simply unaware of their influence? Once again, my training as an art historian guided me. From it I knew that lack of awareness of an object's power to persuade is no gauge of its persuasiveness. On the contrary, its impact may be all the greater for it. A message can become "naturalized"—that is, seen as inevitable or obvious—when its form becomes so familiar and integrated into routines (like dining out) that we no longer perceive its arbitrariness and artificiality. In the case of a menu, naturalization would mean that the choices a menu presents seem to be as we expect them and what we wanted all along. With the possibility of naturalization in mind, I resolved to find out if and how menus steer consumer satisfaction and choice.

To be sure, this book makes the persuasiveness of menus a central concern. But it encompasses more than just the diner's perspective. I start with the premise that a menu's main function is to broker the interests of restaurateurs and us diners. A successful menu convinces us we like the choices we find while ensuring (by influencing our choices) the restaurateur a profitable and smoothly running business. Thus, my ultimate goal in this book is to reveal what makes menus effective as mediators of the restaurateur-diner relationship. To the restaurant as an enterprise, nothing is more vital than the health of this social bond. The two parties involved might be individual or aggregate. By *restaurateur*, I mean not necessarily one person but everyone who, together, decides the character of their establishment. Likewise, I think of *diner* as anyone or all who hold sway in the dining party.

Like all people, restaurateurs and diners carry complex and varied motives, but we can generalize about where each party stands vis-à-vis the other. For example, unless diners go to a place unwilling, we can assume a high degree of accord—after all, picky eaters are unlikely to choose a restaurant that offers only a surprise prix fixe menu. But, even when diners and restaurateurs share interest in a type of experience, the potential for discord lurks.

Restaurateurs bring to the table distinct motives that can interfere with ours. We don't worry as they do about profit margins on items, attracting and keeping talented staff, turning tables, or whether the offerings take logistical and financial advantage of constraints in funding, staffing, equipment, space, buying ingredients, or the law. Concerns like these require that restaurants limit our freedom of choice in how we dine, for how long, and what we buy for how much. Such limits can conflict with desires unique to us—such as getting the best value, staying as long as we want, receiving the utmost hospitality, and having what we think is enough choice.

A good overall business model minimizes tension on multiple fronts, and the menu is often paramount to the task: it attempts to influence our desires and choices—even our contentment with those choices.

A menu works hard before, during, and after a restaurant visit. Our first contact with one—in a case near a doorway, through a window and above a counter, or on a mobile screen—often occurs before we commit to dining somewhere. A menu then signals whether or not the restaurant is our kind. Must we order family style? Are we comfortable with the foreign words? How much is a main course? What the menu says filters the public for sympathetic people, determining whether or not we patronize the restaurant in the first place.

At that point, it also sets expectations, which affect our dining satisfaction in the end. The promises a menu makes about its offerings—typically in images or words—can dictate how gratified we are by our eventual selections and, by extension, the chances we come back. So, at least for the sake of repeat business and good word of mouth, a menu must be careful what it makes us wish for. A menu sours us on a place if it overpromises. Conversely, it can calculate pleasant surprise.

When we're on the premises and considering what to order, a menu nudges us in more ways. By how it sequences courses, or organizes and names the item headings, a menu attempts to direct the event of our meal. With statements of rules ("No substitutions, please"), it may even try to modify our behavior in minutiae.

Not the least of a menu's jobs once we cross the commercial threshold is to sell us items, including the restaurant as a whole. The latter task doesn't end at the physical or virtual doorway. Once we're inside a restaurant and searching the menu for items we want, verbal and visual features get another look. Then, the menu can reinforce (or undermine) the scenario that unfolds as we dine. In that way, the menu helps us judge the credibility of the brand and, in some cases, the entertainment value of the restaurant. Also on closer inspection, the material qualities of a menu—beginning with its cleanliness—affect our impressions of quality. Finally, at every point of purchase, a menu uses verbal and visual devices to make individual items attractive.

In turn, in all stages of our restaurant encounter, from our resolve to visit through each decision point in the meal, we use a menu to gauge where and to what extent we have room to negotiate for the variations we want on the restaurant's offerings and rules.

You may have noticed that, in the effort to elicit our cooperation and satisfaction, menus rarely work alone. They partner with other features of the restaurant's mis-en-scène. Consider the servers. Menus come to life in the hands of waitstaff, who may orient us to them upon arriving at our table, point to parts of the menu not to be missed, and make recommendations: "The cheesecake here is to die for!" Servers are a menu's wingmen. When reciting specials or answering questions about how a dish is prepared, they're also its missing pages.

Menus conspire, too, with seductive features of décor. At upscale-casual eateries, we might find a wall of wine bottles or a romantic view of the rotisserie—sure signs the menu sells wine and slow-roasted meats. Any salad bar is always its own menu-within-the-main-menu. At fast-food outlets, the windows display posters reproducing their TV and social-media ads. These, with furniture-sized photos of hamburgers or tacos, are menu megaphones. Have you seen the colorful collection of plastic food samples in the shop windows of Japanese restaurants? They're captivating and informative, lures for the printed menus inside. In cafeterias or buffet restaurants, the dishes themselves, tempting in trays, contribute to the sales pitch of the menu.

Some menu supplements do more menu-like work—informing, appetizing, entertaining, and steering customers—than the written menus of the same establishments. At A'Float Sushi, a busy place in

Old Town Pasadena, California, there's a printed menu, but the real attraction is the center of the restaurant, where diners sit around a large boat-shaped station of sushi chefs and a conveyor belt on which the chefs continually deposit dishes. The items rotate, passing within arm's reach of diners charged by the number and colors of plates they take. The last time I ate at A'Float, I barely glanced at a printed menu.

At The Gardens of Taxco, a Mexican haunt in West Hollywood, all dinner options (from its opening in 1971 until 2016, when it closed to change location and concept) were sing-sung by the waiters.

The spoken menu has an infamous past. Students of American history remember the unexpected civil rights hero Booker Wright, a black waiter at Lucso's restaurant in Mississippi who startled everyone in 1965 when he told NBC News about his treatment by the white customers. Before speaking out in a way that cost him his job and, some say, his life, he demonstrated for the camera the rapid-fire recitation of the menu—there's no written menu, he said—that was Wright's routine shtick.

Although we can't be sure they're as old as restaurants themselves (which archaeologists date back to ancient Greece), or even as old as written menus (the earliest of which was discovered on the wall of a bar in second-century-BCE Pompeii), we do know that restaurant-menu supplements and alternate forms have existed for a remarkably long time. The first evidence I found was in Sung Dynasty (960–1279) China, principally during the Southern Sung (1127–1279) period. Some large restaurants frequented by prosperous merchants had, in addition to written menus, so-called "viewing dishes." As soon as guests were seated, waiters would bring to their tables prepared examples of items from which the customers selected. They promptly swapped out the viewing dishes for ones the guests could eat. More than one contemporary chronicler described this menu-like practice, if only to point out that the less sophisticated diners who began eating from the viewing dishes were mocked.

The multiplicity of menu forms, today as in the past, begs the question: What is a restaurant menu? I found no definition broad enough to encompass the likes of server recitations and displays of real food. I propose this: *A restaurant menu is a communication of the establishment's offerings. In most cases, the offerings are presented as options from which the diner may choose.* I say "most" because there's one exception, increasingly prevalent in recent decades in gourmet places: the set tasting menu, which I discuss in chapter 1.

When I began my research for this book, the question of how menus influence consumer choice had already received a great deal of attention. Since the 1920s, a deep reserve of English-language manuals on menu design for would-be restaurateurs had amassed. Journalists sometimes repeated their dicta, spreading them further into popular consciousness.

But I questioned their advice. The literature teemed with bold, yet rarely supported, directives for designing profitable menus. Although they sometimes disagreed, the manuals all recommended specific tactics, from where to place high-margin items on a page to sell more of them to how to write dish descriptions and prices. Advising restaurateurs to place items they want to sell most where the diner looks first, and then claiming the diner looks first at the upper-right portion of a vertical-fold two-panel menu, is just one example of the manuals' penchant for promulgating concrete and rigid design principles.

Because they're some of the few books with *menu design* in the title, they were the first I read. But, as I did, I grew skeptical. My own experience as a diner contradicted not just particular points, which I take up in subsequent chapters, but also their general implication that people perceive and use menus in uniform and predictable ways. At my most disillusioned, I questioned their fundamental premise—that menus influence us, period.

I thought about my visits to restaurants, especially fast-food places, with Jamisin, my significant other. We process information on a signboard and make a selection as if we're two different species. In less than a minute, Jamisin figures out the optimal combination of items he likes that get him the best deal. On occasion, he even outsmarts the restaurant, recognizing that two separately listed dishes add up to something less expensive than an advertised "combo" with similar contents, or that the addition of one à la carte side dish to a bundle is a better deal than a running promotion. Meanwhile, especially if I'm new to the place, I get overwhelmed by the cacophony of colors, pictures, and scripts. It takes me a couple of minutes to catch on, if I ever do, to the intended information hierarchy, and sometimes I don't read the menu in any of the orderly schemes claimed by the menu manuals. Because I'm impatient when I'm hungry, I feel pressured easily in a queue, and I don't frequent fast-food places often enough to get used to the style of their menus, I tend to hunt quickly for something I know I like and just go with that. That's when Jamisin, always looking out for me, tells me there's a better version of what I want in a section of the board I didn't see.

This recurring scenario showed me how variously people perceive and respond to menus. It certainly cast doubt on universalizing declarations by experts about what techniques of menu design "work." Recognizing the discrepancy between my experience and the experts' statements, I also knew that, to properly examine what makes menus persuasive, I needed to refer to personal experience for at least one source of truth.

That's one reason I dined at more than sixty different restaurants (listed in Appendix A, see page 209) and documented my experience of the menus in each case. I generated the list based on every menu type I could conceive, a list that encompassed all of the characteristics that my review of the popular and scientific literature (and a few hunches of my own) convinced me were the most consequential to menu design.

My list included concepts that were single- and multi-unit; chains regional, national, and international; eateries of varying ethnicities and cultural fusions; kid-friendly and catering to the elderly; vanguard and traditional; historic and new; full-service, half-service, and self-service; with set tasting menus and with food choice; specialized and catchall; casual and formal; more and less "themed"; and for differing times of day. To avoid trying just places fitting my personal taste, I made sure to go to many restaurants I had to steel myself to visit. In the process, I was careful to ensure that my sample ranged widely across neighborhoods. I wanted my restaurant sample to represent the broadest possible range of menu styles. I hoped that, through encounters with a gamut of types, I would increase my chances of noticing facets of menu design and their impact previously ignored.

Because I decided to consider such a vast spectrum of menu examples—what's more, at my own expense and in the gaps of university teaching—I had to be pragmatic. I confined my restaurant outings to my home base of LA and surrounding municipalities. Occasionally, I share my experiences of menus elsewhere, especially where there's no local equivalent or I had a noteworthy firsthand experience. Inevitably, I draw as well on my own menu memory bank—the cabinet-sized menu collection I accumulated over decades. But my main focus is on the menu experiences I had with this book in mind.

Thankfully, my reliance on the LA region isn't too compromising. The extraordinary ethnic, cultural, and socioeconomic breadth of its residents and tourists as well as the range of restaurants seeking their business make the LA environs a valid locus for studying menus of the widest variety.

Owing to special circumstances, such as a fascinating menu change during my research period, or to differing conditions, such as the presence of a drive-thru menu in addition to an in-store, I visited a few places more than once. At each location, I made sure to document and, if allowed, collect all menus for that meal service. I noted their physical placement in the restaurant as well as their verbal and visual design. I observed how servers and features of the dining room aided menus by highlighting or recommending certain items or introducing or re-introducing menus to the table throughout a meal. To determine what expectations menus created—and what promises they did or didn't fulfill—I also documented how pictures and descriptions of items compared with the dishes served.

To supplement firsthand documentation of menus in restaurants, I delved into scientific studies of menu design and related topics. To better understand the restaurateur perspective, I also interviewed owners, chefs, managers, menu designers, restaurant consultants, and auxiliary folks. Most of the book's insights have national relevance. Where research permitted, I made cross-national comparisons.

Although Jamisin doesn't share my fiendish enthusiasm for restaurant-going, we made a deal that he would accompany me on most of my restaurant outings. I'd pay and he'd stay alert as an extra pair of eyes and ears. The fact that he could be helpful—his skill with cameras, he conceded, might come in handy under low-light conditions—and the prospect of being treated to at least some places that appealed to him sold him on the time-consuming idea.

I figured that dining out as a couple would normalize my presence and make my photographing of food, menus, and features of décor less disruptive and, with Jamisin sitting across from me, partially obscured. I also imagined that a higher check would ingratiate me to the establishments from which I would eventually ask to keep the menus. In addition, with him ordering too, I could see more dishes. Only in a few instances did I go to the places on my list solo or with a good friend who knew what I was up to. The outing for Chinese dim sum was exceptional. To be worthy of cart service, I assembled a party of five.

I see the irony that conscripting my significant other creates for a book about choice. At the same time, the situation is instructive. Jamisin's deference to my needs is just an extreme and protracted example of the compromise that regularly occurs among members of a dining party (as in other social groups). The consumer choice I speak of isn't always individual. I agree with sociologist Daniel Miller, who, in *A Theory of Shopping*, asserted that purchases, while seemingly individual acts, are deeply social, affected by our relationships with others. We consider what other people think, need, or want even when we buy things for ourselves. Miller didn't have restaurants in mind, but his point is apropos.

Nevertheless, except when a selection among tasting menus required the whole table to pick the same one—an occasion of some tension between Jamisin and me that I'll comment on later for its relevance to menu design—Jamisin could order whatever he wanted, while I maintained a certain methodological rigor: I always ordered whatever the restaurant tried hardest to sell through graphic or linguistic devices of the menu, server recommendations, ads, or prompts in the décor.

I imposed this discipline for various reasons. I wanted to familiarize myself with the items the house wanted me to buy—what was in *its* interests. I also needed to create the potential for conflict between what I wanted and what the restaurateur hoped I'd order. If I found myself ordering against my will, I'd know that the menu failed to persuade me. Under normal circumstances, I'd have followed my own inclinations. Finally, I followed this practice to best assess how well the menu kept its promises. For instance, if the menu featured an alluring photograph of a dish, I wanted to know how well the item I received measured up. By ordering the dishes the menu most hyped, I would test the menu's credibility.

Throughout this book, I find and interpret patterns in these experiences. Part I, Directing Events, uncovers how menus of varying formats and structures attempt to orchestrate our courses of action in a restaurant, including how we build a meal. Part II, Selling Items, investigates how menus use a variety of devices to try to influence purchases, including the total restaurant experience. In each chapter of the book, I highlight a distinct menu feature—verbal, visual, material, structural, etc.—and the various design approaches to it that I discovered. In the process, I not only evaluate the persuasiveness of design methods but also explore why restaurateurs make particular choices in menu design. The two lines of inquiry intertwine. To judge what makes menus successful, we must identify the problems restaurateurs want menus to solve, not just what gratifies diners. In my Conclusion, I articulate what determines choices—and, thereby, stylistic differences—in menu design as well as what makes menus of any style persuasive.

Diners, restaurateurs, and students of both: join me to find out how it is that, while we order from menus, menus try to order us. If you share my interest in the workings of restaurants, the experience of dining out, the rhetoric of things, or the matter of consumer choice, I expect you'll find something illuminating and even amusing in what follows.

PART I

DIRECTING EVENTS

CHAPTER 1

The Privilege of Submission

AFTER ALL TWENTY-TWO COURSES OF THE SET MENU, MY FRIEND Chari and I were finally released from Nozawa Bar—a ten-seat sushi counter, walled off for reservation only, at the back of the walk-in restaurant Sugarfish. We were woozy and bloated.

At Sugarfish, we could have ordered sushi and sashimi à la carte. We would have stopped eating as soon as we were full. Nozawa Bar served only omakase.

It wasn't omakase, or "chef's choice," in the usual sense. Normally, the sushi chef selects for the diner the best from the market while considering her tastes. The more frequent the customer, the better the chef learns them. Finally, the diner decides when to quit. With so much custom tailoring, the price of omakase also varies.

At Nozawa Bar, Chef Osamu Fujita served the same set of dishes to all guests at a uniform price. He determined the course number and sequence and the meal's pacing. We ate very well—a wider range of seafood and more rarified and complex preparations than we could have had at Sugarfish. In return, we surrendered our wills. Our only choices were between sparkling and still water and from a brief list of sakes, wines, and beers.

What we experienced was actually a *tasting menu*. This format requires diners to submit to the will of the chef. For the privilege, diners typically pay a premium, and the price, too, is predetermined. Our meal at Nozawa Bar was $212 per person, including the tip (we had no choice in that, either). Since the tasting menu fixes what diners eat in what order and, finally, what they pay, it exemplifies the menu "directing the event" of a meal in the extreme.

As you might imagine, the severe restriction of diner choice, including in matters of cost, makes the tasting menu one of the least popular and therefore rarest menu types. But it does thrive in a small slice of the restaurant marketplace, where chefs with the rare license to be creative constantly and without compromise—a privilege normally hard-won through professional distinction—find support among diners able and eager to pay for extraordinary and surprising culinary art.

Finding perfect agreement between the two parties, however, isn't easy. As we'll see, even among adventurous gourmets, including professional restaurant critics and me, fits of discomfort and complaint arise. And, among all but the most renowned chefs, the entitlement to serve only a tasting menu, let alone one that's totally free of creative restrictions, remains an elusive prospect.

In recent years, the professional culinary world has given restaurants with tasting menus some of its greatest honors. Restaurants with the highest rankings on the world's most anticipated annual lists have been predominantly tasting-menu-only. In 2017, for example, nine out of the top ten on The World's Fifty Best Restaurants (TWFBR) were. Even though the more established *Michelin Guide* differs with TWFBR's estimation of particular places, Michelin, too, gave restaurants with only tasting menus the lion's share of top spots.

The ratings organizations offer little insight into why their contributors disproportionately celebrate the form. TWFBR's website claims no standardized criteria for judgment. It reveals only that, each year, TWFBR relies on seven nominations for best restaurant from each of its over 1,000 sources, comprised of "industry experts"—meaning, chefs, restaurant owners, food writers, and other distinguished gourmands. They must have dined in the restaurants they choose in the past eighteen months and they may not nominate their own restaurant. No genre—not even the casual bar and grill—is off-limits. Michelin does have exact criteria for judgment, but keeps them close to the vest. Nevertheless, Michelin's general methodology, which is common knowledge, is totally different from TWFBR's. Anonymous staff "inspectors" must repeatedly visit the restaurants they rate. According to Michelin's website, what distinguishes a three-star restaurant from a two for Michelin is that the cuisine is "exceptional" as opposed to merely "excellent." Given the divergent rules, it's no surprise that TWFBR and Michelin have different lists of the best restaurants. But it makes their agreement on the value of tasting menus only more mysterious.

Because it gives them maximum creative control, perhaps the tasting menu serves the interests of chefs especially, at least those who want their cuisine deemed "exceptional." If so, the willingness of diners to cede so much power to chefs arose fairly recently. Several decades ago, restaurant chefs couldn't assume so much authority over our meal experience. Their use of the tasting menu for artistic expression is inseparable from their rise as tycoons, celebrities, and heroes of innovation.

Their path to total creative control began in the early to mid-1970s, as international media heralded the French revolution known as *nouvelle cuisine*. Paul Bocuse, Michel Guérard, Alain Chapel, brothers Jean and Pierre Troisgros, and Roger Vergé were the first in a long line of revered French chefs to own their own restaurants and become a fascination of mass media. Some, such as Bocuse and Guérard, even expanded their business portfolios to include other products such as wine and health spas. These precursors to today's brand-building "super chefs" established what we now recognize as a tasting menu: a prix fixe ("fixed price") multicourse *menu dégustation* ("tasting menu").

Nouvelle cuisine's chef-controlling menu format was strongly influenced by the centuries-old Japanese formal meal known as *kaiseki*—specifically the luxurious variant served in restaurants that may consist of as many as fourteen seasonal courses. French chefs were exposed to kaiseki when they traveled to Japan after Chef Tsuji Shizuo opened Japan's first French culinary school in 1960.

Nouvelle's version of the multicourse menu was typically half of kaiseki's length and more idiosyncratic in the types of dishes, revealing an even greater creative license for chefs. According to kaiseki historian Eric C. Rath, contemporary and historical kaiseki chefs—about the latter we can only guess from the scant evidence of old menus—have had a lot of latitude in creating individual dishes; however, diners can expect certain preparations: for example, a sashimi dish and a simmered dish. The order of these is also traditional. Nouvelle chefs valued breaking with the past in more ways and more rapidly—using new cooking methods and drawing on international cuisines to an unprecedented degree.

Those borrowings included one more aspect of kaiseki: the chef's composition of food on the individual diner's plate. The idea of serving dishes in a sequence had been the norm for fine dining in Europe since the medieval period. However, the composition of the individual diner's plate was largely left to either oneself or fellow diners, who took for themselves or served each other helpings from nearby dishes. With plated dishes, nouvelle expanded the chef's dominion.

In the United States at the same time, some of the most esteemed of the new breed of chef-proprietors also specialized in tasting menus. Arguably the most important was Alice Waters, who, with the help of chef Jeremiah Tower in the midseventies, quickly became the most influential chef-owner in America for a novel paradox in restaurants. At her Berkeley, California, establishment, Chez Panisse, Waters combined relaxed service and homey décor with a formal menu—the main dining room served a single tasting menu only.

In the 1980s and 1990s, some of America's most internationally reputed fine-dining chefs, including the late Charlie Trotter in Chicago and Thomas Keller in California, distinguished themselves first and foremost through the conceptual and aesthetic brilliance of their tasting menus. Trotter's introduction of an all-vegetarian menu now seems prophetic, as does Keller's use of the tasting menu for witty storytelling. Keller's notorious amuse-bouche of smoked salmon and crème fraîche "cornets" in the shape of ice cream cones—an ironic nod to childhood wishes for dessert before dinner—added meta-commentary on the meal to the chef's growing toolbox.

To be sure, not all innovative or celebrated chefs since the seventies have expressed their ideas solely or even mainly in tasting menus. As I demonstrated in my book *Smart Casual*, there was an increased tendency among the most venerated restaurants to borrow features of décor, service, cuisine, and—yes—menu structures from "casual" eateries. In this way, the line between fine dining and everything else blurred and the gourmet style spectrum got wider.

It's fair to say, then, that the tasting menu became the ultimate incubator of chef innovation only at the more formal gourmet restaurants. That's where we find what continues to separate "fine" from "casual," even as other marks of that distinction—such as white tablecloths and concealed kitchens—faded: intricate and precisely composed dishes with greater refinement of ingredients, more ritualized and exacting service, lengthier meals, and higher-than-average checks.

Over the 1990s and the first decade of the 2000s, the tasting menu was once again the eye of the fine-dining brainstorm. Chefs of a new culinary revolution made it their format of choice. The international innovators of "modernist cuisine"—from Ferran Adrià and Heston Blumenthal in Europe to Grant Achatz and the late Homaro Cantu in the United States—were the most radical since nouvelle.

Modernist chefs used the tasting menu to experiment with meal structure. Some stretched dinner to thirty or forty briskly paced and tiny courses. Or they upset the conventional order of sweet following savory.

The chefs' structural provocations were part of a larger project to rethink—and, by default, expand control over—every possible dramatic and sensory element of a meal. This included inventing new kinds of service ware for unconventional food forms—airs, foams, and flavors or temperatures or textures for the diner to encounter in a prescribed sequence. Vessels and implements were sometimes so strange that servers would have to instruct diners in their use, thus coaxing them into novel performances.

Modernist chefs played with the ways other senses affect taste. They augmented dishes with visual and olfactory stimuli, such as captured and released smoke or steam, even sound. In 2007 Blumenthal created a dish called Sound of the Sea, which paired seafood with a recording of lapping waves and seagulls. Diners heard it through earbuds coming from an iPod lodged like a hermit crab in the accompanying conch shell.

In essence, the modernists threw themselves into gastrophysics. In their books on the subject, Charles Spence and Betina Piqueras-Fiszman define *gastrophysics* as the multisensory science of how we perceive food and drink. Perfecting a meal, they say, is an ongoing object of research that takes into account the full range of cognitive, sensory, and contextual factors affecting the diner. From the modernists' gastrophysical perspective, the chef's artistic reach over their guest's experience knows no limits.

Proclaiming allegiance to modernist cuisine is no longer in fashion. But the modernist idea that the chef's art extends to every facet of a meal still prevails. And, while not all top restaurants serve forty courses, the tasting menu's status as the chef's crowning Gesamtkunstwerk in fine dining remains.

It's easy to see from this history how the tasting menu serves the occupational interests of today's fine-dining chefs. But how does it appeal to diners?

"Does it, even?" I might have answered, if asked, as we exited Nozawa Bar and re-entered Sugarfish at the peak of its evening din. In that moment, the energetic room and the breeze from the front patio were a relief. Not just for me. Chari, who for years had been game to go to whatever restaurant I suggested we try next, gave me a look at once pained and bubbling with laughter: "No more tasting menus."

We took a stroll in the soothing August air outside the restaurant and compared notes. Our stomachs are robust, but we both found every bite after course fifteen painful.

We knew we'd have no choice in food. But we didn't anticipate the mismatch between the chef's plan and our appetites. Discomfort only intensified with the trappings of fine service. The mindful rituals of presenting, explaining, and clearing away dishes; intervals for changing dishes; and pauses for topping off water glasses and wiping away spills all seemed to protract the experience. We endured out of respect for the chef's skill and ingredients; out of curiosity, of course; and so as not to disturb other diners by the scene that leaving early would have made. That we were spending a lot might have also factored in; although, I like to think we wouldn't be so foolish as to aggravate our condition mentally and physically just because we paid monetarily.

With our feelings, we weren't alone. In fact, our reaction to that night's meal echoed what others had been saying about tasting menus. Especially in the 2000s, as dinners reached extremes of over thirty courses and three hours, newspaper critics and bloggers alike had been questioning their value for the diner.

After noticing a wave of top restaurants nixing à la carte offerings and a set of intrepid chefs opening places with nothing but tasting menus, *Vanity Fair* critic Corby Kummer published, in late 2012, the now-infamously cantankerous "Tyranny—It's What's for Dinner." It began: "The reservation was nearly impossible to get. The meal will cost several hundred dollars. The chef is a culinary genius. But in the era of the four-hour, 40-course tasting menu, one key ingredient is missing: any interest in what (or how much) the customer wants to eat." In his article, Kummer aired every common complaint to that point about the contemporary tasting menu: It's too often too much food for too much money to bolster the self-expression of the chef over the satisfaction of the diner.

But is it fair to demand that a tasting menu satisfy the appetites and tastes of us all? Isn't incompatibility a hazard of anything that standardizes? And gastrophysics aside, the success of the tasting menu from our point of view depends on factors outside any chef's control. Appetites and tastes are variable and unpredictable. It's worth mentioning that, nine days before our visit to Nozawa Bar, when I checked the site, the biggest complaint of Yelp reviewers since the restaurant's opening wasn't that there was too much food (our feeling), but rather that the pace of the meal was too rushed (which we didn't sense at all).

My experiences have differed from other diners' accounts of the same tasting-menu restaurants on plenty of occasions. A year later, for example, after dining at Maude, one of the buzziest debuts on the Los Angeles restaurant scene at the time, I thought that, unless all of the reviewers were just brownnosing its celebrity-chef owner Curtis Stone, Jamisin and I were surely in the minority when we felt alarmingly underfed after its nine-course menu. I hate to admit this—for it doesn't reflect my appreciation of the restaurant's gorgeous interior design and warm, knowledgeable, on-point staff; nor does it duly credit the chef's imaginative concept of featuring one seasonal ingredient each month that made a surprising appearance in every course—but, after the prolonged progression of sparse plates, Jamisin and I came to a swift agreement. Thirty minutes after leaving, we were at Five Guys rushing into the arms of a cheeseburger. Shamefaced, but with zeal, I ate the entire thing. He did too.

Was our lack of satiety the chef's fault? Not unless a critical mass copped to the same truth. If one had, Stone may have rethought the trade-off I assume he made with substance in pricing his menus relatively low. Ours, featuring berries, was $95 per person. This was on the high side for the restaurant's monthly menus that year, but a hundred dollars less than other, more filling, tasting menus in town at establishments of equal vanguard stature, with comparably competent staff, serving a similar number of courses.

You might think that, if a restaurant offers a choice of tasting menus, varying in length or theme, the likelihood of incompatibility goes down. But such a choice can only make matters worse if there's more than one person in the dining party and, per the usual rules of restaurants with tasting menus, the entire table must choose the same one. It only invites conflict among companions.

When we visited Providence, an elegant seafood-focused restaurant then ranked number one on *Los Angeles Times* critic Jonathan Gold's list of best restaurants in the greater LA area, Jamisin and I had to wrestle toward a consensus. The restaurant had just turned tasting-menu-only. Jamisin was, as usual, motivated by a desire to save me money while also hoping to get out of spending three hours in a fine-dining restaurant. He saw the three choices of tasting menus on the menu and immediately fixated on the six-course *Signature and Seasonal Menu*—by far the shortest one. I think I gave him a look of impatient incredulity and made an ungracefully stern suggestion that we order a longer one, either the *Providence Market Menu*, at nine courses, or the *Providence Chef's Menu*, with eleven. I reminded him that we were there for research, and it was imperative that we witness the restaurant's full ballet. I felt badly about my sadism-by-generosity, though we both got over it quickly enough.

It's unavoidable: the tasting menu will cause tension and dissatisfaction. But I also know that that statement can't fully account for the genre as a social compact. Haven't we diners, restaurant critics among us, been crucial accomplices in exalting the form? Where would the tasting menu be without accolades? While the critics lambasting it did capture how Chari and I felt that one August night, I concede that they represent a limited view of the genre's satisfactions—even for me in other instances, even when I was just as overfed.

I agree with the tasting menu's defenders when they claim that the form surprises and enlightens us as no other menu can. Diners won't order what they don't yet know exists. And, since the tasting menu is aesthetically and conceptually coordinated as no other restaurant meal, it can do so across multiple facets of experience. The best chefs use the format to inspire thought long after digestion.

Tasting menus can lead to unforeseen gustatory pleasures. I can still recall an amuse-bouche I had in 2010 at the Oakland, California, restaurant Commis. It looked like a garnished sunny-side up egg lying at the bottom of a small brown bowl. Inside the ceramic was actually a poached egg yolk perched above the center of a shallow pool of cream of white onion, under which was an invisible mound of ground medjool dates. On one inch of the edge of the white cream was a layer of chives on top of another layer of steel-cut-oat granola. The dish was craftily balanced—savory, sweet, creamy, herbaceous, and crunchy—and complemented with a pairing of fruity hard cider.

Four years later at Coi in San Francisco: an equally surprising dish also featuring egg. The menu called it "California Sturgeon Caviar—egg yolk poached in smoked oil, crème fraîche, chives." A layer of caviar covered the cap of a gravity-defying yolk, which sat, without breaking, half-on and half-off a ball of crème sprinkled sparingly with chive. Scooping everything up, I tasted one rich bite reminiscent of a classically dressed baked potato—smoky, salty, creamy, tangy, and with an allium kick—but with a mouthfeel more viscous, denser, and practically magnetic, as if made on a planet with more gravity.

I mention these dishes not just because they were delicious, delightfully disconfirming of visual cues, and original, but also because I don't like eggs. I never would have ordered them.

The tasting menu is also uniquely capable of creating drama throughout a meal. I still marvel at the exceptional examples of pacing I was fortunate to experience. Only the prospect of a set menu could have given Chef Grant Achatz and his team at Alinea in Chicago the chance to play with foreshadowing in a 2008 meal I will never forget. The dish "WAGYU BEEF maitake, smoked date, Blis Elixer" appeared in stages, but very mysteriously at first. After course fourteen (out of twenty-seven), the server placed what looked like an abstract sculpture on the table at a distance from me that signaled it wasn't to eat. An elegant metal stand balanced a smooth piece of wood, barely a foot long, at a forty-five-degree slant. In a clothespin grip, the wooden object held a hard, square, pink sheet. The server allowed the curious sculpture to linger for two more courses without explanation. In that time, the object deepened in color and softened, eventually drooping. Its culinary function became clear in the plating of course seventeen, when the server picked up what I finally recognized as a sheet of lusciously fatty Wagyu beef, draped it over a plated maitake mushroom and date, and dressed it with Blis Elixer.

In 2010, at the original incarnation of chef José Andrés's minibar in Washington, DC, I witnessed a different marvel of pacing. Remarkably, I wasn't overstuffed or exhausted eating thirty courses. I believe that's because all were served in just two hours—a rate of one course, on average, every four minutes. Actual variations in the timing, which corresponded to the size of the courses, ensured that the meal wasn't monotonous. The tight choreography by the three chefs working behind the six-seat counter that composed the restaurant then—with each presenting a course to two diners at a time and all in unison—ensured a lively rhythm throughout. The meal was like a splendid firework display: no lags and a satisfying crescendo. After a rapid-fire series of sweets to end the meal, the bill came in an "egg" that the chefs shattered open on the countertop in one final "POP!" Andrés and his team showed the importance of avoiding the gaps in service that turn a tasting menu into an ordeal of fatigue and captivity.

Tasting menus can also offer unparalleled opportunities for communion and culinary understanding. Social bonding among guests who are strangers happens when a tasting menu occurs at a uniform seating time. All encounter the meal's surprises simultaneously and can enjoy others' delight in discovery as much as their own. Eye-opening dialogue between kitchen staff and diners about the chefs' methods and ideas also happens in situations, such as seating at kitchen counters or other arrangements, where guests can freely speak to the people preparing their food and overhear others doing the same. Because they created both of these conditions so invitingly, I'll never forget dining kitchen-counter-side at minibar and at the original Momofuku Ko in Manhattan, or the pop-up dining events in LA known as Wolvesmouth and the Amalur Project. Places where customers order individually and come and go as they please are less conducive to these rewarding dynamics.

Tasting menus allow for all-encompassing concepts that provoke thought about the definition of a meal. To offer a nonalcoholic beverage pairing with a tasting menu is increasingly common. But it was still rare—and revelatory—when I opted for one at the late Chicago restaurant Charlie Trotter's in 2010. It's customary for tasting-menu restaurants to offer wine pairings. Chef Trotter must have realized that not everyone wants to or can drink alcohol, and that liquor isn't the only drink that complements food. The beverage menu explained that its concoctions—"created using juicing, infusing, and brewing methods"—were specially designed for the evening's dégustations. You can sense the marvelous range of this menu-within-a-menu's palette—extending from cool and carbonated to milky and piquant to woodsy and warm—just by reading the list:

> Sparkling Pear
> Young Coconut & Lime
> Sour Cherry & Mint
> Redwood Infusion
> Black Tea & Sage
> Cranberry Clove

I love wine, but I found this every bit as stimulating as a good wine pairing and I didn't miss the wearying effects of alcohol. More than that, I appreciated the restaurant's challenge to conventional menus everywhere.

In rare cases, a chef turns the tasting menu into a test bench for a revolution. It imagines and launches alternatives to how we, as a society, raise and consume food. So it is with Dan Barber at Blue Hill in Manhattan and Blue Hill at Stone Barns in Pocantico Hills, New York. The latter is attached to a farm and laboratory called the Stone Barns Center for Food and Agriculture, which both restaurants rely on for ingredients as well as the research and development related to them.

Barber upsets even the most eco-conscious menus of the moment, which attempt to source ingredients from farms that raise livestock humanely and everything organically. In his manifesto on farming, cooking, and eating entitled *The Third Plate,* Barber pointed out that even these conscientious practices are ecologically unsustainable, so long as chefs still dictate what ingredients they want to use regardless of their impact on farming ecosystems. The result, Barber argued, is that farmers must produce for a market unaware that it's furthering ecological imbalance and soil depletion.

Barber told the story of the Blue Hill menus' evolution in response to his growing desire to support what an entire farm requires to replenish itself. At his restaurants, and with the help of his staff at Stone Barns, he aimed for seasonal menus that make use of all the ingredients that sustain a farm. He wanted to make it financially viable for the farm to engage in optimal practices, including judiciously rotating the specific crops necessary to maintain soil health, planting complementary companion crops (nitrogen users with nitrogen capturers), and bringing animal rotations in tune with crop rotations (they, fertilizing the soil after grazing on rich terrain)—all the while adapting techniques as conditions change and innovations in breeding occur. Per Barber: "In order for these farms to last, I needed to learn to cook with the whole farm."

Whether or not the farming and eating methods Barber promoted in the book are in fact sustainable or can be scaled up enough to impact the titanic modern food system isn't my purpose or capacity to judge. What's impressive in this context is that Barber harnessed the uniquely authoritarian powers of the tasting menu to provoke worthwhile thought. He challenged a common assumption we make when beholding a restaurant menu: the consumer is king, entitled to as much choice as the market will bear.

When menu concepts are as upending as Barber's, they prod us into deeper reflection about what satisfaction, in the context of dining out, really means. They encourage us to measure by standards beyond our preconceived wants and knee-jerk consumer habits. I haven't been to Blue Hill since Barber started his magnum opus, but I hope I can revisit it soon to sample a draft.

In addition to being able to appreciate the enlightening powers of some tasting menus, I can sympathize with defenders of the form who delight in how it relieves them of choice. Blogger Allison Levine expressed the sentiment most glowingly in a 2014 review of Maude: "What I love the most about tasting menus is that you don't have to do any thinking about what you want to eat. The chef makes all the decisions."

Given how common it is to identify consumer choice with liberty and the pursuit of happiness, satisfaction from having no choice is unexpected. But when the choices people face on a daily basis become too numerous and too trivial—we didn't always have twenty different kinds of yogurt in the supermarket—it can feel luxurious to put the fate of our dinner in the hands of a master. And surely, those who can afford to dine by tasting menu have more consumer choice than most.

In form and content, every tasting menu is an effort to resolve the conflict that the restaurateur may sow by restricting choice: On one side is fine-dining chefs' interest in their own creative and career progress and some diners' willingness to trade agency for new artistic experience. On the other is the diners' wish to determine the duration and contents of their meal.

So, then, how do tasting menus reconcile these divergent interests?

To answer this question, we might consider the market logic of tasting-menu-only restaurants. While it's true that the outsize prices of dégustations are the biggest markups in the business, the demands that tasting menus place on diners—in cost, time, and attention—make the customers for restaurants featuring only them, especially the experimental menus that tend to be lengthy, sparse. Rare is the place that can attract the constant flow of gastro-tourists that will keep it booked.

When it can, it's by reputation of the chef. The greater and more global the chef's fine-dining renown, the better are such a restaurant's chances of making money.

Tasting menus also lessen the chances of opposing desires by tuning their originality to the adventurousness of their markets. After all, the customer base for avant-garde dining is small. A menu that shrinks it unnecessarily can ruin a business.

Few chefs can attract the capital, media attention, and top sous talent necessary to consistently push the boundaries of ordinary taste. The uncompromisingly creative tasting menus of the world concentrate in very few hands. At this writing, these one-percenters of the culinary field include Daniel Humm at Eleven Madison Park in New York City; Massimo Bottura at Osteria Francescana in Modena, Italy; Joan Roca at El Celler de Can Roca in Girona, Spain; René Redzepi at Noma in Copenhagen; Grant Achatz at Alinea in Chicago; Juan Mari and Elena Arzak at Arzak in San Sebastián, Spain; Andoni Aduriz at Mugaritz, also in San

Sebastián; Alex Atala at D.O.M. in São Paulo, Brazil; and a handful more of the sort who speak at international chef congresses, such as the MAD symposia, and have labs in addition to kitchens where they avoid the daily grind that dulls the edges of other chefs.

The drop from the top to even the best of the rest is steep. Unless uncommonly well capitalized, running ingeniously on an overhead-minimizing business model such as a pop-up, or subsidizing the effort with another business, as Nozawa Bar did by operating inside Sugarfish, fine-dining menus must make concessions to a broader market. They must include more familiar fare or more choice. For restaurants with tasting menus, this means seldom making them the diner's only choice.

When I met them, Charles Olalia and Sergio Lujan Perera were two young, dynamic chefs with already worldly perspectives on fine-dining businesses. They had worked at a variety, including some of the one-percenters'. The resume of Olalia, then-executive chef of Patina in Los Angeles, contained such globally renowned brands as Guy Savoy and The French Laundry. Perera, cofounder of the tasting-menu-only pop-up the Amalur Project, worked at, among other places, Arzak and Mugaritz.

According to Olalia and Perera, the optimal profit-making menu structure for the majority of fine-dining restaurants isn't tasting-menu-only. It's a mix of tasting menu and à la carte. At Patina, Olalia maintained this very combination. It gives the customer maximum choice while allowing the restaurant to use the same stock of ingredients in different ways. As Olalia put it, "The tasting menu one night might have lobster. The next day an item on the à la carte menu could have lobster claws."

Olalia also mentioned that most fine-dining places need enough familiar dishes on the menu to appeal to a range of customers. "Not all diners want to get something they don't expect," he said. At Patina, for example, he claimed a fifty-fifty split: "About half the dishes are surprising and half are straightforward—you get what you expect when you read the description." Thus, he explained, on the menu, "Green Salad and Baba au Rhum identify a dish by a name or familiar point of reference and these things are presented as they are. Whereas [the] dishes [on the menu] that just name ingredients retain mystery and invite surprise upon presentation."

For her book, *At the Chef's Table: Culinary Creativity in Elite Restaurants*, sociologist Vanina Leschziner talked to no less than forty-five "elite" chefs in New York City and San Francisco, and they indicated much the same as Olalia and Perera. Her study of the dynamics of originality in restaurant menus revealed that, in spite of critical acclaim and high restaurant ratings, most of the chefs she studied were caught in some compromise of invention and imitation. In composing their menus, they felt pressure to adhere to a culinary style, even the chef's own "signature." They also had to make dishes that wouldn't alienate too many customers. At the same time, they felt a pull to differentiate their menus in order to attract other customers and critical respect.

Leschziner also empirically confirmed my more loosely formed impression that the higher the chefs' stature, the less they imitate the ingredients, dishes, and even the style of writing on menus. They are more, to quote Michelin, "exceptional."

Of course, that conclusion also suggests that the pressures on top chefs are atypical as well. They're sure to disappoint if they don't constantly astonish.

Clearly, the total submission required to experience the ultimate in tasting-menu art is a rare privilege for chefs and diners alike. But, like the sixteenth course at Nozawa Bar, it isn't always painless.

CHAPTER 2

The Four Faces of Togetherness

WHILE VISITING RESTAURANTS FOR THIS BOOK, IT OCCURRED TO ME that most menus at full-service places, where servers wait on tables, make some sort of proposition about togetherness. The menus try to influence whether and how we diners share food and how we share time.

Why would restaurateurs take an interest in our conviviality? They don't care about our social lives. A more likely motive—conscious or not—is that how we eat together affects the smoothness of their operations and their potential for profits. From commensality comes opportunity.

For suggesting how diners should commune I found four menu stratagems: what I'll call the *family-style* menu, the *shared-plates* menu, the *sequential* menu, and the *flexible* menu. If we go out for table service today, we're sure to encounter one or a hybrid of these. They each use a unique set of rhetorical tools to create a scene of sociability that suits the restaurateur.

Have you had a meal out like this? Your family or friends gather around a table and order a variety of dishes to share. To ensure a complete and interesting provision for all, the selections range in tastes, textures, colors, food groups, and cooking methods. Your place at the table has an empty plate, which you fill with samples from communal dishes set

in the center of the table. Orders come from the kitchen in no set sequence—whenever they're ready. Since you may take from any dish at
any point in the meal, you satisfy your appetite without degrading the
esprit de corps of sharing.

You're most likely to have such a meal in a restaurant serving Asian or
African cuisine, although you may also find it in trattoria-style Italian
restaurants. The most ubiquitous setting in the United States, given its
long-rooted and extensive presence throughout the country, is probably
the Chinese restaurant.

Although not all restaurants serving communal dishes rely on the
menu to communicate that sharing is their custom, I have reason to
believe that what I call the family-style menu encourages compliance
with it. The key is the menu's organization by types of ingredients and
preparations.

The purest example I studied was at Giang Nan, a respected, though
recently shuttered, Shanghainese restaurant in the San Gabriel Valley.
Not counting its last two pages, which listed three pricey, all-inclusive
banquet options, the twelve-page menu contained "House Specials,"
"Cold Plates," "Dim Sum," "Fowl (Poultry)," "Soup & Casserole," "Seafood,"
"Rice & Noodle," "Clay Pot," and "Vegetable" headings. That the menu
divided dishes by food type only—there was no indication of differences in portion size—suggested that to order from only one section of
the menu would be too much of one thing; whereas a variety of dishes
would be too much for one person.

By its structure alone the menu powerfully hinted that diners should
select an assortment of dishes to share. Moreover, with no dessert—in
fact, no temporal categories at all—Giang Nan's menu ensured that
guests would consume all parts of the meal at roughly the same time.
That's the family-style menu in its strictest form.

In less pure versions, it's common to find dessert tacked on to an
otherwise course-less menu. It seems like an afterthought.

So alien is sequence to the family-style menu that the attempt to graft
temporal categories onto them can be inadvertently comical. When we
visited Din Tai Fung, an ever-growing chain of Taiwanese restaurants,
a list of "Steamed Dumplings," a house specialty, preceded "Appetizers"
on the menu, mocking the meaning of *appetizer*. At the venerated Thai
restaurant Jitlada, a menu section entitled "Main Courses" struck me as

the height of irony. I barely noticed it amidst the deluge of course-less categories, which included "Soups," "Salads," "Seafood," "Curries," "Specialty Curries," "Chef's Specialties," "Jitlada Vegetables," "Rice Dishes," "Noodles," "Chef Tui's Jitlada Seafood Specialties," "Beverages," and a two-page menu-within-the-menu called the "Southern Thai Menu," itself divided into nineteen categories. So-called "Main Courses" got no priority by menu location, portion size, or price point, and against the flood of food types, had no chance to stand out. Although trying to be inclusive, Jitlada's menu was family style through and through.

In compelling us to order a variety of dishes to share, family-style menus don't do all the work by themselves. They rely on our pre-existing notions of an ideal meal.

All major world civilizations have defined the ideal meal—not exclusively, but at its most elaborate, for feasts—by variety and balance. Anthropologists and culinary historians alike have noted that, while cultures differ on what ingredients compose a meal and what makes a proper sequence, they agree on certain compositional principles. According to Margaret Visser in *The Rituals of Dinner: The Origins, Evolution, Eccentricities, and Meanings of Table Manners*, these principles include "variety, contrast, and completeness . . . to range from liquid to solid, cold to hot, and through all the flavours from savoury to sweet." Most people confronted with a menu divided solely by food types are likely to feel an inner tug to order more than one dish from more than one section of the menu.

Restaurant décor may reinforce the rhetoric of the family-style menu. The most common feature, in my experience, is the presence of an empty plate—not the "charger" plate, for decoration, but the one to eat off of—at each diner's place before the party sits down. The plate implies that you shouldn't expect a dish to come out of the kitchen composed just for you.

Where family-style menus appear, servers rarely instruct us in how to order. The printed menus do most of the nudging and, since we so often find family-style menus in restaurants where ethnic traditions of communal-dish dining are widely familiar, many of us know the drill before we walk in.

Places with family-style menus, however, don't have them just to further a heritage. They're good for business. For example, these menus incentivize visits by larger parties. For us guests, the larger the group, the more variety of dishes each of us can enjoy. For the business, the larger the party, the bigger the check. While more people at the table might also take longer to dine, especially on the special occasions that might bring a big group together, the higher check mitigates the slower table turn.

The family-style menu gets the most out of small parties, too. Its inducement to order variety leads two or three people to order more than they can eat in one sitting. They can take the rest home. Why Chinese restaurants in America are so identified with Fold-Pak containers might not just be due to their take-out and delivery service.

Meanwhile, the atemporal structure of the family-style menu helps the restaurant on the operational front. Not having to time courses gives the kitchen flexibility. No need for an expediter to sync up the pace of the kitchen with that of us diners.

What I call the shared-plates menu, after the communal dining it encourages, is like the family-style menu in key ways. Organized principally by food type, it urges us to share a variety of dishes in no fixed order. This relieves the kitchen from synchronizing with us, which, in turn, creates informality.

There's a lot, however, that the two menu types don't have in common. That's because the shared-plates menu advertises a very different commodity. Above all: the originality of the chef and director of the beverage program. Dishes, cocktails, wines, and spirits exist to surprise as much as to please. To come up with novel combinations of ingredients, mixologists and chefs ignore boundaries between ethnic traditions and borrow a bit from here, a bit from there. To wit, these entries from a menu I collected while at the vanguardist restaurant Ink. in West Hollywood: "**Hamachi**, whipped olive, orange-soy, coriander, pine nuts"; "**Corn**, housemade doritos, nori, green onion"; "**Lollipop kale**, crème fraîche, pig ears, togarashi."

Also unlike the family-style, the shared-plates menu tends toward offerings of so-called "small plates." The association of shared with small began in the mid-1980s, when shared-plates menus were born as a multicultural spinoff of a Spanish tapas (bar snacks) craze. Subsequently, ethnically eclectic tapas-sized dishes to share over drinks were often listed on trendy menus as "small plates."

Like the tasting menu I discussed in the previous chapter, the small-plates format serves the interests of chefs who want to be known as innovators. Offering many little dishes allows them to invent more in the mode of appetizers—meaning, free from the compositional formulae, such as making a slab of protein the star, that bedevil entrées. At the same time, the fact that we order more dishes to make up for their small portions gives chefs a greater chance to show their creative range.

Contemplating the scores of menus and restaurants I sampled made me realize that, because it has to sell a less familiar product than the family-style menu—one with no single ethnic tradition from which to gauge the dining customs—the shared-plates menu must direct our behavior in more explicit terms. I found clues in the design of menus and in the way other restaurant features cooperated.

A notably aggressive case was at A-Frame in Culver City. When Jamisin and I dined there, the menu couldn't have made the sharing seem more imperative. A bright-orange tagline at the top of the off-white page—saying "Modern Picnic"—announced its casual and communal expectations loudly. The largest heading for food, "On the Table," sounded commanding. A lowercase menu section, labeled "to pass around," gave further instruction. If these messages weren't directive enough, the bottom of the page brought out the big heavy—a quotation by one "Papi Chulo," referring to Roy Choi, the chef-owner rock star enough to have a nickname: "A-Frame is home. It's how I'd cook for you if this was a house party. No ridiculous pretentiousness, no hors d'oeuvres. Straight macking, lip smacking, and big belly laughs." Papi wasn't just branding. He was setting an example.

The décor fortified his message. All tables were picnic benches. Even strangers had to share space, if not food, reminding again of the house concept. What's more, each person's place started off with an empty plate—the food-sharing restaurant's one universal hint.

To a minimal extent, A-Frame also used its staff to train guests on the menu's codes. Our server told us only what the menu and décor couldn't. His small speaking role wasn't surprising given the nightclub ambience A-Frame built with its large bar area, low light, and thumping hip-hop. Nevertheless, once we ordered, our server was sure to tell us that our dishes would come out "staggered." That may seem like a small thing, but his warning was an important act of management. By preparing us to accept the kitchen's prerogative in timing, he guarded that privilege.

Other shared-plates restaurants may give servers a greater role in menu-concept instruction. At The Church Key, a stylish restaurant on the Sunset Strip with rolling carts of novel munchies and cocktails in addition to a printed menu, the servers set the stage at the outset. When Jamisin and I visited, I noticed that, on first approach, servers asked guests if they'd dined there before. If they hadn't, servers told them that the restaurant had dishes to share and proceeded to suggest how many dishes of what type per person they'd recommend. They then forewarned that, besides the menu, dim sum carts would circulate periodically "at the chef's discretion."

At The Church Key and at Ink., another shared-plates venue, the servers supplemented the printed menus strongly. For food, each place had just one tidy, undivided list. By their order and prices, one could, if focused, detect the progression of dishes from smaller and lighter to bigger and heavier, but the servers' more explicit interventions made missing the message to share them near impossible. Family-style menus don't require, by menu or server, such overt direction.

From a restaurateur's perspective, the shared-plates menu also differs from the family-style. Operationally, the ones with many small plates have slightly different requirements. Although the kitchen doesn't have to time courses, servers have to bring out and take away many more plates than for a family-style menu and, because gourmet standards demand it, make more changes of our personal plates and flatware. This means more work for the staff. When I asked her about the challenges of offering a shared-plates menu, Kasja Alger, chef and co-owner of the exemplary Mud Hen Tavern in Hollywood, made me aware of this trade-off.

At the same time, the greater role the bar menu tends to play in a shared-plates scenario rewards the extra trouble in higher checks and tips. Mud Hen Tavern, as I experienced it, was a prime example of a shared-plates restaurant that maximized promotion of the bar. Mud Hen Tavern stood in the place of the same owners' prior shared-plates concept, named Susan Feniger's Street. As if to correct course, the new place had a name that evoked drinking and an interior that gave the bar far more space, and it used drink menus as a central design feature. Names of liquors appeared not only as one would expect, in the menu on the table, but also on tall chalkboard menus specially designed by a hired artist and mounted over the bar. They were the first things I noticed as we entered the restaurant. Add sharp suggestive selling by the waitstaff, and voilà: a recipe for drink sales. When Jamisin and I dined there, our server informed us of new and special beverages to complement our food at every decision point in the meal.

Only several decades old, the structure of the shared-plates menu is understandably more volatile than the more established family-style menu. If one counts Chinese restaurants as the starting point, the latter has had over a century in the United States to smooth out its snags. Conventions have hardened into traditions and we know what to expect. Meanwhile, the shared-plates menu's recent vintage and tendency toward trendiness make it rife with shifting terminology and ways of communicating how and what we're supposed to share.

A flash of the shifting winds appeared in the *Los Angeles Times* in 2014, when Jonathan Gold remarked, in the review "At Porridge and Puffs, Spoonfuls of Devotion in Every Bowl," "dinner out in Los Angeles is starting to look different this year, evolved past the tyranny of appetizer-entrée-dessert and even the forced camaraderie of small plates."

The shared-plates menu was evolving in other ways as well. In March 2015, *New York Times* critic Pete Wells reported on a new iteration in "Small Plates Grow Up." He noticed a nationwide tendency for servers to offer to "course out" dishes ordered in shared-plates restaurants. This broke from the previous practice of allowing tables to become festivals of clutter. I vouch for this. At Ink., when I asked the server about the order in which our dishes would arrive, he explained that he and the chef confer on sequence, so that only some of the dishes, those that harmonize best, go out to the table at one time. It's true that Ink.'s approach and what Wells meant represented more of a trend in service than in menus. But keep in mind that the trend in service arose from a kink in the menu.

In 2015, I noticed that some menus in this genre had themselves begun, if somewhat awkwardly, to do a little "coursing." At République, a Hollywood establishment serving an up-to-date version of "California cuisine" that my friend Chari and I tried, I saw a menu heading called "Starters." Like the "Appetizer" section of the family-style menu at Din Tai Fung, it was comically crowbarred in. It was the third heading down after "Toast" and "Oysters." While the cauliflower dish we ordered from this part of the menu did arrive first, we didn't order any toast or oysters to test whether or not we would receive our starters before those. (This outing wasn't officially part of my study sample.) What we do know is that, in keeping with the shared-plates genre, the order of dishes was up to the kitchen.

In addition to experimenting with sequencing, our visit to République exemplified a shift in the language associated with shared-plates menus. When she introduced herself, the server informed us that the restaurant serves dishes "family style, to share." She didn't say, "we do shared plates" or "it's a shared-plates concept"—a phrasing I heard more of the previous year. In a short span, the words *shared plates* had gone out of fashion, too. At A.O.C. Wine Bar & Restaurant, a renowned Cal-Med place where Jamisin and I dined in courtyard plein air, the menu had, at the bottom of the page, a category called "Platters," suggesting sharing in new words. By the time you read this, the terminology on shared-plates menus, and their introductions by servers, may have changed yet again.

The currently volatile shared-plates menu has also yet to settle disagreements between the artistic ambitions of chefs and the appetites of diners. This is particularly true of menus full of small plates.

Evidence of a tug-of-war is legion. Complaints about "small plates" by professional critics and others on social-media sites have been rearing up since the trend reached critical mass in the 2000s. *LA Weekly* critic Besha Rodell dubbed the commotion the "Small-Plates Debate." Over the years, articles in the *New York Times* ("In Defense of the Entrée"; "The Big Problem with Small Plates"), the *Washington Post* ("The Case Against Small Plates"), and even a Chowhound thread begun in 2014 ("Are 'Small Plates' Just a Trend [I Hope]") indicate the rising frustration of diners forced to split a set of culinary haikus that don't fill their stomachs.

Yet those who prefer the collective adventure of sampling a variety of dishes, and care less about getting full, have stood up for the besieged little dishes. See, for example, the 2013 *Slate* article "In Defense of Small Plates" and "The Importance of Small Plates" from the blog *The Bad Deal*.

Like Betty Hallock in her 2013 *Los Angeles Times* article "Small Plate

Dining: Train Wreck or Terrific?," the rest have taken a bystander approach, reporting on the passions of others. Given their timing, I suppose that the upsets to shared-plates menus and their service routines have in part been responses to the herk and jerk of public opinion.

The sequential menu is much steadier, a fixture in US restaurants since the likes of Delmonico's under Charles Ranhofer in the nineteenth century.

The sequential menu doesn't care whether or not we share food. It's keen to decide how we share time. By its temporal structure—the division of foods into, say, appetizers, main courses, and desserts; or *antipasti*, *primi*, *secondi*, and *dolci*—the sequential menu recommends that we dine lockstep in a progression. It implies that a party skipping a course falls short of the convivial ideal—represented as a dramatic arc— and that only a heel leaves her tablemate to the awkwardness of eating a course while she watches. The sequential menu conflates leaving our companions in the lurch with spurning the restaurant's commercial advances—deserting by not ordering dessert.

I notice a variety in sequential menus. The marathon tasting menus I discussed in chapter 1 are the most unusual, in that they don't leave the choice to participate in every course up to us. Atypical for the same reason are those prix-fixe bundles that some restaurants offer not so much to show off the originality of the chef as to avoid disturbing featured entertainments. At the Moroccan and Tunisian restaurant Moun of Tunis in West Hollywood, we had to choose a set menu as soon as we were seated on our pillowed banquette. How else to avoid untimely calls to the fez-wearing server interfering with the belly-dancing show? At Opaque: Dining in the Dark, a traveling concept at which people dine in pitch blackness, we likewise had to choose a multicourse menu upfront. We would no longer be able to see a menu once led into the lightless dining room by our blind guide.

To get us to participate in every act of the dining drama, all other sequential menus, where courses are optional, need to do some persuading.

On a dinner outing to Patina, a landmark of fine dining in downtown Los Angeles, I witnessed a vigorous and elaborate example of that salesmanship. Not only were the choices of food and drink laid out in courses, the sequential menu's typical nudge to follow a storyline, but there also was an extended series of discrete presentations of separate printed menus for almost every course plus intermittent propositions by auxiliary menus in nonstandard forms.

Holding cocktail-and-beer lists, our server introduced himself and made the first overture: "May I interest you in a cocktail? We also have a full bar."

Jamisin asked about nonalcoholic options. That triggered the presentation of a printed coffee-and-tea menu. His choice of tea, in turn, prompted the revelation of a rolling menu, a cart displaying varieties of tea in a gallery of transparent cylinders. (Another cart sold coffees the same way.)

After bringing my cocktail and properly steeping Jamisin's pot of tea, the server reappeared with a food menu. He highlighted items in the appetizer and main-course categories, ensuring that we took both courses seriously.

The next menus came in human form. These were customized recommendations through a back-and-forth with the sommelier and passes by a gentleman selling varieties of bottled water.

Once our main courses were cleared, our server returned to tempt us with a printed menu of desserts and after-dinner drinks.

Well, almost. Actually, when he approached our table after the main courses, our server had the dessert menus tucked under his arm. He was keeping an intervening option open. This became clear when he asked us not only "May I get you dessert menus?" but also "May I offer you cheese?"

"Yes, cheese!" I beamed. That produced the magnificent cheese cart, which occasioned a leisurely discussion of goat, sheep, cow, and blue.

So, the dessert menu actually appeared twice—at first tentatively, then fully, after the cheese cart finally exited the stage. That was near the end of hour three. There was still time for offers of coffee and a digestif.

Our meal at Patina was a master class in amplification by protraction and variation. By dividing the menu into submenus, as well as meting out and diversifying its presentations, the restaurant ensured our full attention to the advertisement of each course. Some credit should also go to the dining room's comfortable seats and low decibels. It made us all the more amenable to staying for the whole show.

Ironically, such scenes of *luxe, calme et volupté* have a tendency to turn each offer of a course or a drink into a high-pressure situation. I suspect that how prepared you are to pay for the full gamut of courses and how hungry you are for the same determines whether you perceive the elegantly extended propositioning as polite service or hustle.

Also, these scenarios make the choice to sit out a course your companion will have really unappealing. It's easy to assume from the pacing of service that such an abstention would make the gap in shared action feel infinite for you both.

Although most aren't as ceremonious as they were at Patina, sequential menus are historically associated with the fine-dining arena Patina represents. That's to be expected. The multiplication and prolongation of service rituals that coursed meals require sets a more formal tone than bringing food out all at once or in a haphazard order.

From the standpoint of restaurateurs, the pomp and circumstance of a sequential menu has the downside of slowing table turns. Yet the sense of occasion the format engenders allows them to charge a premium for the time. The course structure has another advantage: the bringing and clearing of plates allows servers to sell us dessert or more drinks at times that feel authentic to the situation.

Not all is traditional with the sequential menu, however. The tendency in recent decades for expensive gourmet restaurants to have ultra-casual atmospheres has changed some sequential menus' game. Clamorous spaces with open kitchens, no tablecloths, and come-as-you-are dress codes are home to many sequential menus now. Indeed, the high-low combination of formal food service and informal digs is typical of this contemporary style. In these louder and less physically comfortable contexts, sequential menus can't rely on the old devices of protracted pacing and hermetic setting, lulling us into a multiple-course meal. They require new approaches befitting a bustling environment.

I found a creative one at the original location of Salt's Cure. The shoebox storefront in West Hollywood was nothing more than an L-shaped dining counter overlooking a busy kitchen surrounded by one clothless layer of tables. It wasn't the kind of ambience that automatically exhorts one to stay for a meal in multiple phases. But each set of offerings was presented in a way that made saying "no" to any one seem like missing the point of being there.

The restaurant's website let me know the point on its home page. A paragraph on the "Salt's Cure Philosophy" stated a commitment to California-sourced, organic food and biodynamic wine, as well as a thoroughly artisanal approach: "We make everything ourselves, from the ketchup to the bacon." The pride in house-made charcuterie is in the restaurant's name.

Thus, Salt's Cure made it seem like an abnegation of enlightened consumption not to order from the two menus on a cork clipboard that the server brought to our table as we sat down. The card featuring "Snacks" included the vaunted charcuterie. The page lying under that had, among other locally sourced products, the touted list of biodynamic wines. Because both were proclaimed specialties of the house, they were more difficult to resist than wine and snacks otherwise would be.

At this point, however, Salt's Cure had only begun to play on our fear of missing out. The restaurant made its main menu—which on our visit listed five appetizers, five entrées, and three sides—a real challenge to turn down. It was, after all, the most distinctive feature of the restaurant's interior design and a centerpiece of its branding effort on social media. Salt's Cure boasted a daily changing menu in the form of a chalkboard built into the restaurant's back wall. Anyone wanting to know the daily specials—and every set of daily specials in the restaurant's entire history—could find out on the Salt's Cure Facebook page, where the restaurant posted a photograph of the chalkboard on a daily basis. In this way, the chalkboard menu became so characteristic of the restaurant that to not order from it would be the equivalent of never having dined there.

Finally, the server conveyed the few dessert options in person. This spoken menu, which emphasized house-made ice creams, maintained the artisanal angle that made the house's other menus such cunning dares to decline.

Not all of us who go out to eat want to have the same series of courses as our companions. Nor do we all want to share the same food. Even those of us who do might not want to every time we dine out. Fortunately, we don't have to. We can refuse to give in to the social pressures of sequential, shared-plates, and family-style menus by ordering what we want and eating how we want as much as the menu and service will accommodate. Or we can go somewhere with a flexible menu.

An event involving the latter might go this way: A family of three goes out for a meal at 6:00 p.m. Dad's having the sandwich-and-salad combo. If his order sounds like lunch food, that's because he works the night shift and, for him, it's lunchtime. Mom's had a late-lunch meeting with colleagues at work, so she's not very hungry yet. A cocktail to unwind and an appetizer will do it for her. But their teenage daughter has to eat a full dinner now. She's still growing, after all, and she has to digest her food before dance class at eight. Going out to eat at six was the only way the whole family could get together.

A similar scene could happen among friends: A group goes out to catch up. Everyone can do a full dinner and beers at seven, except one. He has to squeeze the outing in between appointments he has with his personal-training clients. While the rest of the party has another round, he'll be nursing a smoothie until he has to bow out. At least they all found some time to meet and a place that could satisfy differing needs.

Where can we go where we feel welcome to structure our meal independently of our companions, where we can convene in spite of differing schedules or meal plans? A good bet is restaurants with extended opening hours. The flexible menu goes hand-in-hand with restaurants of this type.

Across the United States, big-box casual-dining chains may be the most ubiquitous sites, but we also find the combination of extended opening hours and flexible menus in restaurants that have sufficient consumer traffic throughout the day for nondining reasons, places where people might think to sit down to eat on an impulse and, then, don't always want a full meal.

Such eateries abound in tourist locales. A case in point from my field study was Ray's and Stark Bar, the full-service gourmet restaurant and bar attached to the Los Angeles County Museum of Art (LACMA). Museum visitors passed by it continuously. Anyone could have gone there with the intention of having a full meal or just a snack and a cocktail. The restaurant was distinguished enough for its cuisine to sustain dinner service when the museum was closed. But, during the day, it kept its options open while the museum was.

We might also have a meal like this at a place designed for multiple uses. An example in the modern-brasserie vein is Bottega Louie, where I lunched in downtown Los Angeles. On the way to my table, I passed through its gourmet-specialty and pastries shop. Another from my rounds was the historic midcity Los Angeles landmark Canter's Deli, with a restaurant and a crowded bakery and deli open all day. The casual-dining chains I visited had their own mixtures of restaurant and retail. At Marie Callender's, a family-friendly chain with units throughout the western United States, a bakery near the entrance sold the restaurant's signature pies. The more upscale Cheesecake Factory, a nationwide casual-dining chain, likewise featured a glass case of cheesecakes.

The casual chains I visited in the bar-and-grill style—such as Applebee's, BJ's Restaurant & Brewhouse, and Claim Jumper—took a different approach to multi-use. They divided their interiors into zones of table dining and bar dining, so that the latter could profit from snackers, drinkers, or three-course eaters who, unlike other visitors, want to watch sports or enjoy a grown-ups-only environment.

Flexible menus work hard to make us feel that it's okay to commune in diversity. They make a variety of meal structures possible without showing favoritism toward any one. To do so, they have listings of "appetizers" and "desserts," and, in some cases, the option of multicourse deals. These suggest the possibility of course structure. But any bias in that direction is counterbalanced by course headings with plenty of atemporal categories. Flexible menus also typically list a wide span of beverage types—say, milkshakes, juices, wines, cocktails, and coffees—all at once. Simultaneous choices of drinks belonging to differing meal times and times in a meal make it easy to find the right lubricant to cover any lulls in the communal action.

Before visiting Ray's and Stark Bar at LACMA for a Saturday brunch, I noticed that the restaurant's menus for lunch, brunch, and dinner on the restaurant's website had slightly different nomenclature—for example, brunch had "Snacks and Sides," whereas lunch and dinner had "Bites"—but every menu could just as easily have been used for a complete shared-plates experience, a complete sequential meal, or simply for a good time with a snack and a drink. All had "Small Plates" and "Large Plates"—except brunch, which swapped "Small Plates" for "Brunch Plates" but kept "Large Plates"—to satisfy the inclination to share. At the same time, someone opting for courses could have started, in all cases, with a selection from "Garden," proceeded to "House Made Pasta," and moved on to "Large Plates." The same menu also made ordering just one dish of "House Made Pasta" or only one of the "Wood Fired Pizzas" just as plausible, as these lists of pasta and pizza were substantial sections of the menu.

The staff didn't advocate any particular dining arc, either. My server let me choose which of my two dishes I wanted brought to the table first.

At all-day diners or delis or at casual-dining chains, we likely find a similar menu structure. There are multiple pathways toward a meal. When Jamisin and I went to dinner at California Pizza Kitchen (CPK) in Glendale, I could have had a taco from the "Tacos and Sandwiches" list while he indulged in one of the signature "Pizzas," or we could have ordered two entrées and had a pizza to share (this we did). Alternatively, we could have shared a "Small Plate" as an appetizer or had an "Appetizer" as an appetizer—sharing or not. I could have eaten a large "Salad" while he put two "Small Plates" together. The salads came in "full" and "half" sizes, accommodating any plan. There was also a menu separate from the main menu, entitled *Be Adventurous*, which highlighted its own program of small plates and a wide range of drinks. The CPK menu was flexible in the extreme. Some foods or combinations on the menu looked perfect for a light and cold lunch, while others seemed better for a hearty and hot dinner. Still others made the place seem like the perfect after-work spot for cocktails and bar snacks.

Reports on trends in the casual-dining-chain restaurant segment, a fixture of industry press and research firms, have shown a movement toward flexible menus several decades long. Yet the past several years have brought a deluge of these reports. Trend-spotting outfits—such as the market-research and consulting firm Technomic, Inc., and the magazine *Nation's Restaurant News*—have revealed a ratcheting up of tactics to increase meal-structure flexibility. The last recession was one of the catalysts industry experts cite for speeding up the trend toward widening meal options.

Reporters have noticed a rise in offers of multicourse bundles at attractive discounts. At the same time, following gourmet fashion, the same restaurant segment dramatically increased its offerings of "small plates" along with other little dishes, such as "starters" and "sides." Lewis Lazare, who reported on a 2014 study by Technomic for the *Chicago*

Business Journal, quoted the company's executive vice president. Tellingly, Darren Tristano's statement stressed the dishes' flexibility: "These items can deliver add-on value or can be mixed and matched to function as a meal or a standalone snack."

Customers have responded in kind. The same report mentioned a Technomic survey of 1,000 casual-dining-chain consumers, which found that "38 percent of respondents ordered small plates as starters, while another 30 percent ordered them as the main part of their meal."

Casual-dining chains also have sought to widen their appeal during daytime hours traditionally less trafficked. Some have extended their opening hours to take advantage of late-night snacking and drinking. No longer were many units of BJ's and Applebee's closing at ten or eleven. According to Ron Ruggless, writing for *Nation's Restaurant News* in 2011, they began to stay open until midnight or 2:00 a.m.

Meanwhile, casual-dining chains promoted bar menus and drinks to boost the happy hours that precede the traditional dinnertime. Catching the beginning of the trend in 2012, James Scarpa reported in his *Nation's Restaurant News* article, "Building Momentum," that their advertisements had the desired effect of increasing high-margin orders during less-crowded times.

For restaurateurs, flexible menus have special powers. They make it possible for a restaurant to appeal to the broadest possible market for the restaurant's niche in price point and taste. Also, they're uniquely positioned to take advantage of impulse decisions to dine out. Savvy restaurateurs know that not all ventures to a restaurant are reserved or planned in advance.

This is what Daniel R. Scoggin—president and CEO of T.G.I. Friday's from approximately 1971 to 1986—told me about the history of Friday's, the first of the casual-dining chains in the bar-and-grill style. In the advent of new competition in the mid-1970s, he revamped the food menu. To do so, he explained that, among other considerations, "We looked at our business and noticed that the people who came to the restaurant did so as an impulse decision. They didn't wake up in the morning and plan to go to Friday's, but decided to go more or less spontaneously. We looked at that." That's one reason Scoggin fashioned a menu for broad appeal—a hallmark of casual-dining-chain menus to this day.

More than other kinds, restaurants with flexible menus can capture what Scoggin called the "veto vote," the industry term for that one person in a group who doesn't want what the others want. A group can be confident that such a restaurant has a meal plan to suit everyone.

All four types of menus thrive side by side today because they serve a diversity of restaurant-goer occasions, lifestyles, budgets, and tastes. Nevertheless, the relatively recent vintage of flexible and shared-plates menus—the former, in embryo in the mid-1970s; the latter, born in the mid-1980s—is noteworthy because it indicates that the interests they serve are fairly new. As a result, these menu structures may prove especially malleable in the near future. Any changes we see will likely stem from shifts in the conditions that prompted the menu formats' initial rise.

Flexible and shared-plates menus represent adaptations to recent societal trends, including nonstandard work hours—shifts that fall outside of typical daytime, Monday-through-Friday hours—a resurgence of snacking, and the rise of foodism.

The trend toward nonstandard work schedules began in the 1960s as a by-product of what social scientists call our evolution toward a "24-7 economy"—a confluence of growth in the service sector of the labor force and the globalization of business operations. If a significant percentage of people have been working nonstandard hours, they might have wanted to eat at nonstandard times. Clearly, restaurants with flexible menus stand to profit from work schedules that deviate from industrial-age norms. But that's not all. A parallel trend in people's eating habits compounds that advantage.

Snacking—eating in between main meals or eating small amounts at frequent intervals instead of big meals spaced out—has become increasingly frequent. Historians of meal patterns, such as Megan Elias and Abigail Carroll, point out that not eating three principal meals a day has actually been the norm for centuries. But Carroll, in *Three Squares: The Invention of the American Meal*, demonstrates that the recent surge in snacking is still striking because it deviates from a preceding interlude—in the United States, from the mid-nineteenth century to the 1950s—when snacking was frowned upon. A combination of developments since then—increasing nonstandard work schedules, more people eating alone or on the go in vehicles, food manufacturers developing and marketing ever more snack foods, and occasional claims that eating more small meals is better for your health than fewer big ones—encouraged snacking and resuscitated its reputation.

Consumer research has shown that snacking's recent ascendance is dramatic. A series of surveys of more than 5,000 adult Americans by the US Department of Agriculture revealed that, while 59 percent of respondents over 1977–78 reported snacking, 90 percent did over 2007–8—a jump of 31 percent in thirty years. A Technomic survey of 1,500 adults from 2014 gives more recent, if not directly comparable, data. It shows that 51 percent snacked at least twice a day, up from 48 percent in 2012.

A meaningful amount of this snacking happens in restaurants. A 2009 report by the market-research firm NPD, reported the same year by Fern Glazer in "Snack Occasions Grow Faster than Any Other Daypart," found that visits between main mealtimes accounted for 15 percent of all restaurant traffic. In a 2017 article entitled "Restaurants Rethink Menu Strategy as Snacking Spreads," Glazer documented the persistent impact of snacking on the restaurant industry. She conveyed the results of a 2016 survey by the same firm that found snacking at restaurants on the rise from the year before. For the year ending in September 2016, visits to restaurants in the hours between conventional mealtimes rose 3 percent while visits during lunch fell 2 percent, the growth in breakfast traffic shrank to 1 percent, and dinner visitation remained as it was.

The shared-plates menu, largely aimed at adventurous diners, exploits a different set of new social dynamics. Principle among them is the rise—starting in the mid-1970s in the United States—of the chef as a creative-class hero and business mogul. Some chefs' status as tastemakers and economic leaders gives them the authority to set restaurant terms in line with their own interests in culinary self-expression. The proliferation of small plates in the shared-plates menu genre testifies to this license.

Of course, chefs wouldn't have such entitlement without the parallel rise of foodism, gourmet consumerism that celebrates the creativity of chefs. Gastronomes define themselves by their adventuresome approach to dining and by putting dining at the center of social life. The shared-plates menu, which encourages trying a wide variety of dishes, is well suited to their consumption and socializing preferences.

The shared-plates menu also benefits from a central tenet of gourmet culture in more politicized form—the belief in the moral value of communal eating. The most vocal source of this ethic in gourmet culture is the slow-food movement, born of the late 1980s as a reaction against the alienation effects of modern industrialized society. According to it, taking time to break bread with family or friends is palliative.

As I've shown, however, the shared-plates menu is still working out an ideal agreement between restaurateur and diner. This fact indicates that gourmets aren't completely different from other restaurant goers. They too have appetites that can be frustrated by small plates, and they have the same individualistic tendencies as other contemporary consumers. Think about it this way: Would restaurateurs have to communicate the sharing rules of shared-plates menus so explicitly if food sharing were the default mode of their (gastronomic) customers?

CHAPTER 3

Assembly Lines and Conveyor Belts

AT NINE ON A SATURDAY NIGHT, JAMISIN AND I STOOD ON THE BUSY urban edge of UCLA in the dinner line at 800 Degrees Neapolitan Pizzeria.[†] Even at that hour, it snaked out the door, halfway down the block. People throng to this place for the customizable, locally sourced, gourmet-caliber pizza, and because it's fast.

The concept belongs to a growing industry segment called "fast casual." It combines the speed of service of the traditional quick-service restaurant (QSR), such as McDonald's and Burger King, with a level of food quality, supply-chain ethics, and personalized service formerly unknown in that segment.

At 800 Degrees, these came with a process: For first timers like us or those needing a reminder, paper menus lay waiting in the holder outside. Since the queue was long, we had a few minutes to peruse. It was a good idea to get ready. For, as soon as we entered, we were swept up into the single-file flow.

The line was a fast-paced, multisensory, and interactive version of the paper menu. Signboard lists attached to the wall at corresponding intervals, but they weren't as thrilling as what I saw through the glass partition we moved alongside: floury balls of dough in various phases

---

[†] In 2018, the restaurant rebranded as 800 Degrees Woodfired Kitchen.

of flattening, plots of pizza toppings, rows of salad staples, and then the red Ferrari of a prosciutto slicer standing with an eye-catching shine. Nor were they as entertaining as the cooks assembling orders behind the rainbow of ingredients.

As we went from station to station, we might have stuck with the orders we came in with. But the place was exciting, and we could change our minds if tempted by the daily special posted inside the entrance or inspired by new combinations we saw the cooks making.

We had to hurry. The menu was a tightly wound script for us and the staff to enact. Every action had a swift over-the-counter reaction. First, we chose the pizza base—margherita, bianca, marinara, or verde—and then the toppings. One cook prepared the base; the next added the toppings.

We dared not mess up the sequence. If we ordered both at the same time, we'd be promptly redirected by station number one. "The toppings come later," I overheard.

The 800°F oven cooked the pizzas in one minute. So, by the time we reached the cashier, the steward of the oven, who stood past the cashier at the end of the long, straight part of the line—beyond where it veered left into drinks and gelatos—was handing us our pizzas. They were as ready to eat as we were.

While in line, however, there was a hitch. A young woman in front of me was ordering a multitude of toppings and had just as many questions about them. One minute is an eternity in a line with such a swift, methodical pace, and the setback seemed like two. A ten-foot gap opened up in front of her. She seemed immune to the social pressure building up behind, the bodies bending behind me to get a better look at what was holding them up.

I was in research mode, so I found the holdup more enlightening than frustrating. Her refusal to get along by moving along reminded me of what the design of the line was supposed to make us forget: we were waiting. Of course, she made the wait longer. But, really, the whole experience prior to eating—the menu experience—was a form of waiting.

Customer waiting is a business bugaboo. A wait that's unpredictable and feels too long exposes our dependence on sellers. Sellers don't want us to notice the extent of our dependency. Certain types of menus tinker with the experience of waiting, making us think we're more in charge of what's happening than we are and thus keeping the peace. Some really do minimize wait time, but many just create the illusion.

The menu at 800 Degrees was typical of one fashioner of waiting I call the "assembly line." You find it at places where transaction speed is a priority. This includes fast casuals, cafeterias, and the drive-thru lanes at traditional QSRs. There are digital variants, too—online ordering systems for dine-in, takeout, and delivery (on websites and mobile apps) and the guest-facing tabletop tablets in so many casual-dining chains where quick table turns are the rule.

I've personally observed a variety of techniques for managing the experience of waiting.

Among the most important is to minimize the gaps in time and effort between all events of service. Cafeterias, fast casuals, and drive-thru lanes do this by stationing the ordering, paying for, and receiving food and drink into one taut physical line. Along it, the menu proper is physically inseparable from other parts.

Digital "lines" are just as tightly sequenced, but more complex. Take the case of Seamless, a third-party online ordering service that facilitates pickup and delivery from myriad member restaurants. Whitney Hess, the consulting user-experience strategist who directed the design team and masterminded the design process for the app I sampled, the first version of Seamless for iPad (launched in 2012), gave me insight into the mobile app's structure.

From interviews with then-current and likely Seamless users, Hess discerned what she called "personas," consumer profiles of value to the business. She also came up with "user case scenarios," ideal ways for people to interact with the app. The main ones were 1) I'm hungry now; feed me, and 2) I'm curious about what's on Seamless near me; I might be hungry an hour from now.

Within these basic scenarios, she mapped out variables. For example, under "I'm hungry now," there could be a number of possibilities, including 1) I want to re-order what I had last time, and 2) I want to pick up my food on my way home. She then inventoried the high-priority functions associated with these scenarios and charted an efficient series of screen "flows" to move them along. In a blog post about the design, Hess diagrammed the basic scheme as a decision tree.

From the consumer perspective, an effective digital ordering system won't appear as a physical assembly line or the decision tree that undergirds it, but it will shorten the time and motion between processes all the same. At the very least, one should be able to initiate any event by a clickable or tappable button from any screen. The app Hess strategized for Seamless did.

As do the digital tablets that angle up at you from weighted stands on the tabletops of casual-dining chains. Take the seven-inch Presto-brand device that Jamisin and I explored on a visit to the Azusa location of Applebee's. No matter what screen we were on and what stage of the meal we were in, we could tap the screen once to start an order for appetizers or for desserts. Accessing games for $1.49 each, donating to the charity the restaurant supports, signing up for the loyalty program, and paying for the meal were also each only one tap away.

Digital assembly lines have the added benefit of remembering user preferences and identifiers, which can reduce the wait even more. Third-party ordering services, such as Seamless and Caviar, as well as single-restaurant apps, such as Domino's, make the most of previous inputs. Once we, as registered users, sign in, they give us the chance to repeat a past order without going through the process again. By storing our addresses and credit cards, they also speed up checkout.

In April 2016, Domino's took easy ordering to an extreme. It introduced a Zero Click app that requires only opening the app to send a saved favorite order. It gives you ten seconds to opt out before automatically submitting it. Clearly, this was geared to the most habitual users.

For digital assembly lines to work as efficiently as possible, they must also have intuitive interfaces. Hess stressed the importance of conforming to user expectations, including the habits of interaction for a particular device. The iPad, for example, has conventions of usage distinct from a Samsung smartphone. If one designs against that grain—say, by positioning a back button in an unusual place or not allowing a swipe gesture when that's normal for the device—potential customers might get frustrated at having to learn new rules, equate that time and effort with loss of control, and abandon queue.

For user-interface, user-experience (UI/UX) designers, conforming interfaces to user expectations is basic. In the primer *UX 101*, Joseph Dickerson extends this principle to all kinds of controls—tap, gesture, and voice. The design for each means of interaction involves special considerations, but any designer will tell you that all should be user intuitive. Interfaces should also be forgiving. They should adapt to minor mistakes by offering corrections and accepting incomplete information.

I found most of the interfaces I explored for this book intuitive and forgiving, with one exception that proved the psychological importance of the rule. A few months after Domino's introduced "Dom"—the voice-ordering feature added to the mobile app for iPhone in October 2014—I decided to test how intuitive and adaptable he was. Or, rather, Jamisin would do it while I held the camera and recorded.

Thankfully, voice ordering was an optional feature, because Dom was pretty dumb. Ordering from him went badly from the start:

> **Dom:** "Would you like to order your easy order, a recent order, or would you be placing a new order today?"
> **Jamisin:** "New order today."
> **D:** "Sounds good. Would you like delivery or carryout?"
> **J:** "Delivery."
> **D:** "I'm afraid I can't figure this one out. Would you mind tapping your selection?"

Maybe his hearing wasn't so good. Jamisin spoke loudly and clearly enough.

As the ordering continued, we discovered also that Dom's vocabulary was severely limited. Because voice-controlled interfaces are anthropomorphic, I expect them to be adaptable to common variations in speech. Dom, however, had little range. Here's an example of the sort of exchange that happened a few different ways during our session: After finally finding success in selecting an item, Dom asked, "What's the next item you'd like?" Jamisin fished to see if Dom could handle a general proposition. "Something to drink," he tried. But, alas:

> **D:** "I'm sorry. I don't quite understand. Would you try again?"
> **J:** "I'm thirsty." [This was, perhaps, gratuitous.]

> **D:** "Sorry. I'm still having trouble. Try again or ask me for help."
>
> **J:** "Help. Help."
>
> **D:** "Here's some help for you. Take your time. What's the next item you'd like?"

At this point, a sort of user's manual came on screen. Apparently, Dom needed to hear specific words or phrases:

> Tell Dom what you'd like to order.
> Say the name of a specific item or a menu category:
> "A large pizza with pepperoni and onions"
> "14 pieces of barbecue chicken wings"
> "Desserts"
> Or you can also say:
> "Coupons"
> "Menu"
> "Checkout"
> Tip: To edit or remove an item please tap it.

To interact smoothly and quickly, I would have needed a crib sheet or to memorize the list of acceptable terms. And patience. Six months later, we tried ordering from Dom again to see if he'd evolved. In this respect, he hadn't changed a bit.

For UI/UX design, constant iteration is normal. In fact, Domino's iterates or replaces with more resources and dedication than most restaurants. At this writing, Domino's devotes a department of over 200 employees, one-third of its headquarters workforce, to making the brand stand out as much, if not more, for pioneering tech as for food.

Seeing the future, Domino's stopped outsourcing its digital development in 2010. The choice to do all of it in-house has paid off. Journalists reporting on the company's rapid rate of invention since then—to enable ordering not just by desktop, phone, and tablet but also by smart watch, by Twitter, inside a Ford car, and through Samsung's Smart TV, to name a few channels—are challenged to keep up. To create a world in which no place lacks access to Domino's, what are a few glitches along the way?

No doubt, the prototype for the physical and virtual ordering systems I've discussed—the ones that work—is Henry Ford's automobile assembly line. To design it, Ford applied the chief tenet of Frederick W. Taylor's turn-of-the-twentieth-century theory of scientific management, the bedrock of operations management: to be efficient, eliminate unnecessary steps.

Since their beginnings in the 1920s, fast-food operations have used Ford's model for turning out food, but with one important difference. They've given consumers a role on the line.

Today, all restaurants with assembly-line menus merge the functions of ordering, prepping, cooking, paying for, and picking up food. The zipper-like integration of producer and consumer roles not only reduces time and motion toward services and sales. It also plans each action by one party to take approximately the same time as the next action by the other. At 800 Degrees, putting toppings on my pizza took about as long as deciding on a salad. Paying the cashier gave the pizza a minute to cook.

As sociologist George Ritzer suggests in *The McDonaldization of Society*, a landmark cultural study about limited service, having us do for ourselves what employees would otherwise do for us is a clever way for operators to save themselves time and money. I would add that our active role lessens the strain of waiting. By taking action, we feel less dependent.

Attesting to this in industry reports, corporate heads at Applebee's and the fast-casual chain Panera identified waiting for the check as the number-one customer "pain point" they hoped installing tabletop tablets would alleviate. Apparently, where speed of service is desirable, not having to wait is more important than being waited on.

Over decades of studying service situations—including banks, clinics, supermarkets, and restaurants—social scientists specializing in the psychology of waiting, the science of marketing, and a special area of operations management called "queue theory" confirmed the correlation between customer satisfaction and the active involvement of customers who have to wait in lines. They put forward a set of principles that covers this case.

In an often-cited paper from 1985 entitled "The Psychology of Waiting Lines," David H. Maister was among the earliest to articulate them. Of the eight conclusions he drew about perceptions of waiting, three apply well to the case of restaurant menus. The first, "Unoccupied time feels longer than occupied time," relates to customers helping themselves or "coproducing" a customized item; for, to be "occupied" can mean to be doing something. Yet the word *occupied* also signifies the more passive state of being diverted, such as by entertainment or menu information. The line at 800 Degrees occupied us in both senses.

The other two maxims—"Uncertain waits are longer than certain waits" and "Unexplained waits seem longer than explained waits"— refer to the power that knowledge about the length of the wait has on perceptions of it. At 800 Degrees, the visibility of ingredients and their assembly didn't just disguise the wait as entertainment. It let us monitor progress.

Another frequently cited article, from 1991, examined all three principles in a real-world experiment with bank lines. The authors made a succinct prescription that combined the ideas: "Entertain, enlighten, and engage." They meant that, if a customer is distracted from or informed about the length of a wait, even a longer wait may seem shorter than one that's objectively shorter. While admitting the influence of cultural background, individual personality, and situational assessments of opportunity cost on perceptions of waiting—not to mention the subjective and plastic nature of everyone's experience of time—and allowing that management is never in total control of our responses, social scientists have continued to build upon this theory.

One outcome of their efforts is the realization that, as we wait, it matters what we learn about our wait. Most of all, we want evidence that we're advancing toward our goal and that employees are doing what they can to help. As long as we see them preparing our order, we're not just distracted from the wait; we can forgive it. Perhaps being privy to the process pleases us also because it makes us feel we control it.

Based on their insight, social scientists have explicitly recommended that organizations design their "servicescapes" to hide employees who don't assist customers and to prominently display those who do. One study of customer experiences of websites in *Management Science*, entitled "The Labor Illusion: How Operational Transparency Increases Perceived Value," formulated a parallel to this advice for digital environments. The authors found that people prefer shopping sites with longer waits to those with instant results as long as the lagging sites signaled that the business was making an effort. They advocated websites to communicate that employees are working on customer requests.

A 2017 study of perceived waiting time and satisfaction on a simulated online travel site found "exaggeration"—overestimating a wait time and then providing results sooner than projected—to be one example of a labor illusion that worked brilliantly to reduce perceived waiting time and enhance customer satisfaction. Of course, an infinite variety of labor illusions may work, as many as there are ways to design the variables of queue flow, queue architecture, and provision of information.

From my own experiences of assembly-line menus, online and off, I vouch for the labor illusion's charm. I see, for example, why Pizza Tracker, the trademarked feature on all Domino's online ordering platforms, has been such a powerful influence in the field of mobile ordering. Pizza Tracker is a graphic we can watch immediately after submitting an order—an extension of the menu's assembly line. It's a fat blue line divided into five numbered pieces representing phases of employee action. They each pulsate in red for as long as Domino's, we suppose, is doing the indicated task. After we close the pop-up message saying, "Your order has been placed," Pizza Tracker keeps us apprised.

The first moment is particularly ingenious. Pizza Tracker makes an instant graphic leap from section one to section two. Clearly, section one has no function except to be skipped over—purely psychological. The red begins pulsating at section two.

What happens next is also clever. As soon as a section goes red, a reassuring phrase appears. Set in all caps and punctuated with an exclamation point, a textual display of extra effort: "WE'RE FIRING IT UP!" After a few minutes, the message changes to "YOUR ORDER IS IN THE OVEN!" A sucker for the tracker, I was excited to see the chipper "QUALITY CHECK COMPLETE!" and, finally, "WE'RE ON THE WAY!" Bravo, Domino's! You filled my horror vacui between order and delivery.

Well, not entirely. There was still a dreadful void between "WE'RE ON THE WAY!" and our pizza's actual arrival. Luckily, I found another app to fill it. Caviar, a third-party service specializing in delivery from a select group of restaurants, kept a GPS tracker on its drivers. Every time I tried out the service, I watched it on my iPhone like a rat in a lab experiment. I constantly refreshed the screen to follow the orange symbol representing the Caviar driver until she approached my block on the map. Finally seeing the driver made me happy in a way I'm convinced I wouldn't have been had I not known where she was at all times.

For showing effort in a physical line, the drive-thru lane at In-N-Out Burger in Hollywood, at the corner of Sunset Boulevard and Orange Avenue, deserves special praise. If left unattended, the cars that queued up the day I pulled into the long driveway might have taken (heaven forbid!) a few minutes to reach the menu stand and speaker for ordering. But employees relieved customers of this uneventful stretch. There were two working the lane, approaching cars at intervals well before the menu stand. They carried portable tablets for tapping in orders and driver-facing menu boards that hung from them. This service occupied me for a part of the line during which I was trapped and gave me the impression that In-N-Out was doing its best.

The service at the In-N-Out drive-thru not only altered my perception of waiting. It likely lessened my actual wait. The spacing out of order inputs that the driveway attendants did probably preempted a bottleneck in the kitchen that would have jammed up the cars. I think their work compensated for bad lane design. This In-N-Out had its menu stand and speaker far too close to the pickup window.

Clearly, assembly-line menus do a lot to affect our experience of waiting. But that isn't their only rhetorical ploy. They can also structure the wait to sell us more stuff.

If we have to follow a scripted sequence—because we're stuck in a physical line or navigating a virtual trail of screens—we're a captive audience for advertisements. For example, by having to stop at the salad station at 800 Degrees, I was more likely than otherwise to consider a salad. Likewise, if my normal tendency is to overlook the french fries on a Burger King menu, the drive-thru lane at the location on Sunset and La Brea in Hollywood did its best to compel me to think about the "Satisfries" they were promoting at the time I passed through. A poster for the product showing a giant close-up image and claims of health benefits got plenty of my attention while I stalled behind another car.

Something similar occurred while Jamisin and I were at Applebee's in Azusa. Our tabletop tablet took advantage of our seated position. It pushed us ads for appetizers, desserts, and games—a perpetual rotation of food porn and trivia questions—throughout our stay. I can only imagine the pressure on parents to keep kids occupied by buying games. Applebee's surely knows that young children especially get restless when forced to sit through a meal with adults.

I experienced a more complex version of this captive-audience scheme when exploring the Taco Bell mobile ordering app on my iPhone. With every tap of a menu item, a screen popped up that tried to upsell or cross-sell. To see what would happen, I tapped the "Doritos® Cheesy Gordita Crunch" button. The screen that followed suggested I "Make It Supreme." Another button promoted "add-ons." I pressed it. Up came a list of additional ingredients, such as cheese and sour cream, which I could pile on for extra charges ranging from 35 to 60 cents each. The Taco Bell app was relentless. It suggested additional items once again at checkout.

These upselling, cross-selling, and ad-pushing tactics have proven successful. An industry report from February 2015 disclosed a statement from Taco Bell that the bills on its app averaged 20 percent higher than orders at stores. The company attributed the overage specifically to people adding on ingredients. The author of the report insightfully noted that, on in-store menu boards, the extras can get crowded out of view. But on the app, where options appear sequentially and with pictures at a noticeable scale, the offers have more impact.

Pushy tabletop tablets have had similar success. One senior vice president for the casual-dining chain Chili's told a reporter that, before adopting its Ziosk system, the restaurant tested the effectiveness of showing people ads for food items on the tabletop tablets as they dined. Chili's found that sales from desserts featured this way increased by almost 20 percent.

A study of similar tablets at forty-five outlets of a full-service casual dining chain in Southern California (the name undisclosed) likewise showed their check-raising power. After an examination of point-of-sale (POS) data from all of January 2016, researchers found that the average check at tables not using tablets was $39.56. The average among tables ordering their entrées via tablet, however, was $46.86.

The profitability of tablets increases exponentially when we factor in the devices' ability to speed up table turns and offer the opportunity for savings on labor. In a related study by the same researchers involving one unit of the same restaurant chain before and after it adopted tablets, both occurred. The investigators observed that the time guests spent occupying a table was 17 percent less when they used tablets for payment only and 31 percent less when they used them for ordering as well. Meanwhile, servers spent 36 percent less time tending to tables using the device just for payment and a remarkable 65 percent less time on tables using it also for ordering.

In how they affect profitability, physical and virtual assembly-line menus do have differences. For instance, only with people behind us in a physical line can there be social pressure to keep up the pace, an aid to the restaurant's volume of sales. As the woman in front of me at 800 Degrees showed, however, not everyone is so susceptible.

Tablets and mobile apps can use social pressure to increase revenue, but through the tipping process instead. By including a default suggestion at checkout, these systems regularly nudge us to tip on their market's high side. Our Applebee's tablet recommended 20 percent. In a 2014 *Bloomberg Business* article, "The Waiter's Role Changes as Restaurants Encourage Ordering via App," Vanessa Wong reported that restaurateurs using tablets—including Applebee's, Chili's, and the casual-dining chain BJ's—admitted to her that suggestive tipping works. I've yet to see reliable data showing how often and how much the practice increases gratuities.

Restaurateurs using digital ordering devices have one more advantage in the profitability game. They can use the rich data and analytics available with many digital systems to prevent losses and find sales opportunities. Knowledge of inventory trends can guard against over-buying and running out of popular items—small sources of lost revenue that may bankrupt a place over time. Information about customer traffic can help refine staffing schedules. Server scoring that shows who sells how much of what can identify staff training needs or inspire performance incentives. Meanwhile, evidence of how we navigate their digital menus can help operators refine the menu designs. Among other things, that means ameliorating our impressions of the wait.

Online ordering apps have the distinct advantage of pacing their lines to the restaurant's benefit without appearing unserviceable. To avoid overwhelming the kitchen during peak traffic hours, a digital service can specify pickup or delivery times that spread the stress of increased traffic over times less busy for the staff. Meanwhile, because they need not stand in a physical line, customers retrieving food by appointment may feel privileged to bypass one. If choosing delivery instead, app-using customers—in keeping with Maister's maxim regarding "explained time"—may feel less anxious about their wait while the restaurant gains from their additional business.

When full-service restaurants offer mobile apps, even meals eaten in house can beef up sales while allowing the restaurant to pace its work. In June 2014, BJ's launched such an app. Customers could order before arriving at the restaurant and pay as soon as they were ready.

These benefits to the customer present an operational challenge to restaurants. Orders by app might overwhelm the kitchen or cause food to be prepared too far in advance. BJ's forestalls these problems by firing up an order only when the party who placed it via app sits down. By carefully pacing digital orders, BJ's shaves satisfying minutes off the wait for diners while maximizing its per-table yield.

I would be remiss if I didn't tell you, before leaving the topic of menus that tailor waiting, about another discovery I made in my fieldwork: the assembly line's structurally inverse twin. I'll call this menu type the "conveyor belt" because, instead of us moving along a line to choose food and drink, the conveyor belt circulates the options throughout a dining room to us.

I've seen literal conveyor belts used in restaurants for this purpose in self-serve sushi places—my old hangout A'Float Sushi in Pasadena comes to mind—where popular plated items pass in a loop like airport baggage in front of counter-seated guests. But there are less literal forms, too, such as cart service in dim sum restaurants and roving gauchos with meats for tableside carving at Brazilian *churrascarias*.

Since customers in these situations remain stationary, and because one finds these menus mostly at full-service restaurants (self-serve sushi the exception), conveyor-belt menus may seem unrelated to the assembly-line variety. But, as with assembly-line menus, waiting—and the effort to disguise or minimize waiting—undergirds all conveyor-belt menus.

The chief challenge they must overcome, however, is unique. Conveyor-belt menus must manage the discrepancies that arise between the illusion they create—that we don't have to wait long to satisfy our appetites; after all, carts with food abound—and the reality of the situation—that we get our hearts set on just a few items and can't predict when they'll come our way.

Nevertheless, conveyor-belt menus share some of the assembly line's devices for managing the waiting-related stresses that this discrepancy creates. Prescriptions to "entertain" and to "engage," for example, apply as much to conveyor belts as to assembly lines. In my outings to restaurants, I noticed a range of devices that fulfilled these functions.

The Brazilian *churrascaria* chain Fogo de Chão attempted to bolster our sense of control over the wait by engaging us in an active role. Like every other table, ours came with a green disk that said, "Yes, Please!" and a red one with, "No, Thanks!" If we put the green disk facing up on the table, gauchos knew to come by. If we displayed the red disk, they passed us by. The disk system was supposed to give us a sense of command, even though we weren't in charge of when or how often the gauchos approached. The restaurant's provision of an all-you-can-eat salad bar offered another sense of agency, a way for us to help—and thus "occupy"—ourselves.

Everyone who goes to Fogo de Chão, however, knows that the main attraction is the meat; and, over its rotations, the restaurant keeps control.

It's difficult for conveyor-belt menus to strike a balance between circulating a dish seldom enough to keep it in demand—or, in all-you-can-eat situations, from depletion—and frustrating us by too-sparse offers of what we want. For me, Fogo de Chão lost that balance. The kind of meat I preferred came by our table so infrequently that the restaurant's promise of "all you can eat" seemed more like "all it will offer whether I want it or not." The restaurant's website and the brochure the host gave us after leading us to our table represented thirteen varieties of meat. Throughout our meal, I counted a total of eight in circulation, and noted that just seven came to our table. After sampling a bit of each, I realized I craved only one.

Because I constantly scanned the room in the vain hope of signaling the gaucho with the desired selection, the meal irritated me. And because I kept one eye on the gauchos at all times, I too often felt neglectful of my companion. The gauchos, meanwhile, maintained schedules I couldn't predict. In the end, I reckoned that, for the set price of $58.50, I would have rather had one dish with a substantial portion of the meat I wanted and be able to remain sociable and calm.

My friend Chari told me that, when she dined at Fogo de Chão, she called a server over and requested the meats she wanted to come to her. We should have such gumption. But I doubt the owners want requests like hers to become the norm. If they did, they would design a different kind of menu.

I suspected that the set-price, all-you-can-eat structure of the menu was part of my problem with the format. It's a disincentive for the house to circulate gauchos at a faster pace or to have them cut more gratifying portions when they arrive. Other restaurants with conveyor-belt menus stand to gain from the chance I overorder. I did find that the ones I visited were more forthcoming.

In keeping with social scientists' advice to entertain and engage waiting customers, a key device of most conveyor-belt menus is to create a stimulating environment. The one at NBC Seafood Restaurant, where Jamisin and I went for dim sum with friends as a party of five, succeeded in this respect. The place was positively hectic. NBC Seafood is a popular, highly regarded restaurant for dim sum. As the first place to serve it in the San Gabriel Valley, it's also an institution. The restaurant was so crowded on the Sunday afternoon we visited that we waited for an hour for our number to come up on the electronic screen. Meanwhile, the dining room was the size of a banquet hall.

Filling it were carts hawking all manner of dishes, from pastries to pigs' feet. I counted fourteen unique carts in circulation and duplicates enough to cause traffic jams two carts deep between the large round tables. The carts moved quickly. As soon as we were seated, we began accumulating plates.

Clearly, at NBC Seafood, business meant busyness. The constant action also mitigated some of the ennui that might have otherwise overwhelmed the experience of waiting for the carts we wanted most.

In recent years, a spate of gourmet restaurants, beginning with State Bird Provisions in San Francisco, adopted the traditional cart service of Chinese dim sum restaurants to serve decidedly nontraditional, ethnically eclectic fare. In my restaurant sample, The Church Key was a notable example.

In keeping with its famously splashy surroundings on the Sunset

Strip, where the line between restaurant and nightclub has blurred for decades, The Church Key went well beyond the dim sum restaurant's usual means of creating an entertaining and engaging environment. When we dined there, cart service was circus-like. In addition to carts with food, some proffered cocktails and a show. At one, a server stirred up clouds of liquid nitrogen as she whipped up campy retro drinks— the Lemon Drop, the Appletini, the Sex on the Beach—in the surprising form of freeze pops. As part of the performance, we were supposed to suck them through the plastic sleeve. Did I mention that one of the cocktail carts was a repurposed vintage Pan Am Airlines drink cart and that the server who worked it donned the authentic Pan Am uniform?

The phasing of offerings on carts also kept things lively. They changed not only daily but also over the course of a single evening. Despite our three-hour stay, we didn't exhaust the possibilities. We left, in fact, before the canned cocktails for which the place is notorious began its rounds. To open these drinks, I'd read, the servers gave you a tool called a church key. It was a nod to the pre-1960s way of opening a can before the pull tab. As we settled our check, I asked our server about the canned-cocktail cart. She said it had yet to make an entrance.

Although cart service was the main event at the restaurant, the setting contributed much to its sensory hype. The sprawling space prevented monotony with multiple decorative zones and something new to look at on every surface. There were mismatched stools at the bar and plates of differing color on the tables. Oversized chandeliers grandly tied the jumble together, as did the interior's central point of focus: a metal tower of dramatically lit bottles and glasses reaching from inside a surrounding bar to a high ceiling. All the while, a soundtrack of electronica pulsed just under danceable volume.

Although conveyor-belt menus entertain and engage in ways comparable to assembly-line menus, they differ when it comes to the social scientists' prescription to "enlighten." Their design can uniquely benefit from the minor discomfort of our never knowing when we'll get what we want. Because the conveyor-belt menu keeps us passive, dependent on servers to come to us on their schedule, we're likely to assume that the things we want are hard to get and that we better stock up on them when we have a chance. What if the server with the item we're pining for doesn't return, or does so seldomly that we blink and miss her? The conveyor-belt menu can manipulate our fear of missing out, tempting us to order more.

I liken this tactic to what social scientists call "scarcity messages." These are promotional signals by marketers that an offer is in limited quantity or for a limited time. Since the late 1970s, researchers have studied such promotions and noted that, when issued just prior to stated deadlines, they dramatically increase sales. Scholars argue that scarcity messages induce our urgency to buy by triggering feelings of "anticipatory regret" as we imagine the aftermath of not buying. One study in a grocery store further found that, when people thought an item would soon be unavailable, they bought more of that item than people unaware of such restriction.

Although the study wasn't in a restaurant, let alone in one with a conveyor-belt menu, I find it applicable. Even at NBC Seafood, which had an abundance of carts, I felt that the dishes we most wanted constantly eluded us. This made me a bit frantic, and inclined to order an extra helping when the opportunity arose. In the end, we selected twenty-two dishes, even though only thirteen unique carts came to our table. I assure you that a few of our dishes were duplicates.

Some scholars have suggested that limited-quantity messages are more persuasive than limited-time. But, for conveyor-belt menus, this doesn't matter. Since the impression they give of limited quantity is predicated on our assumption of a limited offering time, these menus create the conditions of both.

Assembly-line menus can issue scarcity messages as well. They can announce or display evidence of an item's limited availability along the line. But how they do so isn't fundamentally different from an advertisement by other means, whether via store window or text message. Conveyor-belt menus, on the other hand, can play hard to get just by the special way they make us wait.

PART II

SELLING ITEMS

CHAPTER 4

The Right Amount of Choice

HALFWAY DOWN A DIM SIDE STREET IN LA'S KOREATOWN SITS HANBAT Shul-Lung Tang. With a front entrance befitting a back alley, the restaurant looks undistinguished. In fact, it's remarkable—a triumph of radical simplicity.

In purely utilitarian digs, a plain box of bare blond tables and black chairs, this establishment serves little other than a comforting beef soup. It has since 1988. The menu is so short I can list all the contents without straining this paragraph:

Shul-Lung-Tang (Beef Soup) $8.72
Mixed
Brisket
Flank
Intestine, Tripe & Spleen

Soo-Yook (Boiled Beef) $17.44
Mixed
Flank
Intestine, Tripe & Spleen

Hanbat Shul-Lung Tang is beloved. The last time I checked, in April 2018, 1,756 Yelp reviewers gave it an average rating of four and a half out of five stars. If longevity and low overhead are also clues, the place is self-sustaining, if not lucrative. Considering the restaurant's short menu and long life, I wonder if it would be just as successful if it offered even one more item or one fewer.

No expert I read or spoke to denied that menu size is consequential—with good reason. If a list feels too long, we're daunted by the thought of reading the whole thing, then merely scan and miss things. Or, we seek out only what's familiar. There's a limit to the time we'll spend before hunger or a tight schedule hastens our pace or we no longer want to push other people's patience.

It's also safe to say that menu variety makes a difference. It affects whether the restaurant sells us anything. A menu without sufficient span won't lure a group with divergent desires—including the proverbial veto vote who wants fish when everyone else craves steak. Nor will it tempt a repeat customer with a case of monotony coming on.

It's easy to see that menu length and breadth matters to customers. But, let the case of Hanbat Shul-Lung Tang caution us: it's tricky to pinpoint what, exactly, is the right amount of choice. A 2013 article entitled "Menu Choice: Satisfaction or Overload?" in the *Journal of Culinary Science & Technology* demonstrated this well. The authors tested the "choice overload hypothesis" of psychologists and economists—the idea that there's a range of choice at which satisfaction with decision-making is greatest—on perceptions of restaurant menus.

After studying examples and consulting with chefs, they drafted two series of menus: one in the style of a fast-food restaurant; the other, fine dining. They approached members of the public, most of them parents and their college-age kids at a university open house, as they dined in the school cafeteria. On a nine-point scale, 202 participants for the fine-dining condition and 241 for the fast food rated the menus as having too little, just enough, or too much choice.

While no meaningful differences by sex or age emerged, the responses starkly split on the basis of restaurant genre. In the fast-food scenario, subjects thought the optimal number of dishes for all parts of the menu was six. But, in the fine dining, that number differed and depended on the menu section. People most wanted a list of between seven and eight appetizers and desserts and ten entrées.

The experiment showed that satisfaction with choice depends on restaurant genre. But I don't think we should see the number of choices respondents preferred as universal or absolute. The authors themselves pointed out key limitations of their study, including the singular cultural context (the United Kingdom) and that subjects might not have been typical consumers of the kinds of menus they assessed. Even more compelling: people might have simply picked numbers in the middle of the range. If they'd seen one hundred fine-dining entrées instead of fifteen, they might have said fifty was best instead of ten.

I'll qualify the influence of genre further: what seems appropriate by restaurant specialty or style can change. Sirio Maccioni, the New York City restaurateur and maître d' who rose to fame as impresario of his fine-dining restaurant Le Cirque, boasted in his 2004 autobiography that, in 1974, he kept at least fifty-five items plus specials on the Le Cirque menu. He was proud, too, that his kitchen could meet guests' extra demands.

Maccioni was the last gasp of the standard that a great fine-dining restaurant should encompass many tastes and satisfy diners' whims. Today, comparable establishments get more respect for representing the style of the chef. Due to a transformation of gourmet culture since the mid-1970s, at least in the United States, today's fine diner willingly defers.

This gives restaurateurs of the genre the opportunity to make their operations—famously high in labor and food expenses—more cost-effective by limiting the menu.

Now it's common to find well-regarded fine-dining menus with less than half of Maccioni's ideal, or in cases of the set-price dégustations I discuss in chapter 1, with no food choice at all. Luckily for the restaurateurs, the shorter menus have positive connotations. They signify chef authenticity, expertise, and focus.

By way of fashion, then, genre molds our view of choice. But it's not the only force. Consider the local restaurant landscape. How much diversity is there in our midst? If we have a plurality of dining-out options, a place with a limited menu may feel less restrictive than it would in a town with slimmer pickings.

Hanbat Shul-Lung Tang benefits from an extremely varied field. In Koreatown alone, there's every sort of Korean restaurant, and, in LA as a whole, the ethnic and stylistic variety is second to no city. Unless brought there unaware or against her will, no one who enters the place is disappointed that all she can order is boiled beef or beef soup.

Furthermore, doesn't our assessment of the size and range of a menu also hinge on its contents? Are they familiar? A long menu with more items we recognize will make choosing less stressful than a same-size menu with a novel list. Former *New York Times* restaurant critic Frank Bruni put it best in his 2005 review "Read 'Em and Weep," a sweeping critique of "the sprawling menu problem" he then found at a crop of trendy Manhattan restaurants: "Expansive, elaborately segmented menus are hardly new. Many traditional brasseries have long had them. But then those restaurants present carbon-copy compendiums of familiar dishes, reducing the possibility of confusion."

In 2014, taking aim at a related trend of gourmet menus, *Washington Post* critic Tom Sietsema sharpened the point in his article "Menu Confusion: Plates of All Sizes in Quirky Categories Befuddle Hungry Diners." He recounted how ingenious headings—such as "Foraged" and "Coast & Plains," which befuddled him in one case; and "Nibble," "Chomp," and "Feed," which perplexed him in another—drove him to servers for explanation. Justifiably, Sietsema gave his equally "frustrated" dining companion this last word: "If you have to explain how the menu works, perhaps the menu isn't working."

As an art historian who has long taught students of communication design, I know that, if a menu is overwhelming or confusing, the layout might also be to blame. How easy is it to find what we're looking for, or to notice something that distinguishes the restaurant? Are graphics and language legible? Are items of the same category grouped together? Are distinctions among sections clear? If designers don't address these matters, particularly in long menus, the likelihood of confusion increases.

Design solutions to the problem of information hierarchy abound. On a visit to the Sherman Oaks outpost of the casual-dining chain Marie Callender's, I was struck by the use of labeled tabs to separate parts of the menu, which amounted to a spiral-bound book. The tabs made navigating the long list easy.

To keep people turning the twelve pages of the Dave & Buster's menu, designer Shannon Phillips worked with the gaming-and-dining chain to devise a smart solution. She kept the textual descriptions of dishes

toward the vertical central fold of the pages and David Chasey's alluring food photography near the edge. I agree with Phillips that this pulls
diners' eyes in the direction of the next page, prompting a page turn. To
prevent the scheme from getting dull, she varied the number and size
of images.

In print alone there are countless ways to lessen confusion and hold
interest. The possibilities expand with interactive mediums. For example, using touch-screen tablets to show only one part of a menu at a time
can stop us from feeling overwhelmed. The sections of a large menu can
be advertised enticingly—and succinctly—on an introductory screen.
We can then tap through to the parts that interest us.

Some research has shown that clarity, aesthetic appeal, and hierarchy
can strengthen a long menu's sales. Several years ago, the parent company of the International House of Pancakes (IHOP) chain saw checks
slipping. In response, it conducted extensive research on, among other
things, the menu. Using eye-tracking technology to test variations in
the display of the same items, they found not just that the selection was
too big but also that people didn't notice the menu's breadth. It had as
wide a selection of burritos and burgers as pancakes and waffles, but
people weren't buying from the former.

Therefore, in 2012, the company overhauled the menu's design. While
it decreased the number of items somewhat, from 200 to 170, it made far
more dramatic changes to their presentation. Designers gave pictures the
advantage over text, used color-coding to draw attention to the company's priorities, and created a clear grouping system—separate pages for
pancakes and for burgers—to make it easier to notice the menu's scope.

In early 2014, the company declared a 3.6 percent rise in sales. Tellingly, diners were buying the very dishes they hadn't noticed before.
Since the menu remained, by the standards of most genres, large, it's
unlikely that the new appeal of old items was due solely to the menu's
reduction. Rather, the change in design led people to process the large
number of choices differently, and in a way that better attuned them to
the menu's variety.

A 2017 study by hospitality-management scholars Eunjin Kwon
and Anna Mattila helps explain the psychological dynamics at work.
Through a survey of 166 US adults recruited from an online consumer
panel, they tested how much variety subjects perceived on the same

assortment of twenty teas on a menu in differing labeling schemes and page layouts. The labeling of the tea categories and the layouts of the twenty items influenced how much variety respondents perceived. When the teas were divided by attribute (black tea, green tea, etc.), subjects sensed greater variety than when they were organized by benefit (energy boosting, stress relief, etc.). And yet, when the menu in either labeling style was displayed on four digital pages, subjects perceived greater variety than when presented on one digital page. Meanwhile, in the four-page layout, the difference between the two labeling schemes on perceptions of variety went away.

The authors interpreted the findings in compelling ways. First, they suggested that, when many items appear all at once, as on a single page, we feel overwhelmed and mentally organize the multiplicity into a more unified whole ("gestalt" processing). This tendency makes items seem similar. They then reasoned that a benefit-based labeling scheme likewise enhances the sense of unity because we don't readily break down benefit-based labels (as opposed to attribute-based) into further subcategories in our minds. That's because attribute-based categories, such as "black tea," have more universally recognized subcategories, including country of origin (China, India) or tea type (Lapsang souchong, Kangra). But benefit-based labels, such as "stress-relief," are more ambiguous and subjective. The authors' findings show that the layout of long lists and their labeling impact our estimations of variety—and, by extension, sufficient choice.

Extrapolating carefully from the research of consumer psychologists, I also suppose that our notions of enough menu choice depend on individual personality. Studies of consumer variety seeking have long established that individuals have differing optimal stimulation levels (OSL)—preferred degrees of environmental arousal. When stimuli dip below our OSLs, the reasoning goes, we'll try to restore it by pursuing novelty or variety.

Although the theory of OSL has yet to be tested with restaurant menus, it has been examined in other contexts of consumption that apply. The work of hospitality-management scholars Jooyeon Ha and SooCheong Jang, who've looked at the variety-seeking intentions of restaurant patrons, is especially relevant.

In a 2013 survey of US subjects, Ha and Jang found that differences in

OSL affected variety seeking so strongly that it modified other motives, such as how frequently or recently a person visited a site of consumption, how satisfied she was with the last experience, and what values—eating for enjoyment or for a practical purpose, such as nutrition—she hoped to get out of a purchase. Controlling for all of these factors, the investigators found that people with high OSL were far more likely to seek novelty or variety in their next restaurant if their satisfaction from the last was low and they were strongly motivated by hedonic or practical values. But those factors had almost no effect on variety-seeking intentions in people with low OSL.

Other scientists have shown that, in addition to individual OSL, factors such as age, risk-taking inclinations, customer loyalty, gender, and education also impact novelty seeking in dining out. Confirming the obvious, they've demonstrated that loyal customers and the more risk-averse have less interest in trying new restaurants. They've also concluded that men (versus women), nonseniors (versus seniors), and the less educated are similarly disinclined.

Two years later, Ha and Jang elaborated on their earlier study on the basis of a new survey, which showed that boredom with a restaurant (visited in the last month) significantly alters the previously accepted picture of what factors affect novelty seeking. Their work revealed that individuals' intentions to try a new restaurant when bored with some attribute of the last one (food, service, or environment) varied disproportionately with age—seniors were much more likely to try a new place than nonseniors—and propensity to take risks. It should shock no one that risk-takers were especially keen to visit a new restaurant when bored of the last. Ha and Jang, however, didn't find customer loyalty, gender, or education to be especially influential on the desire for novelty when diner boredom played a role.

Too bad the authors didn't consider the amount of choice on a restaurant's menu as a factor in subjects' willingness to revisit a place. Still, their studies do contribute to our understanding of what shapes our sense of sufficient choice. I can think of no reason why they wouldn't affect our judgments of choice on restaurant menus, especially when deciding if we want to go to a restaurant again.

Successful menu design isn't just what makes us diners happy. It reconciles our wishes with the interests of restaurateurs. Menu choice is certainly a characteristic that requires some balance. Figuring out the ideal amount for a restaurateur, as it turns out, is no less complicated than for us diners. The answer is highly variable, and what dictates the right menu size and scope for a restaurant goes well beyond its operator's ability to match *our* ideas of adequate.

Business-savvy operators usually start by evaluating the restaurant's capacities. To figure out how much choice the menu can offer, they assess the size and equipment of the kitchen and storage, the size of the dining room and takeout/delivery potential, the skills and ambitions of cooks, and the reliability of ingredient costs and supply.

If a menu is too short, patrons losing interest won't be their only problem. The restaurant will also be more sensitive to volatility in ingredient availability and cost. Also, as industry writer Robert Klara counseled in the 2014 *Adweek* article "Are the Salad Days Over for Single-Item Restaurants Like Crumbs," a menu that's too limited won't keep the best back-of-the-house staff. There's not enough opportunity for the kitchen to develop and display talent.

A menu that's too long, on the other hand, wastes or taxes resources. Holding more ingredients than diners consume leads to throwing perishables—and, with them, money—out. Moreover, if rarely ordered, menu items whose ingredients can't all be used for high-demand dishes drag down profits. Finally, a menu too long for the kitchen to execute to standard will slow operations.

Only in rare cases, like the Thai restaurant Jitlada in Thai Town, can a place thrive by slowness where speed is its categorical norm. While there, I noted that the menu had over 250 items, but the kitchen was tiny. Well aware that this isn't a formula for speed, the owners put up warning signs throughout the dining room: "Our kitchen is small. Our love of food is big. Please be patient if your food is a little late. But we promise, Jitlada's food is worth the wait!"

Due to great cooking and rare renown—glowing write-ups by local and national critics, consistent ranking on top-restaurant lists, and more camera time than its neighbors—the local reserve of patience runs deep. Also, because Jitlada's prices are relatively high, the restaurant makes up in bigger checks what it loses in slow table turns. Sure, I could get the cheapest item on the menu, an appetizer, for $5.95. But most dishes on the menu I saw were in the $12-to-$24.95 range, on the high side for the area. A surprising number of items were priced in the forties—none of the nearby Thai restaurants dared do this—and there were standouts beyond those: a dish called Spicy Seaside, featuring steak and tiger prawns, for $64.95 and the most expensive, a seafood platter, for $119.95.

Speed, however, is essential in places that rely on low prices and high volume—including many large restaurant chains—and this shows in decisions about menu choice. In recent years, a number of such chains have put their lists on a diet. According to market research by Datassential, the average menu size of US chains increased from almost eighty-three to nearly ninety-eight items between 2005 and 2008, and then fell to just under ninety-three in 2014. Research and consultancy firm Technomic found that the 500 largest chains in the United States had cut more than 7 percent of their food items in 2014 alone. This may not seem like a great reduction, but given the tendency of the large-chain menus to expand, a small percentage decrease represents noteworthy discipline.

In the few years prior, many chains in the full-service, midscale market trimmed their menus, some dramatically. Casual-dining Tony Roma's dropped its selection from ninety-two to sixty. BJ's went from 181 to 150. IHOP, Olive Garden, Red Lobster, and Chili's made similar cuts.

In 2017, Chili's made news again when, in an effort to pull out of a deepening sales slump, it cut its menu drastically, deleting 50 of its 125 items. According to *Nation's Restaurant News* reporter Ron Ruggless in "Chili's Streamlined Menu Speeds Up Service Times," six weeks after thus downsizing and putting the focus back on the chain's signature burgers, fajitas, and ribs, ticket times declined by 12 percent—allowing more table turns—and selections of signature entrées rose almost 40 percent. Moreover, tickets taking longer than fifteen minutes—which Chili's had identified with the most customer complaints—dropped 40 percent.

Several years earlier, so-called "limited-service" chains (those with reduced or no tableside service) underwent a similar spate of cuts, and company heads likewise touted their aid to the bottom line. In 2014, the CEO of Burger King gloated about a 3.6 percent rise in US and

Canadian sales that he attributed to a recent menu trim. In an interview from the same year, the COO of McDonald's spoke of lightening its list to good effect. He admitted that, in 2013, the restaurant "overcomplicated" matters by adding "too many new products, too fast." The menu at McDonald's had in fact been growing for years. Between 2004 and 2014, it expanded 75 percent, from 69 to 121 permanent items.

We should be careful, however, when interpreting the menu purges. They were neither universal nor merely a matter of item subtraction. Wise restaurateurs, including those operating chains, don't consider the size of their menus apart from the complexity of producing items on it. They ask, *What's involved in preparation?* If the execution of food and drink is efficient, a menu with more items can yield a higher volume of sales than a smaller one filled with intricate builds.

A report in the *Wall Street Journal* on a bout of menu expansion at Starbucks between 2009 and 2014 demonstrated the point. It revealed that the company increased its menu from 181 items to 255, and productivity rose. The report included an interview with the company COO, who pointed out that the correlation between menu size and customer traffic is never straightforward, and that Starbucks excelled by increasing efficiencies.

To his point, when BJ's pruned its menu, it also reduced readying times. The restaurant shaved valuable seconds by, for example, cutting onions more roughly and returning to serving pizza in the pan. BJ's tried serving pizza on a dish because management thought it looked better that way, but in the end, the transfer from pan to plate proved one move too many.

In any case, cuts in the size of chain menus aren't always desirable. If they were, the menus wouldn't have ballooned in the first place. Collections of historical menus and decades of industry journalism attest that the size of chain menus has fluctuated. Company executives and consultants explain this as an ongoing balancing act. The restaurants need to simplify their menus to speed up service, yet they require menu innovation to fuel consumer interest. Confirming the point, the COO of McDonald's attributed the robust growth of the company's menu between 2004 and 2014 to additions it deemed necessary in response to food fads, pressure to add healthful items, and the recession-era demand for more low-price options.

Chain-menu growth has also come from battling the competition. A common tactic is to imitate. If one chain in a market segment offers a chipotle chicken sandwich, another adopts one in self-defense. That's probably how, at one time, the Southwestern brand Chili's ended up serving pizzas, the Italian-style Olive Garden acquired hummus, and seafood-themed Red Lobster came to list tortilla soup. I doubt it was a coincidence, either, that T.G.I. Friday's announced its partnership with low-carb brand Atkins in 2003, the same year Applebee's put out the word it was teaming up with Weight Watchers. Incidentally, these deals added a whole section to both chains' menus.

The more market share a chain wants, the more susceptible it is to menu "broadening"—increasing variety. It has to win the veto vote. The BJ's menu at the Burbank location that Jamisin and I visited declared its aim to please all on the first page: "Today, you will find something everyone will love on the menu. . . ." Take a look and you'll see that the largest casual-dining-chain menus today—the likes of Applebee's, Chili's, and T.G.I. Friday's—and those, perhaps like BJ's, targeting a similar market, are a mix of crowd-pleasing favorites, trendy additions, multicultural accents, power-brand partnerships, healthful alternatives, and budget-friendly deals. Options like these tend to accumulate, and while their selections may please the greatest number of potential patrons, they make it a challenge for restaurants to keep costs down and service speed up.

If you ask me how big and diverse a menu should be to satisfy diners and profit-motivated restaurateurs alike, I'll propose this general rule: The most rational strategy for all types of restaurants is to simplify the menu, including the production of items, as much as possible while meeting the expectations and preferences of potential diners. Of course, the latter vary widely by diner and restaurant type. As we've seen, many gourmet diners today don't mind, even relish, restriction of choices on a gourmet menu as long as they're the ideas of a respected chef; whereas the diners at many large-scale casual-dining chains tend to expect those menus to cater to the full range of standard cravings.

The trick is to maximize, without overwhelming, the diner's experience of choice, yet minimize the costs of offering it. Easy to say. Hard to do. But many restaurateurs, including some in my study, have come up with crafty solutions.

First let's talk about water—a menu item many of us take for granted, as our cups are often filled before we even ask for it. When it comes to water, the most choice many of us ever experience is that between "tap" and bottled "still or sparkling." But not at Ray's and Stark Bar, the restaurant attached to the Los Angeles County Museum of Art, where I went for brunch. There I found an entire menu of waters, what struck me as an ingenious way to offer variety.

This novelty, bound in blue leather, had a table of contents dividing twenty bottles of water into ten countries of origin. Against crisp white pages, each bottle got a two-page pictorial. The monumental profile of each bottle took up the entirety of the right pages. The left neatly displayed tasting notes and numbers—on volume, nutrition, and price—and dot-mapped the water on two elegant graphic keys ranging from sweet to salty and smooth to complex.

While there, I asked then general manager Martin Riese about the menu. He claimed he brought the concept from his home city of Berlin, where the trend in water sommeliers precedes us. A true enthusiast, Riese made his own award-winning California brand, on the menu as 90H20. As he went through oenophile rituals—presenting the example I bought, pouring the chilled drink into a wine glass, and resting the bottle just so—he taught me the basics of water connoisseurship. I appreciated the effort all the more knowing that, with the LA sun penetrating the glass wall by my table, he was probably baking in his suit.

His cleverness impressed me. Riese pointed out that, in the United States, the Food and Drug Administration regulates water as a food. Therefore, it has to have an expiration date. Water's is two years from production for glass bottles and one year for the faster-deteriorating plastic. In essence, Riese had bought the luxury of at least one year to sell his stock—far more time than the chef had to sell food ingredients. Since the restaurant didn't have much of a wine list, the other type of list with a comparable shelf life, and its food menus fit easily on brief single-panel cards, another forty-five stunning pages added heft, beauty, and a sense of variety to the restaurant's portfolio for an excellent cost-benefit balance.

By rolling out Shakin' Flavor Fries in 2015, McDonald's did something similar. With a purchase of fries, customers could choose one of several packets of seasonings. The availability of Garlic Parmesan, Zesty Ranch, and Spicy Buffalo enhanced the guest experience of choice for a pittance. The spices cost the company next to nothing and, like Riese's waters, could hold long.

I can't say how much these tactics influence purchases. But we do have some evidence that our perception of variety on a restaurant menu—which is tied to our estimation of choice—influences how much, and how much variety, we're willing to select. Building on prior consumer research, which shows that increased variety perception prompts the purchase of a greater number and variety of items in nonrestaurant contexts, researchers Hee Jin Kim and Song Oh Yoon confirmed the same dynamic in the case of restaurant menus. In 2016, they studied 105 South Korean students' selections from and evaluations of variety on differing versions of a mock menu. The menus all contained forty-five dishes divided into "Appetizer," "Main Dish," and "Beverage & Dessert" categories. They learned that the subjects perceived greater variety on the menu when those categories weren't divided further and that, when told to react to the same ordering scenario, the subjects who perceived greater variety mock-ordered more dishes and dishes of a wider variety. Perhaps restaurateurs should refrain from dividing up their menus into more categories than they must.

If ingredient prices and supplies are steady, restaurateurs can try another cost-saving, choice-enhancing tack. They can expand the use of the same few ingredients. When restaurateurs use beef or mushrooms or mozzarella in myriad ways, for example, we diners can have a wide selection while they enjoy economies of scale.

Daniel R. Scoggin, a captain of casual-dining-chain industry for decades, calls this technique "crossover" and considers it golden. In an interview, he told me that, as president and CEO of T.G.I. Friday's from approximately 1971 to 1986, this is one way he profitably expanded the Friday's menu. In 1976, the business effectively changed from a singles bar that offered some food to a full-fledged restaurant. The menu, in turn, transformed from a short list on a chalkboard, a mere appendage to the bar, into sixteen pages. Friday's had a few choices of burgers, steaks, egg dishes, salads, sides, and desserts on the old slate menu when Scoggin posed the bankable question: What else can we do with these ingredients?

Lately, a favored way to maximize the experience of choice at minimal cost is to offer customizable menus. Smart. These create as much an illusion of choice as the real thing. Since, with customization, we create our own combinations from the parts that make up a dish—say, a hamburger or a burrito—a few components seem like infinite possibilities.

Although it wasn't the first to create this type of menu, the fresh-Mex fast-casual chain Chipotle, whose sales quadrupled between 1999 and 2015 (before outbreaks of the norovirus beleaguered the business), was the most widely copied model of it. When Jamisin and I visited the Larchmont Village site, an assembly-line structure led us through the decision points literally step by step. Following the order of the signboard on high were trays of food along a counter. Behind it, servers built the works to our specifications. The first fork in our road was burrito versus bowl. About a foot down the line: white or brown rice. Next were several fillings to choose from—a few long-cooked meats, a vegetable option, and a vegan tofu scramble. A selection of black or pinto beans followed that and preceded an array of toppings—salsas, cheese, guacamole, and sour cream. Drinks and chips capped the line. By chain-restaurant standards, the menu was miniscule. And yet, a daily customer could, in theory, go for weeks without repeating an order.

The Counter, a full-service chain with a build-your-own-burger theme, actually specified the number of combinations possible from the choices of three buns or no bun, four proteins in three different weights, ten cheeses, eighteen regular and ten premium toppings, and eighteen sauces that I counted when we went to the mid-Wilshire venue. At the time of my visit, the restaurant's website claimed over 312,120 unique burgers.

Chipotle and The Counter, with units and imitators proliferating, found a sweet spot between supply and demand. They also set the stage for "memorable experiences," the holy grail of experiential marketers.

In their landmark text, *The Experience Economy*, marketing consultants Joseph B. Pine and James H. Gilmore argued that consumer experiences become memorable when they're personalized. They then recommended many experience-enhancing practices for maximizing business success, including the "mass customization" used by Chipotle and The Counter.

By "efficiently serving customers uniquely," the authors said, not only do brands lessen the gap between what customers want and what they can get; they also allow attachment to the brand to become deeply personal. At Chipotle and The Counter, the burritos and burgers we concoct can seem as singular as signatures.

There must be many more ways to guarantee the cost-effectiveness and marketing power of a choice set. But there's no common calculus by which restaurateurs arrive at their idea of the right amount of choice. Moreover, as I learned by talking to restaurateurs, not all pursue a profit-optimizing path, and those who do—even in restaurants of the same style, structure, and market—don't all agree on strategy.

Unless you knew the personality, expertise, history, and life goals of one Allan Tam, owner of J&K Hong Kong Cuisine in Chinatown from 2011 to 2015, you'd never guess the logic behind him keeping a menu with 265 items plus a two-sided table tent with a trial list of about 20 more. True to the fashion of Hong Kong–style cafés, his menus were long and broad, with lists of Western dishes—from spaghetti to steak dinners—as well as Chinese. But fidelity to genre explained only so much.

I became privy to Tam's thinking through Jamisin's introduction. Arguably the restaurant's most loyal customer, Jamisin had earned the privilege. He'd been eating there since 1998, when the place was under different ownership and another name. Since my move to Los Angeles in 2001, I would accompany him on occasion, so I knew the place. But I hadn't been back since Tam had taken over. In the meantime, he and Jamisin had become acquainted. Would he talk to me for my book? We would come for dinner. He obliged.

Throughout the evening, I noticed how much Tam bothered about the quality of his restaurant, especially the food. When guiding us in what to order, he explained how the Hong Kong dishes were prepared. He pantomimed every step.

Tam knew how to make the dishes because he actively reviewed and revised the kitchen's recipes and ingredients. For the pan-fried noodles the menu advertised with beef brisket, he said he used only the plate—the fattiest part. When I complimented him on the White Wine Pork Chop we tried from the table-tent menu, he informed me that he made it with chardonnay. "Rich." He spoke as if he were the executive chef. To some extent, he was. The items on the table tent were largely his invention. His latest experiment, which we were game to try, he called Garlic Butter Shrimp. He made up the name right then.

Tam liked pleasing regulars. In addition to what was on the printed menus, he kept a stash of pork belly, off menu, just for his Chinese customers. He claimed it sold out in two to three days every time.

I meant it when I told Tam how much I liked the food. His dedication—and the experienced chef's ability to realize Tam's vision—really showed. "I have many demands," he responded. "You care," I repeated. "Yes, care," he nodded.

Given his intense interest in—some might say, micromanagement of—the kitchen, you'd think his background was culinary. You'd be wrong. Before he owned J&K, he'd spent twenty-seven years rising through the ranks of the Hong Kong telecommunications industry. His only previous restaurant experience was working as a waiter at a Panda Inn while he attended college in the United States. That's when he learned how to make so many Chinese dishes.

At the base of Tam's newly adopted role was a dogged work ethic. Like the servers, he bussed tables, took orders, and served food. His fusion of executive and server roles showed in his dress. The neat slacks and striped, button-down Oxford shirt with a pen in the breast pocket said, "I'm the manager." The black sneakers squealed, "I'm on my feet all day." Jamisin told me that Tam wasn't just there all day. He was there every day.

What Tam didn't attend to, however, was just as revealing as what he diligently watched. Like the restaurant's website, the main menu remained unchanged from the previous owner. Tam didn't think it worth his time to evaluate the contents. Why not? He didn't want to spend the money to print new menus. When he wanted to change the table-tent offerings, which he did quarterly, he had his wife graphically design them for free.

At first, his disinterest in analyzing the main menu and his justification for not doing so baffled me. Unsurprisingly, my questions about his use of menus as merchandising tools led nowhere. Tam's main means of marketing was to put an ad for the restaurant in the local paper. Beyond that, he thought it best to just always be there, observing what people liked. He could tell me that 90 percent of his business was from regulars and that his Filipino, Mexican, and policemen customers loved steaks the most.

Few professional restaurant consultants would approve of Tam's disregard of the menu as a sales tool. Either he didn't know about menu analysis and design or didn't consider them important. I suspect it was both.

But before we judge Tam's management style, we should realize that he wasn't trying to maximize profits. As he explained, the restaurant was, for him, a hobby in semiretirement. He started it to keep busy while his daughter went to college in California. He got into the restaurant business because the threshold for entry was low and J&K was, to him, inexpensive. In addition, he saw his involvement as temporary. If a more attractive opportunity arose, he'd change course. He might even go back to "telecom." In the meantime, his goal was to drum up a little more business, but he didn't want "crazy." He said he was "satisfied with the business size."

Having spent the bulk of his career in another industry, he may not have been clued in on restaurant menu design. But, as a former vice president of a company, he wasn't a total business naïf. Nor was he completely impractical with respect to his personal goals. Even though it wasn't textbook standard, whatever he did probably worked well enough for him.

Maybe it's not farfetched to imagine idiosyncrasies of management on the part of independent restaurateurs. Should we then assume that the managers of big chains, in contrast, go by the book? If that's true, they don't all read the same one.

Illustrating the point is the difference in philosophies of menu management that emerged in the formative years of T.G.I. Friday's. In one corner: Daniel Scoggin. He became involved with Friday's as a franchisee in 1970, but by the midseventies had merged with founder Alan Stillman when the company Scoggin worked for, Carlson, bought the business. Scoggin left Friday's in 1986 to sail around the world, but soon resurfaced to continue a stellar career. By 1995, he presided over the Ground Round chain. In 1998, he led a venture-capital group to purchase the Houlihan's Restaurant Group. Scoggin developed multiple concepts for the group until his retirement in 2000.

In the other corner: Frank Steed. He, too, played a part in the early history of Friday's and went on to an illustrious industry career. At Friday's, he began as the doorman of the second store and rose to executive vice president over the next eighteen years. He moved on from the chain in 1989, but by then Steed had helped to implement the approach to Friday's management that fundamentally persists to this day. After many years serving as president of several major franchisors and chains, he founded The Steed Consultancy, which advises a client list that includes some of the biggest chains on all matters of national and international franchising.

I haven't done justice to either man's resume. Suffice it to say that the views Scoggin and Steed shared with me derive from loads of experience and long trails of success in the chain game.

Scoggin's management style was immediately apparent from how he approached the challenge of Friday's first flagging sales since its founding in 1965. It was the early 1970s—a challenging period given the onset of a recession, an oil crisis, and the fact that, by then, Friday's had spawned a cadre of imitators-turned-competitors. Scoggin took a sober look at the business. When it came to food, he noticed that the restaurant was "an impulse buy." People didn't usually plan a visit far in advance. He then understood that, to make Friday's the choice of a spur-of-the-moment dining party, it had to satisfy the veto vote.

Scoggin was proud of the path he took to win it: It was too easy, he realized, to compete with Friday's on the bar front, so the business had to excel in food. A menu makeover was in order. He insisted that it have maximum range. Scoggin came up with a system he called the "palate profile." He made sure the food on the menu contained a wide spectrum from light to heavy and bland to spicy.

The competitors at the time were taking a different approach, trying to come up with a common denominator and ending up, in Scoggin's opinion, with something that excited no one. He was proud that Friday's appealed to a variety of tastes.

Scoggin also looked at the restaurant's use of resources. In time, he said, the menu evolved and added more items, but he never approved of a product that didn't have potential for crossover. Crossover is how, in 1976, the brief list on a chalkboard grew so suddenly into a sixteen-page book. Don't eliminate menu complexity if there's no difference in the buying—in Scoggin's words, "what's coming through the back door"—or the kitchen-line layout! Also under Scoggin, if there was something the customer wanted that wasn't on the menu, yet the restaurant had the ingredients, the cooks could improvise. If the item became popular, it went on the menu.

As he made these adjustments, Scoggin insisted no corners be cut on quality. Everything would be fresh and made in-house. "For our brunch menu on Sundays, we even made hollandaise from scratch," he said. "We were committed to that! People would say that's too hard. But we came up with systems to make it work." Invest in personnel and challenge them, he advised. Don't do what the others do: simplifying menus to make work easier, spending on advertising, doing discounting and happy-hour promotions.

Scoggin testified that market research at the time was proving his emphasis on quality correct. As he remembered it:

> We would do focus groups at the restaurant and do blind taste tests of our fresh-made products and the stuff that supply-chain product manufacturers were trying to sell us. We said that, if, in a blind taste test, we couldn't tell the difference or liked the product they were selling better, we'd buy. But that never happened. The fresh product won every time.

Scoggin was thrilled to say that he was able to pull off "white-table-cloth food in a high-volume restaurant." The bottom line with any food operation, he declared, is quality. If you can produce it with a large menu, you will increase your customer base and frequency. However, a limited menu of high quality will always outperform a large menu of mediocre product.

Scoggin was sure to explain that his emphasis on quality wasn't just good for customers. It made the soundest sense for business. By following his plan, he said, "Friday's became the highest volume-per-unit chain in the world with no advertising, no discounting, no happy hours."

Artistic menu design likewise expressed the quality focus under Scoggin. Woody Pirtle told me how much he loved designing menus for Friday's—something he did between 1976 and 1985, while Scoggin called the shots—because Scoggin gave Pirtle free reign. Pirtle's designs weren't the most practical—in an email to me, James Robert Watson recalled from his time as a server that the sixteen-page menu of 1976 was exceedingly hard for customers to read in the dim light—but they were playful and memorable. In my own collection, I have two of Pirtle's 1976 menus, which were designed to look like a kid's school notebook.

They have differing illustrations and one has red and gold star stickers next to certain items. I also have an example of the dictionary-themed menu he did for Friday's in 1981, for which the entries are in alphabetical order and look like definitions. Both impressed me as unusually experimental—and in the case of the notebook menu, unstandardized—for a chain restaurant.

Pirtle's design for the company stopped after 1985. According to Pirtle, the trust in the designer and the willingness to experiment artistically left when Scoggin did.

Scoggin claimed that Friday's culture started to change as early as 1983, when Carlson, who till then had been a passive owner, asked him to take the company public. At that point, Scoggin recalled, Friday's became stock-price driven and bent on building units as quickly as possible. The menu went from big and all from scratch to a narrower list and microwave production. The tragedy from Scoggin's point of view, besides the decline in quality, was that, as these changes occurred, the business didn't alter the economies of the line or the product buying. Mournfully, Scoggin added, "I was heartbroken when they eliminated the test kitchen and began buying from frozen-food suppliers."

I asked if the savings was in labor. Not really, he confided. The problem, he said, is that anything the business might have saved by cutting costs, it was spending on advertising. For him, the choice is this: you can focus on the bottom line, cut costs, focus on the best deals on purchasing, or you can invest in your cooks, your servers, and your customers. Give high quality to customers, he pressed, and they'll reward you with word of mouth—the strongest advertising there is.

Already in the 1970s, he recalled, most chains had started going in the other direction. This was the supply-chain-efficiency model of chain-restaurant management that Tracie McMillan chronicled in depth in her 2012 book, *The American Way of Eating*. She went undercover as a kitchen expediter at Applebee's. Except for grilled items, she found no cooking there. Everything was portioned in "baggies," reheated, and assembled according to "recipes." This system, she said, requires little experience on the part of the staff, allowing the company to hire less-skilled cooks, and it takes maximum advantage of economies of scale derived from partnerships with suppliers and delivery services.

It's true that, over the decades, auxiliary companies such as Sysco and Sygma have evolved to provide a wealth of services for indepen-dent restaurants and chains. They offer everything from business con-sulting to recipe design to logistics management. They'll deliver cooked food for you if that's what you want.

Was there a contemporary chain that Scoggin considered to be car-rying on his philosophy? Yes. The Cheesecake Factory! He described a recent tour he got of one outlet. "It was doing great volume. They were making from scratch several hundred different sauces, each with a three-day shelf life." A new manager came in, Scoggin was told, who said something like, "That's too hard. Reduce the fresh sauces. Take it down to one hundred." Scoggin relished hearing that the company fired him.

After hearing Scoggin's testimonial, I was compelled to experience The Cheesecake Factory for myself. Indeed, the menu was huge, from scratch, and the chain was proud of both facts. On the Our Menu page for the Glendale location Jamisin and I went to, the website announced, "The Cheesecake Factory menu features more than 250 menu selections made in-house each day, using only the highest quality ingredients. . . ." Page one of thirty-five in the main menu went further:

> We are committed to quality, value and your complete sat-isfaction. We prepare our food fresh each day in our own kitchens using the highest quality ingredients available. We use all-natural chicken with no added hormones, premium Certified Angus Beef®, American Style Kobe or U.S.D.A. Choice, fresh fish that is either Longline or Hook & Line caught whenever possible, cooking oils that contain zero grams of trans fat per serving, and much of our produce is sourced direct from premium growers. We offer a variety of substitution options and will always do our best to accom-modate special requests to ensure we prepare your meal just the way you like it.

Our experience of the restaurant supported the menu's claims. The food tasted and looked scratch prepared. Possibly due to the prejudice of many food writers against chains, its hamburger has never been listed in rankings of the best in town, but should be.

The staff was attentive, flexible, and educated about the menu. Our server accommodated requests for modifications and could explain individual dishes. At Applebee's, by contrast, our server, though as nice as she could be, was clearly restricted in her parameters by corporate systems. It was symptomatic that, when we asked to take home our leftovers, she told us she would bring us boxes because the servers weren't permitted to handle food.

Other people like The Cheesecake Factory, too. Every time I visit or pass by one, the waiting room is packed and the wait for a table over an hour. But that's just anecdotal. According to a 2014 report by Market Force, which polled more than 1,600 consumers to get their ratings of the service, food quality, and value of casual restaurants in five categories—breakfast, steak, Italian, seafood, and general menu—The Cheesecake Factory won first place in the general-menu category.

Frank Steed was well aware of Scoggin's viewpoint. According to Steed, the two men have an on-again, off-again friendship that goes through cooling phases over differences in their approach. Nevertheless, Steed gave Scoggin credit for many good things about the early Friday's culture, including the creation of the "palate profile."

But Steed found Scoggin's menu management otherwise problematic. He pointed out that Friday's wasn't getting any credit for all of the extra work it did to produce an all-scratch menu and one so large. Things got "out of hand" by the early eighties, he recalled: "We shot ourselves in the foot" by offering too many items and complicating procedures.

Steed said he'd learned a lot about customers' tastes from market research: most like the food that's not from scratch just as much as the scratch product. (Steed's account contradicted Scoggin's on this point!) If so, it's foolhardy insist on the latter. Better to make use of supply-chain efficiencies such as preparation in central commissaries. I can see his logic this way: Applebee's didn't become the largest chain in America, almost twice the size of its nearest competitor, by people rejecting its food.

The other issue for Steed was consistency. Contra Scoggin, he remembered Friday's as having the best burger and the worst. It was inconsistent. Product is more consistent, he assured me, when you uncomplicate the menu. If a menu is too big and too broad, it can't be prepared from scratch unless it takes longer, and the quality is unpredictable. "Why do you go to McDonald's?" he asked, rhetorically. For consistency and speed. It's not going to be the best burger in the world. But it's good enough and you know what you're going to get.

Steed argued that consistency matters more and more as a business scales up. There's a big difference, he stressed, in what you can do if your goal is to have 20 stores from what you can do at 200, and there's a difference, again, going from 200 to 2,000. The more of the market you want, the more you need a menu that captures a broader market. But you also need consistency and speed. Without it, he insisted, you can't get big.

One consideration, he mentioned, is personnel. You have to be practical regarding the skill level of the staff you'll find. If you want to grow, make it easier for more people to do a consistent and speedy job.

These values, he suggested, were even more important in today's marketplace, in which casual-dining chains are losing market share to fast-casual operations that do good food faster. Restaurateurs would be wise to listen to Steed, a successful and seasoned franchising consultant, on the dynamics of scale in the restaurant business.

On the question of how scale affects operations, Scoggin and Steed actually agreed. Unprompted, Steed, like Scoggin, made an example of The Cheesecake Factory. He didn't discount the value of the chain's quality. He just explained it as a function of the chain's smaller scale. As I write this, it has fewer than 100 units. "Cheesecake is what Friday's used to be," Steed asserted. Those words could have come from Scoggin.

He and Scoggin converged on one more point: the ownership structure of a restaurant affects every aspect of a restaurant's operation, including menu complexity. Unlike private companies, for example, those owned by venture capitalists (VCs) can make shortsighted decisions. VCs tend to sign on for short-term contracts and want to see a quick rise in profits. As a result, they make three-year decisions, not long-term brand-based decisions. A company that's publicly owned operates with selling stock in mind. This encourages maximizing supply-chain efficiencies and dumbing down systems, cutting corners, etc.

When Scoggin said this, I mentioned that The Cheesecake Factory was, as he spoke, publicly owned. Yes, he knew. But as soon as a speed bump comes, expect "cut, cut, cut."

In spite of these points of agreement about realities of the business, Scoggin remained less amenable to the interests of scale. He refused to value growing units over maintaining his all-scratch ideal. Steed questioned whether Scoggin's customers care as much about his ideal as he does.

Each side of the argument has its sympathizers and its legacy in the restaurant business. The conflict between them may never be resolved. For me, it's yet another reminder that the right amount of choice on a restaurant menu is a calculation of the utmost import, but is neither standard nor simple.

CHAPTER 5

Secrets

ON AN ORDINARY AUGUST AFTERNOON, I TURNED INTO THE DRIVE-thru lane at the In-N-Out Burger on Sunset and Orange with a special mission. I wanted to see what it was like to order from the "secret menu"—the set of items not on the menu, but available to those in the know. I was also keen to find its limit. Where would the restaurant draw the line on special requests?

In-N-Out's secret menu was legendary. For decades, it had been so widely publicized, mostly by fans customizing their orders and spreading the word, that the company listed six of the most famous off-menu items on its website. With *Not-So-Secret Menu* as the title, In-N-Out clearly saw the irony.

In spite of that, further layers of secrecy—and secret telling—remained. Longer lists with dozens of variations on burgers, fries, and shakes circulated in the press, on blogs, and on social media. Conflicting accounts about what In-N-Out would or wouldn't serve kept things speculative. They also gave my outing a tinge of adventure.

Once I reached a signal point in the lane, a uniformed employee approached my car with a menu hanging from her POS. To establish trust, I dutifully ordered from the laminated list first. Then I asked for the 3 × 3. This cheeseburger with three beef patties and three slices of cheese was on the not-so-secret menu. If my location were up to the chain standard, the request would go smoothly.

The item was firmly in the system. Submitting the order took no extra typing, and my bill would show a computer-generated "3 × 3."

I threw the curve ball last. I planned to ask for something I hadn't seen on any list. I knew that a grilled cheese was on the not-so-secret menu, and I'd read that some customers who requested a cheeseburger with french fries inside had been turned down. I made up a hybrid just as likely to fail.

"Can you do a grilled cheese with fries inside?"

"We can't do that."

Aha!

"Okay, how about with onions?" I countered.

"Sure."

This exchange confirmed my dawning realization about secret menus. Like my grilled cheese with onions, they have to be negotiated on the spot.

Sometimes we're the first to chart an off-menu course. More often, we're standing on the shoulders of countless prior negotiators, whose efforts have solidified into that rumored list. Secret menus foster incessant bargaining because they depend on uncertainty. We can never predict the extent of a secret menu, and there's always some doubt about what will be available to us.

Why does the custom persist? I would argue that keeping the limits of hospitality veiled, no matter how lightly, serves the interests of restaurateurs and diners alike.

Customers make off-menu requests for a variety of reasons. If not purely for research, my motive at In-N-Out, we do it to have our tastes accommodated, to appear in the know, or to get superior treatment. In those cases, ordering off menu makes us feel special. The belief that there's some risk of rejection—even if only for other people—gives special orders a further air of triumph.

Restaurateurs who offer unlisted items also have several possible motives. They may want to exceed diners' expectations, reward valued patrons, or prompt positive word of mouth for the restaurant. If those items were fixed, explicit, and promised to all, they wouldn't serve these purposes. They'd also belong on the regular menu.

Keeping off-menu lists in the shadows also makes them easier to contain. If special ordering goes unchecked, it could jeopardize the economies of the regular menu. In essence, for secret menus to be socially and economically valuable, they must appear mysterious and negotiable. In dealings, however, not all follow the same rules.

So much depends on the way an establishment structures the relationship between restaurateur and diner. The kind of service a restaurant provides—not by vagaries of server personality or diner traffic, but at the planning level where the bones of a restaurant form—determines nearly everything about its off-menu deliberations. It can dictate how and why a menu deviation starts, who gets it, the composition of the item itself, and whether and how rumors about it spread. It can even decide the tattle's tone. The chasm lies between standardization and personalization.

As you might guess, chain restaurants with units in the many hundreds or thousands lean toward standardization. The larger the chain, the more it regulates everything from menus to service, which creates the public perception of a homogenous and regimented operation.

This is the strongest at limited-service chains because every segment of the company-designed encounter between patron and server is at its most rote. Regulars are supposed to be addressed the same way as first-timers. Managers don't encourage servers to recall a repeat customer's favorite dish or how much ice she likes in her tea. That would only slow operations down—the kiss of death for a high-volume operation. If a server does become familiar with a repeat customer, that relationship could lead to special treatment, such as extra generous provisions of fries or special sauce, but interactions like these stray from the company line. Even when a menu allows customization, the protocols of the assembly line don't waver, and while loyalty programs tailor offerings to individuals, these propositions are algorithmic, not improvised.

I don't think it's a coincidence that variations on the expression *to hack the menu* have been used to describe off-menu ordering at fast-food chains almost exclusively. This language, derived from computer hacking, encapsulates the secret-menu subculture that revolves around them.

When I hear the verb *hack* used this way, I picture someone trying to game a system. Convinced that an organization can't be trusted to act in her interests, she resorts to work-arounds and trickery. At the root of her approach is a reciprocal alienation: the system treats the individual as faceless and interchangeable, so the hacker views the system as a monolithic adversary.

The subculture of menu hacking has this mentality in less grim form. But its logic is basically the same. The fast-food chains relate to their customers in a depersonalizing manner, so their customers' attitude about off-menu ordering follows suit.

Menu-hacking chatter teems with symptoms. In how and among whom information spreads, I notice a pattern. Messages by and for consumers that are insensitive to the burdens of restaurant owners—and, by extension, servers and cooks—run virally amok. Fan websites I examined most closely, including HackTheMenu.com, SecretMenus.com, and the "Secret Menu Items" section of Ranker.com—offer extensive pages of secret-menu lists. These lists include names of items, photos, descriptions, and tips for ordering—and all of the usual links for sharing those and one's own on social media.

For some menu hackers, consumer-to-consumer sharing is a matter of principle. At this writing, the welcome page at HackTheMenu.com includes a section at the bottom entitled "Why #HackTheMenu?" Seamlessly promoting its hashtag, the site declares: "Great food is meant to be enjoyed and shared. The secret menu community has uncovered some amazing variations of regular menu items that are sure to excite the taste buds. . . . Chefs experiment and so should you!" The home page of SecretMenus.com offers a similar message of diner empowerment:

> For decades your choices at your favorite restaurants were limited to what was on the menu. If it wasn't listed in black and white on the menu, you would have a hard time ordering it. The increasing popularity of secret menus has changed all of that. . . . At SecretMenus.com, we compile secret menu items from people just like you. The community then votes and weighs in on items to make sure the best always comes out on top!

Perhaps the bloggers and press journalists who report on secret menus have different motives from the hacking fans, but most amplify their efforts. Like the fans, bloggers and journalists use their platforms to inform consumers about available items and where and how to order them. They assume the patron's point of view. Rarely did I see an article like Simonetta Wenkert's "Going Off Menu Can Cause Problems for Both Kitchen and Proprietor," published in *Independent*, in 2015. Most were like Lucy Meilus's 2015 *Huffington Post* article, "We Ate (and Ranked) Everything on McDonald's Secret Menu."

The menu-hacking conversations on social media aren't just one-sided. They're far-reaching. When I investigated the Twitter feed for #HackTheMenu, I encountered a variety of languages—English, European, and Asian—suggesting that the phenomenon was as international as the restaurant chains themselves. All together, the hackers' chatter gave the impression of ganging up.

Amid the din, once in a while, I heard a different voice. On social media, a restaurant worker would chime in, usually to counter a myth or plead for patience with or politeness to the restaurant staff. Here's "Kathryn Erwin" setting customers straight in the comments section of the "Nachos" listing for Chipotle at HackTheMenu.com on December 2, 2015:

> I work at a Chipotle and if you ask any of our crew members we will tell you that we do not have nachos. Nachos normally mean that the cheese is melted and we cannot melt the cheese for you. We can however put chips at the bottom of your bowl and then build a normal bowl for you. They are not called nachos though.

It's really her final line, however, that drives home the annoyance that menu hacking can bring for restaurant workers: "And please," Kathryn implores, "do not be rude to an employee if they refuse to call a bowl with chips nachos." In the conversations of menu hackers, I seldom heard such a distinctly labor point of view.

For the most part, the content of messaging reflects its unilateral shape. Much of it is trophy display. On Twitter, Instagram, and the like, consumers share comments and pictures of their gets. The postings of structurally unsound mega-burgers and flavor-combining shakes are low-cost, high-volume versions of the hunter's moose head on a wall.

Bloggers and journalists make trophy shows of their own. But, due to their lengthier formats, they often showcase them in listicles. Dan My-ers's 2013 compilation, "The 14 Wildest Fast-Food Secret Menu Items" in *The Daily Meal*, is the stock-in-trade.

Some writers dramatize their catches with tales of adventure. In "McDonald's Secret Menu Baffles Restaurant Workers in Manhattan, but They Were Willing to Try," which appeared on *Daily News* in 2015, Jea-nette Settembre told a humorous story of misunderstandings. James Kenji López-Alt brought suspense to his quest to order every item on In-N-Out's secret menu. As he recounted in "The Ultimate In-N-Out Secret Menu (and Super Secret Menu) Survival Guide" in 2011 on *Serious Eats*, the clerk became an enthusiastic collaborator . . . before finally drawing the line.

Others prove their mettle by issuing an early scoop. In the 2013 *Eater* article, "Customers Are Lining Up for This Secret Menu Item at In-N-Out," Elie Ayrouth relayed her success in ordering a burger "Monkey Style"—topped with french fries, cheese, grilled onions, and spread—but warned that, due to the item's recent vintage, "many cashiers aren't familiar with the name."

Like many menu hackers, most journalists reporting on secret menus seem unconcerned with whether or not they tax the restaurants. In the same sentence that Ayrouth said few In-N-Outs knew about "Monkey Style," she also mentioned that many locations might "simply shy away from creating it due to its possible disruptive nature to the back of the house." Mentioning problems for the kitchen was not to dissuade din-ers but to warn of an obstacle to overcome.

Not surprisingly, then, menu-hacking reportage is also full of tips for taking advantage of a restaurant. When suggesting that people be pa-tient during busy times and that they bring a list of ingredients in case the staff doesn't know the item name, some writers almost seem con-siderate of operators. But their advice is just a means to the consumer's end. Others show their connivance overtly.

Malcolm Bedell's "11 McDonald's Menu Hacks That Will Change Your Life," which came out in *LA Weekly* in 2013, did so in the extreme. In addition to listing a variety of McDonald's off-menu dishes, Bedell boasted a suite of payment-evading ruses. These included what he called "dollar menu hacks," for which one had to order two of the least expensive items on the menu and combine them to approximate the contents, but not the cost, of a regular-menu item. Below is the author recommending a Budget Big Mac:

> It's a little known fact that any sandwich on the McDonald's menu can be ordered "Like a Mac," as in, "Let me get a Mc-Double, but make it like a Mac." There's even a button on the register devoted to this task in some locations. So you can order the lower-priced McDouble—hold the ketchup and mustard, add lettuce and Big Mac sauce. Total price, with substitutions = $1.49, $2.40 less than a Big Mac and all you'll be missing is the third slice of bun, some sesame seeds, and most of your dignity.

The latter didn't really bother Bedell. The gamesmanship was too much fun.

That menu hacks are generally customer imposed, not instigated by the restaurants, shows in the character of the items themselves. They tend to be things that only those who don't work in the kitchen would come up with. Such are composites of menu ingredients or entire items. At Taco Bell, one secret-menu item, known as the Incredible Hulk, consists of a five-layer burrito with guacamole instead of nacho cheese. That's nothing but an ingredient swap.

Some well-known McDonald's mash-ups are especially clunky. Secret-menu items such as The Pie McFlurry, a pie blended into a McFlurry shake; the McCrepe, a pancake filled with McDonald's fruit-and-yogurt Parfait; and the McLand, Air, and Sea Burger—the innards of a burger, a chicken sandwich, and the Filet-O-Fish between the buns of one—are Frankensteinian.

Note that the secret menu at McDonald's involves the kitchen very little. All except the Pie McFlurry requires the customer to assemble them. Can such machinations even be called a secret menu? They're more like playing with food.

That customers are the instigators is clear also from the menu-item names. What corporate office would approve calling anything—even the penetration of a double cheeseburger by a Junior Chicken or Mc-Chicken sandwich—"The McGangbang"? If you ask for this in the wrong store, you might be asked to leave.

Some concoctions are so ridiculous that the McDonald's secret menu has attracted parodies. "McDonald's Unadvertised 'Secret Menu' Offerings" in a 2013 issue of *Mad Magazine* included one "Grimace's Lament," made from "equal parts creamy strawberry shake and Filet-O-Fish tartar sauce," and the self-explanatory "Sausage McMuffin with Sponge." Author Scott Maiko captured the clownish monstrosity of a menu with no kitchen sense.

A 2015 spoof in *Lucky Peach* entitled "The Real McDonald's Secret Menu, Revealed" struck right at the hackers' delusion that, in the face of so much contradictory evidence of self-service, they're imposing their will on the restaurant. Explaining what it means to order "Derrida-Style," Lucas Peterson wrote: "At McDonald's, we know that people don't go to restaurants to just enjoy their food—sometimes they want to have to put it together themselves! That's why, at every one of our locations, you can order a deconstructed version of any of our menu items." The nearby photo, showing a dish's components dispersed on a tray, clinched the joke.

The DIY approach of some menu hackers is funny because it exposes the limits of their power. Still, the force of menu hacking has compelled the chains to react.

When put in the position of responding, chains have often revealed the limits of their own power. Asked by journalists if their restaurants have secret menus, the chains' company spokespeople have tended to respond as if in damage control. When *BuzzFeed* reached out to McDonald's for comment on the existence of a secret menu, the representative said, in a typically oblique fashion, that "Our fans like to customize our menu in many unique ways. It's important to remember that participation varies from restaurant to restaurant as McDonald's franchisees are independent business owners." It looks like the company wanted to have it both ways. It didn't want to invite special requests—after all, they're disruptive to operations timed in seconds—and it didn't want to seem unserviceable, either. Loss of market share to a more yielding chain, after all, was at stake. Also, it's hard to resist the free advertising that menu hacking brings for the length of the rumor mill.

Restaurant-industry analyst Bonnie Riggs, in a 2014 interview for BBC News with Debbie Siegelbaum, plausibly suggested one factor that might exacerbate chains' willingness to accommodate. Companies like McDonald's and Taco Bell have been facing stiffening competition from the quickly growing sector of "fast-casual" concepts like Chipotle, where customization is part of the menu structure. Customers, Riggs explained, have grown used to personalizing orders. The traditional chains have struggled to adapt.

Although often on the defensive, some restaurants make attempts to capitalize on the hacking culture as well, and some are more proactive than others. In-N-Out's principal approach, to add a not-so-secret menu to its website and give some of the items on it registered-trademark symbols, is probably the most passive. But that's no surprise. In-N-Out is famous for a less-is-more philosophy of marketing.

Other chains are more assertive by, for example, posting ads for their regular menus on menu-hacking websites. As of April 2018, HackTheMenu.com included a section called "Coupons & Deals," which announced discounts and limited-time offers, some at restaurants with secret menus on the same site. At the same time, the Twitter feed for @HackTheMenu contained regular-menu promotions from a variety of restaurants.

Recently, some restaurants have also crowdsourced patron-inspired variations of items as a way of evolving the regular menu, and have used that process as a marketing device. In 2015, Canada's South St. Burger started a *Not-So-Secret Menu* consisting of four new items inspired by photos that patrons had posted of their customized orders. This is the kind of action that restaurant-marketing guru Paul Barron, in *The Chipotle Effect*, advised brands to take to leverage the power of social media. Borrowing a phrase from Alex Wipperfürth's landmark book, *Brand Hijack*, we might call this ploy the menu-hack hijack.

Standardizing restaurants rarely initiate secret-menu items. When they do it might be to test-market something for a niche too small to justify a full menu redesign and promotional campaign. A well-publicized example is Panera Bread's 2013 decision to use its Facebook page and Twitter account to (unironically) announce a "hidden menu" of six low-carb items. A year later, Panera deemed two of the dishes—the Power Chicken Hummus Bowl and the Power Breakfast Egg White Bowl with Roasted Turkey—sufficiently successful to join one season of the regular menu.

The restaurants' responses to the menu-hacking phenomenon complete the cycle of impersonal relations they start. Whether cagy statements by spokespeople, parasitic advertisements on hacking sites, menu-hack hijacks, or niche-marketing tactics, the actions of the chains appear to be as one-sided as the hackers'.

At sit-down restaurants where skilled, attentive, face-to-face service is a priority—anything from a four-star destination to a casual bistro, usually with one or a low number of units—secret menus normally follow a different code. This is consistent with their restaurants' more personalized and spontaneous hospitality.

While the movements of the waitstaff may be highly ritualized in these restaurants, ideally, they're also attuned to individual preferences and adjusted to behavioral nuances during a meal. Variations in patron status likewise trigger changes in tack. Are you a loyal customer? A VIP? The staff shall treat you accordingly. This personalized approach extends to their secret menus.

Steven A. Shaw characterized these secret menus perfectly in *Turning the Tables*, a book of advice on how to enhance the customer experience of full-service, especially elite, gourmet restaurants. Although it wasn't his objective, Shaw captured the customs of off-menu dining at the personalizing restaurant in their purest form. Dining off-menu, he asserted, is one of the rewards of a prolonged positive relationship with a restaurant. "Most every restaurant is really two: the one the public eats at, and the one where the regulars dine," he wrote. "Being a regular affects every aspect of the dining experience, from getting that tough-to-book table on a busy Saturday night, to getting the waitstaff's best service, to getting special off-menu dishes and off-list wines."

To reap these rewards, Shaw advised, you must pay your dues to the restaurant. Follow the dress code. Learn the name of your server, maître d', or manager. If your interest in the cuisine is genuine, be inquisitive. "Be nice." Repeat these steps regularly. In time, you'll be recognized as the valuable customer you are. Restaurateurs will show appreciation by offering you items off the menu, and, as long as you remain reasonable, you may, after that, make special requests.

Shaw warned, however, that your newfound familial status comes with a grave responsibility. You must keep the gifts you receive to yourself. Don't abuse the privilege by trumpeting them to your friends or, worst of all, by asking the restaurant to extend them the same favors. These acts violate the sacred trust.

In the strict form Shaw portrayed, off-menu negotiations at personalizing restaurants are the polar opposite of menu hacks in every way. They're not supposed to be accessible to everyone. They're built on layers of reciprocal respect. As the recipient of special favors, the customer's allegiance is first to the restaurateur, not other customers. In addition, off-menu items first appear as gifts from restaurateurs, not requests from diners. As a result, the dishes are the sort that cooks, not customers, would conceive: a rare product the kitchen was fortunate to get, something being tested for the regular menu, a childhood favorite of the chef.

The relationships that beget these offers warm the heart, but, justifiably or not, ordinary customers may perceive them, if peripherally glimpsed or overheard in the dining room, as snubs. They can cause envy and make us wonder if the restaurant is unfair.

Several years ago, at the Manhattan restaurant Atera, I found myself on the spectating side of another diner's gift. To understand the potential impact, you have to picture the situation: All twenty of the tasting menu's courses were served at the same time in the same sequence to thirteen guests seated at a U-shaped kitchen-side counter. For this reason and because, as often happens in these situations, I ended up talking to the people next to me, it was hard not to notice a disparity of service. About three-quarters of the way through the meal, the party of two guys with whom I'd been chatting, pals of the kitchen I'll call "Damian" and his chef friend, were slipped an extra plate. Probably realizing that hiding it was impossible, Damian told me the item was from the chef's special stash, a steak he'd dry-aged for fifty-nine days. At this stage of artful rot, Damian whispered, the steak develops rare hints of blue cheese and popcorn. He gave me a bite to confirm.

Had Damian not been generous, and had I not known that he and his friend had history with the chef, I might have felt the exclusionary nature of his offering more. Yet, even with that knowledge, and despite Atera's extraordinary meal, I couldn't avoid the thought that the restaurant ranked its customers. Even if such distinction was deserved or to be expected, it's never pleasant to be reminded. Paying hundreds of dollars makes that worse.

Many personalizing restaurants, however, don't keep their secret menus in such a strict condition—for most-valued patrons only. These days, I notice a growing muddy zone of exceptions and gray areas in which customers initiate off-menu requests—and they're not VIPs or regulars. This happens when publicity about an off-menu item, an inherently depersonalizing force, preempts the unique bonding of restaurateur and guest.

Not all such publicity is planned. Let's say a restaurant discontinues a menu item that had become popular and identified with the place. New customers who learn of the dish or old customers who used to order it keep asking for it. The restaurant obliges. A case in point in Los Angeles is the Smoked Salmon Pizza at Spago. In the early 1980s, when the restaurant achieved world renown, the dish was a signature. Even though Spago has since changed and added locations, and revised its menu countless times, requests for the dish persist.

An avalanche of customer-instigated special ordering can also follow from one customer seeing another with an off-menu item and asking if she, too, may have one. Not wanting to upset her, the restaurateur acquiesces. A chain reaction ensues.

At my favorite modest sushi haunt in Little Tokyo, I was once complicit in such a process. One night, I overheard a guy call out "Obama Roll." I'd been patronizing Hama Sushi for almost ten years and had never heard of it. The order stood out, too, because the restaurant is resolutely purist. The chefs won't make the elaborate novelty rolls you find at some sushi restaurants. Nor do they normally name the basics they make. Talking to my counter mate, I learned that the Obama Roll is a hand roll with eel, avocado, and a crab mixture instead of rice. It wasn't very exotic, after all. But it sounded tasty, so I ordered, "one Obama Roll, please," for myself. I have, from time to time, ever since. On one occasion, my neighbor heard that, leaned over, and put the question to *me*.

When service slowed one night, I asked my sushi chef about the roll's beginnings. Apparently, it already existed as some customers' special order. But, during the 2008 election season, patrons renamed the formerly "Eel, Avocado, and Crab Hand Roll" after the presidential candidate. I gathered that, since acquiring the catchy name, the item had gained a following.

Although many such off-menu items get publicized without a restaurant's help, in plenty of cases, restaurants of the otherwise personalizing sort make a calculating effort. Partly in response to an increasingly competitive, trend-fickle market, some have purposely developed off-menu items and then planted the news. Because they've done this to attract new as much as return business, we must assume that these restaurants want requests for them to come from any customer. As a consequence, restaurateurs undermine the intimacy of those favors. At the same time, they democratize them.

I first suspected that personalizing restaurants were developing off-menu items for marketing when I read about the Los Angeles restaurant Animal having a Bone Marrow Burger. This off-menu item consisted of a patty made of house-ground chuck, short rib, and bone marrow covered in melted jack cheese, caramelized onions, poblanos, and an ode-to-stoners "420" sauce between slices of marbled rye. I had a hunch that the restaurant created the dish, that it wasn't the idea of a customer; the item had the combination of carnivorous decadence and unexpected ingredients that the chefs, Jon Shook and Vinny Dotolo, are known for, and it was too chemically brilliant to be the work of nonexperts.

Using *Animal* and *Bone Marrow Burger* as well the item's alternate name, *Boner Burger*, as search terms, I found clues on social media. A helpful Twitter post from TurningOffJapanese, @tomokoimadedyen, about the "Boner Burger" from August 10, 2015—which mentioned the dish as a favorite of a friend at the *LA Weekly*'s burgers-and-beers fest "on Saturday"—indicated that the restaurant cooked it for an event. The chefs must have created it.

A similar search on Facebook led me to a post by the ratings guide Zagat, which linked to a telling article it had published on July 29, 2015, approximately two weeks prior, in which the Boner Burger was ranked Burger of the Week. In it, author Leslie Balla quoted the restaurant's "director of operations and wine guru" as she recommended White Ale to go with the burger. That, and the photo of the dish getting credited to the restaurant, left me with no doubt that Animal had campaigned.

Was Animal the only restaurant of its kind trying this sort of promotion? Or did it belong to a trend? The path to an answer began with my discovery of Off the Menu. This mobile app recommends secret-menu specials at restaurants in major cities throughout North America. It's remarkable because it behaves like the menu-hacking sites by spreading the word of unlisted items to customers, and yet it specializes in every type of restaurant that those sites don't: one-off establishments and small chains, hot gourmet places, even sanctums of fine dining—the full gamut of institutions I associate with personalized service. In the section on LA, you'll even find listings for Spago and Animal. Since they can't be filed under any one city, the app has a separate section on fast-food chains. But that's it: just one, vastly outweighed, section.

When I explored the app, aspects of it suggested that the featured restaurants were coconspirators: It was free. There were no ads. The pictures of featured dishes were magazine quality and, in many cases, didn't show the items on a dining table. It seemed plausible that the restaurants paid for the listings and supplied the photos. If not, did they at least approve their inclusion in the app? How did the app make money?

Talking to Mike Stasyna, director of operations for Off the Menu, eliminated any doubt that the restaurant's secret-menu promotions were deliberate, and that Animal was part of a larger trend. The fact that Off the Menu had a director of partnerships—charged with talking to restaurant groups and restaurants, getting pictures, and sustaining restaurant relationships—instantly clarified that the content on the app had not only each restaurant's approval but its full-fledged participation. I learned, moreover, that how much a restaurant pays Off the Menu depends on how much business the app brings it and how much marketing on other platforms the restaurant wants Off the Menu to do on its behalf.

Just within the first two months of the app's launch in October 2015, Off the Menu had grown even more collaborative, developing ideas for off-menu items with the restaurants from the ground up. Per Stasyna: "We were thinking, if a restaurant has tomatoes left over at the end of the night, why not create something with tomatoes, a little of this and that, and they can sell what they'd otherwise lose money on? And we could help market these items."

Meanwhile, the Off the Menu app itself revealed that the scale of that trend was growing. Between October and December of 2015, the number of restaurants represented there jumped from roughly 20 to 120 in the section on Los Angeles alone!

How long restaurants of the personalizing type have actively marketed secret menus I can't be sure. But I do know that the unlisted dishes at establishments of this kind have never been so visible or viral as they have since the rise of social media and digital marketing. Only in the last several years has the great gap between the secret menus of personalizing and standardizing restaurants begun to close.

CHAPTER 6

Dinner in Pictures

WHILE SECRET MENUS ENTICE US THROUGH INTRIGUE AND EXCLUSIV-
ity, regular menus rely on artful description. How menus characterize
their establishments and the items they sell varies markedly by restaurant type. Listing dishes by just a few ingredient names is anathema
where large photos of plated entrées abound. The place with a laminated
booklet differs in more ways than just menu aesthetics from the one with
a paper sheet printed daily or the cool cast of a digital signboard.

So pronounced are visual, material, and linguistic distinctions like
these that even a casual observer can detect them. But we need more
than a passing glance to grasp where and why restaurants draw the stylistic lines.

Little defines a menu's sales pitch more than its choices regarding imagery. Image size and layout convey sales priorities and item comparisons,
and the images themselves testify to the character and appeal of the offerings and the restaurant as a whole. The use of photos brings considerations of staging, framing, and lighting. If a menu uses illustrations,
formal elements such as line, color, and texture highlight particular
qualities. The absence of images is just as significant as their presence.
It might indicate a greater reliance on other descriptors, such as words.

It might also work to distinguish the restaurant from the sorts of establishments that let us preview the appearance of our meal.

My field study of menus revealed that the choice to not only identify dishes by photos but to do so on the main menu, as opposed to just a specials or dessert list, was the most polarizing of all image-related practices. This wasn't clear right away, however, because the places that used photos this way were diverse. Chain restaurants with no gourmet or fine-dining aspirations were typical sites. But so were some single-ethnicity restaurants that might well attract gourmet diners.

Their approaches to photography also varied.

The menu for the dining-and-gaming-arcade chain Dave & Buster's represents one common type. In the example I studied, the photos aimed to titillate. The camera took the viewpoint of a ravenous diner. Dishes and drinks were in tight close-up. Only one edge of a plate or glass fit into any frame. Over a dish, the camera hovered at a forty-five-degree angle—the point at which a heap of salad, fried chicken, or fries looks the amplest.

The images accentuated surface sensuality. Among the cocktails, they highlighted condensation on glasses, salt-crusted rims of margaritas, and the pulpy flesh and squeaky skins of limes. All items struck alluring poses. Steak slices were splayed. Desserts were cornucopic. A red berry sauce streamed down a slice of cheesecake, then pooled on the plate over tumbled fruit. The caramel on the Bananas Foster Pie halted on the way down in ballooning blobs.

Shots were high resolution and large—at least two and a half inches across—but they didn't get monotonous because they varied in size and placement. Sometimes, for example, they formed a column along a page's outer edge, and at other times, they took up the top or zigzagged downward.

The imagery on the Dave & Buster's menu is a form of food porn. You can find many variations of this on menus. Depending on the restaurant's branding and the menu's so-called "daypart" (breakfast, lunch, dinner, etc.), the lighting may differ markedly. The spotlighting of cocktails I found on the Dave & Buster's menu, accentuated by its glossy black paper, seemed well suited to the brand's nightclub ambience. But you won't find that high-key theatricality on a breakfast menu. When we visited Carl's Jr., for example, the breakfast and nonbreakfast items appeared all on one board, but I noticed that the breakfast items, on the far-left side of the menu, had a slightly mellower, sunnier cast than the rest of the menu, where the items had greater tonal contrast. Tellingly, the brown of the sausage on the breakfast menu was considerably lighter and less distinct from its surrounding biscuit and eggs than the brown of the hamburger patties was from their framing cheese and buns elsewhere on the board.

Still, all photographic food porn on menus conforms to certain design principles. Image layouts and sizes within a menu vary. Photo quality is high. Food angles invitingly toward the viewer. The photos emphasize bulk and texture—rocky ices, molten chocolate, crispy crusts, gooey cheese—appealing to the desire for abundance and intensity in taste and touch.

The number of restaurateurs who can execute food porn well is limited. High-quality photography and color printing are required for best effect, and they're expensive. Producing the photos is also an ordeal.

According to Shannon Phillips of the Dallas-based Johnson & Sekin agency, the designer of the aforementioned Dave & Buster's menu, the photo shoot required an elaborate setup. At the photographer's studio, the restaurant's chef, a marketing representative from Dave & Buster's, the photographer, and a food stylist all gathered around the staging area. As they worked, the stylist painstakingly directed the chef how to cut and plate the dishes, one by one, and made careful adjustments. For this, the stylist came prepared with a bag of tricks, things like Windex for degreasing the cheese on the cheeseburger and sand for bolstering the body and grit of the chocolate shake. Foods not so doctored would have languished under the lights and constant fussing over the multiple weeks it took to shoot the entire menu.

For Phillips, choosing the right photographer was no less involved. She began by contacting her wide network to bid on the project. Of the bids she received, she presented a short list to the client. In working up recommendations, she took many factors into consideration: who had the most fitting style, working process, personality, and studio space for the job. For Dave & Buster's, David Chasey was ideal.

Given the investment required in talent and time, we tend to find the most spectacular food porn in restaurants with the biggest budgets. The menus at Applebee's, for example, teem with such photos. That the company revises its menus every season makes this especially re-markable. Generally, big sit-down chains, from Dave & Buster's to the Szechuan-style Meizhou Dongpo, and a host of their limited-service counterparts, from Burger King to Taco Bell, make a similar investment. Even some of the smaller chains, like Farmer Boys, appear to follow suit.

A second approach to photography on main menus might best be called quasi food porn. Restaurateurs without the budget, but who want to show customers how their dishes look as served, may struggle to reach food-porn heights, but instead produce a poor imitation. The nine-page menu I documented from the Thai Town restaurant Jitlada, for example, presented vertical and horizontal gangs of photos of plated menu items that resembled food-porn photos in camera angle and proximity to dishes. But, by their dim lighting and tiny size, they looked pretty paltry. The photos that wound down the sides of the single-panel menu at the Moroccan and Tunisian restaurant Moun of Tunis were a bit bigger, brighter, and sharper. Perhaps Jitlada would have done the same if it, too, needed to cover only one page. But even the pictures at Moun of Tunis weren't exactly seductive, too small and distant to com-pete at the level of an Applebee's or Dave & Buster's.

In 2017, restaurateurs with food-porn aspirations and budgets that can absorb an extra $99 to $199 per month learned of a digital app that can extend their capacities, even if not all the way. In a *VOA Newsletter* article called "What's on the Menu? Augmented Reality and 3-D Food Models," Tina Trinh reported on Kabaq, an app that enables restaura-teurs to superimpose 3-D images of menu items on tabletops. Kabaq photographers bring to the restaurant a portable photo booth, which takes a picture of select dishes every second they rotate on a turntable inside. Of course, the quality of the images can be only as good as the portable photo booth allows and the camera readiness of those dishes without professional styling.

Less impressive though they may be, images like these and their 2-D counterparts still fulfill an important function. They describe aspects of dishes—namely, proportions of ingredients and arrangements on the plate—not normally conveyed by text. This information could make all the difference between diners ordering or avoiding an unfamiliar item. Not coincidentally, the many restaurants offering these visual aids tend to target an ethnically diverse audience.

Food porn of high and low quality isn't the only stylistic option for photos identifying dishes on main menus. That's because choice of style isn't only a matter of budget. Some establishments value efficiency in education over sensory stimulation, and take what I call a taxonomic approach.

Some operators that probably can afford high-quality food porn, such as the international dumpling-house chain Din Tai Fung and the San Gabriel Valley's ever-popular NBC Seafood Restaurant, present menu photos in a standardized way. The photos I encountered at these restaurants varied in quality and size—Din Tai Fung's were larger and more tantalizingly vivid than NBC Seafood's—but the layout of images at both restaurants was grid-like and the staging of items uniform. Pictures representing variations of the same dish—say, noodles or dumplings—presented those items in parallel positions. Each of Din Tai Fung's types of steamed buns, for instance, faced in the same direction and showed one bun closed next to another in cross section. Elsewhere, a pair of images showed two types of steamed dumplings, each with the tips of chopsticks picking up one piece from a pile. These weren't the colorful lifestyle shots we find in magazine editorials, just clever ways to show one dumpling from each bunch in greater detail.

What such displays lack in picturesque staging they gain in legibility. Uniformity in layout and imagery make variations of the same dish easy to find. That might matter in places where crowds are diverse, menus are long, there are many similar items, and business thrives on high volume. This style of photography educates—and with speed.

As different as the styles and goals of menu photography can be, it all has one function in common: reassuring the diner. In a lighthearted yet insightful op-ed in the *Ottowa Citizen* entitled "How to Avoid Menu Manipulation," Sara Dickerman gave it the catchy name "handholding." She was referring to menu language, not imagery, but I think her label applies here as well. Handholding in both contexts means mitigating risk, protecting diners from ordering something they might not like. While not all restaurateurs rely on photos to fulfill this function, those who do are probably handholding.

One sign of that intention is the degree to which restaurants with identifying photos of dishes deliver on their pictorial promises. In every one of my visits to restaurants, I made a point of checking for discrepancies between food and photo. I was consistently amazed by the high fidelity. In fact, the more lavish the food porn, the more faithful the items. It's as if the photos upped the ante on the kitchen.

Admittedly, limited-service chains tend to serve their hamburgers more squashed than their statuesque portraits on the menu, but they're usually convincing enough. Any deviation can be blamed on the requisite wrappers and box packaging.

As I explored the menu photography in my sample, I noted that full-service chains à la Applebee's, Claim Jumper, and Dave & Buster's featured the most impressive correspondences. The molten chocolate cake at Applebee's in Alhambra was frosted in the same drip pattern, the scoop of vanilla in the same position. The darkness of the chocolate and the pale yellow of the ice cream matched with the photo almost Pantone-perfectly. Likewise, my Dave & Buster's Chicken & Shrimp Alfredo mirrored in every way—the textures, colors, proportions, even the serving dish—its picture. These places risked no misunderstanding, no disappointment—at least not of the optical kind.

A restaurant's use of photos to identify items on the main menu implies certain assumptions about its customers: they're unfamiliar with the items, they don't want culinary surprises, or they don't arrive with an automatic trust in the kitchen—perhaps all of the above. My sample thoroughly supported this conclusion. The more a place identified with vanguard-experimental cuisine or rarified ingredients, or the more acclaim a kitchen crew had, the less likely it was to identify dishes with photos on its main menu.

Not one of the gourmet or fine-dining restaurants in my study had photos identifying dishes on any of their menus. In restaurants representing the pinnacle of gourmet or fine dining, one can assume diners' confidence in the kitchen most of all. Also, in those places, surprising guests—pleasantly, of course—is part of the point. Where there was any imagery at all on these menus, it was either photography of things other than food or it was illustration that prevailed.

Moreover, instead of explaining dishes, the imagery on these menus enhanced a mood or theme. At the elegant fine-dining restaurant Providence in Hollywood, delicate sepia-toned etchings—of oyster shells, a crab, and the quirkily cropped lower half of a fish—were scattered in unexpected positions across the menu's immaculate pages. They worked brilliantly as quiet reminders of the restaurant's seafood focus and experimental bent. At the same venerated chef's more casual Connie & Ted's in West Hollywood, monochromatic photos conjured landscapes befitting the restaurant's inspiration: a 1947 seaside in Rhode Island, for example, where the chef's grandfather first taught him to fish. Seeing the old man carrying a basket of his catch toward the shore, I could practically hear the ocean behind him.

At the downtown restaurant Rivera, I found the closest thing any gourmet restaurant in my study had to photos of specific items on a menu. The front cover of the cocktail list showed a detail of the restaurant's back-room tequila wall, a place where guests could stow a bottle they bought of the pricey house-made stuff on specially built shelves between visits.

But, as a photo of a menu item, the picture of the tequila wall hardly fit the mold. Because the picture was uncaptioned, it advertised the item only indirectly. Also, at Rivera, tequila was more than just a menu item. It communicated the chef's identity as impassioned producer of the spirit, and it riffed on a distinguishing element of the restaurant's décor. Highlighting the liquor did more than represent an item; it branded the entire experience. In addition, the cocktail-menu cover deviated from the restaurant's photographic rule. The dinner menus took the same approach to photography as Connie & Ted's, evoking the chef's inspirations. One of the several variations of the dinner-menu cover I saw displayed a black-and-white photo of a toreador clashing with a bull. Another represented the famously severe architecture of Brasília. Together, the photos conjured the restaurant's pan-Latin theme.

Curiously, some of the gourmet and fine-dining restaurants in my sample that eschewed photos of dishes on their menus did exhibit such images on their websites. I found it significant, however, that the dishes in those photos went unnamed. That approach jibed with the tendency of restaurants in these niches to limit imagery to branding.

A prejudice persists, at least in the United States, against identifying dishes by photos on menus. I gather this not only from their rigorous exclusion from gourmet and fine-dining menus but also in the overwhelming tendency of establishments aspiring to those associations to marginalize such imagery. This consistently occurs among the more upscale casual-dining chain restaurants—those with higher check averages, more choice ingredients, and more skilled servers—and among brands trying to identify as a quality cut above their market niche.

Of the sit-down chains I studied, California Pizza Kitchen and The Cheesecake Factory distinguished themselves from the likes of Applebee's, Claim Jumper, and Marie Callender's by isolating the very few photos of menu items to separate pages. The latter, by contrast, consistently showed photos of dishes alongside the text. The Counter, the sit-down chain I mentioned in chapter 4, set itself apart from more plebeian burger houses by limiting the in-store photography of its food to a table tent featuring one special. The menu proper omitted photos.

In the quick-service arena, restaurant-class distinctions followed a similar pattern. The fast-casual chain Chipotle marked its superiority to that of traditional quick-service eateries like Taco Bell by confining its photos of dishes to the restaurant's website and leaving the in-store menu board, aside from one panel advertising a catering spread, spare with just text.

The exclusion of dish images, especially photos, from the pinnacles of gourmet and fine dining, and the minimization of these by aspirational brands surely point to a social boundary: a demarcation of the uneducated or philistine who needs handholding from the sophisticate who doesn't. Insofar as gourmet or fine-dining restaurants are exclusionary on the basis of cost and education, differences in menus' use of pictures reinforce social hierarchies.

Of course, the total field of menu imagery isn't that simple. Pictures of dishes on menus don't correspond only to social distinctions, and they don't automatically indicate the presence of lower-income, uneducated, or unadventurous diners. While an element of social exclusion is undeniable in the elite market niches, distinctions among diners can't account for the large quantity and wide variety of imagery on menus that elite diners also consume.

I know from life experience that the same sophisticates who relish a night out at Providence don't for a minute begrudge Din Tai Fung—also a favorite among gourmets—its many photos. They might even find the visual guide to dumplings helpful. I also know that the same diners who want surprise at dinner on Saturday night sometimes like their breakfast more predictable Sunday morning.

The strong correspondence of imagery to restaurant genre, including daypart, across my sample indicates that restaurateurs' use of menu imagery follows conventions—and, by extension, consumer expectations—of restaurant genre and dining occasion. Their use of menu imagery also follows rhetorical function. My sample consistently revealed that each approach to imagery had a distinct business purpose. The imagery (or lack thereof) on the menus I documented was either informing, seducing, hastening the pace of ordering, establishing credibility, maintaining mystery, or asserting brand identity.

At this writing, it's unclear how effective the patterns of practice are for generating sales. Indeed, the general matter of how persuasive menu imagery is remains elusive. Research in this area is still nascent. Unlike pictures in other types of advertisements, consumer information processing in nonrestaurant contexts, and menu language (which has received by far the majority of the scientific attention to restaurant menus), research on the persuasiveness of menu imagery is sporadic and test conditions across studies aren't similar enough to give us broad insights.

Despite this, researchers have positively correlated the use of some types of menu imagery with some people's purchases or intent to purchase the represented items. I hesitate to generalize further from their studies, because they're scant and test radically different kinds of imagery in extremely divergent contexts. Also, their findings come with significant qualifications.

Two recent studies, however, are worth pointing out. While indicative of the dissimilarities and complications involved in this research to date, they offer its most enlightening discoveries. The first, published in 2012, tested the effects of themed menu imagery on the purchases of 342 diners seated alone in a small restaurant in Brittany, France, over a five-week period for six days per week during lunch and dinner. A regular server, instructed to behave normally, presented diners randomly with one of three menus. All offered the same dishes, but one third had seaside-themed imagery (fish on the front page, a boat on the back), another third had countryside-themed imagery (farm animals on the front, a landscape on the back), and the rest bore neutral imagery (tables and chairs on the front, a kitchen cabinet on the back).

The server recorded each order along with the menu theme the customer received. Results showed that the consumption of fish dishes over the test period was significantly higher in association with the seaside theme (43.3 percent of orders) than it was with the countryside theme (13.8 percent) or the neutral theme (21.7 percent). Yet the consumption of meat dishes was barely greater in association with the countryside theme (69 percent of orders) than with the neutral theme (65.2 percent). Meanwhile, the consumption of meat under the seaside condition was only 42.3 percent. Why the seaside imagery, while unable to pull the heavy bias of all customers away from meat, had more swaying power than either of the other themes exceeded the researchers' grasp. I dare not speculate myself.

If anything, I suppose, the study conclusively showed that themed imagery can be persuasive. That's important. But it also revealed that some imagery might be more persuasive than other imagery for reasons we don't yet know.

The second study, published in 2017, produced more definitive results, although not at all comparable with those of the first. It attempted to discern something totally unrelated about a different kind of imagery, in a dissimilar testing situation with another nation's population. What's more, it tested the complicating factor of image perception in relation to text.

The goal, using a hypothetical menu (not in a real restaurant) was to gauge the effects that certain combinations of photography and textual descriptors had on consumers' desire for and willingness to pay for the items they represented.

The researchers conducted a set of two online surveys among adults based in the United States, who were found and paid nominally through the service Amazon Mechanical Turk. In both cases, the respondents first took a survey (with established precedent in consumer-information-processing research) that classified them as visualizers, people with a tendency to form a mental picture of verbal information, or verbalizers, those who code information verbally and tend not to construct mental images from verbal information. In the first case, the researchers randomly assigned to subjects one of four conditions involving either no image or the same photograph of a dessert together with one of two types of textual descriptions for it: the straightforward

"Chocolate Ice Cream" or the ambiguous "Waltz on the Ice." In order to discern the subjects' valuation of the item and intent to purchase, researchers asked them to imagine holding a menu and ordering the represented dessert, then what they would pay for it.

Realizing that the first experiment may have obscured the possible bias of subjects for or against the restaurant genre with which the verbal or visual information might be associated (stylistically, they resembled items on a casual-dining-chain menu) or the food type, researchers produced a second experiment, which was identical to the first in all but two ways. The menu item changed to a lunch salad and the subjects underwent screening before revealing the item price (rather than after, as in the first study) to ferret out their attitudes toward the item.

Both experiments yielded the same results. In the case of straightforward food names only, pictures had a positive effect on all subjects' attitudes and purchase intentions. But, in the case of ambiguous food names, pictures had a positive impact only among verbalizers and a demonstrably negative effect on visualizers.

The most convincing explanation the researchers gave for the discrepancy was that ambiguous names stir the imagination more than common descriptive names, thus creating, for visualizers, the possibility of disappointment when faced with a picture disconfirming their mental images. For verbalizers, the photo simply provided information to compensate for the lack of informative text.

Possible explanations notwithstanding, I believe the larger value of the study is its indication that the effectiveness of menu images as sales tools depends heavily on individual styles of processing verbal and visual information. It prompts us to consider how much innate individual orientation, not to mention the presence of other signifiers (textual, verbal, material, etc.), might affect any attempt at persuasion. Whatever the case, restaurateurs have no control over it.

CHAPTER 7

Defining Mediums

APPLEBEE'S WAS ONE OF THE FEW RESTAURANTS IN MY SAMPLE I VIS-ited twice. The second time was nearly two years after the first. I'd been waiting for the digital tabletop tablets the brand was rolling out to all 1,800 of its stores as a supplement to the main menu to arrive at a location near me.

Although my main purpose was to document the ways of the tablet, during my second trip, I couldn't help noticing that the printed menu had undergone a makeover. I could literally feel it. The earlier Applebee's pages were stiff, shiny, and slick. The newer ones felt softer, more organic.

The interval between my visits had been volatile for the brand. The introduction of tablets, in fact, was one response to an oncoming threat to its market share: the fast-casual segment of the restaurant industry had been gaining popularity. It was swiftly redefining value in casual dining and fast food.

A classic example of this success, Chipotle was advertising and, by most accounts, delivering a higher-quality dining experience for less money in less time than full-service chains such as Applebee's. Aside from savvy marketing, Chipotle's improved product involved more con-scientiously sourced ingredients and fresher preparations, all packaged in an updated store design. Chipotle did away with the clown colors and

hard plastics of traditional chains in favor of a subtler earth-toned palette and materials that looked and felt more natural. Over 2013, the year
I first studied the menus at Applebee's, fast casuals were outperforming
sales in all restaurant segments.

The restaurant's changes to menu medium (materials and forms)
were likely a response to the competition from fast casuals. The tablets,
which allow guests to pay and leave when they're ready and order appetizers and desserts without waiting to be noticed by a server, helped
Applebee's approximate the fast casuals in speed of service. The redesign of the printed menu got the restaurant closer to the naturalistic
style that the new genre was using to promote "healthful" and "artisanal" messages.

Applebee's was probably hoping that the changes in medium would
improve perceptions of the brand's quality. That would be fitting. The
choice of menu materials and forms is paramount for creating impressions of restaurant quality. In this respect, menus are just like other arti-
facts. Among jewels, for example, gold is more precious than silver, and
you'll pay a lot more for some diamonds than others due to superior
cut, clarity, color, and carat. In clothing, certain materials, like cashmere,
and forms, like complex or creative tailoring, are prized above others.

Restaurant quality, however, has more than one definition. It can be
hierarchical—referring to the pedigree of ingredients, fastidiousness in
dining-room upkeep, skill in service, or recognitions of the chef. Yet it
can also mean brand integrity, the degree of alignment with a promised
service or experience. In either case, menu mediums impact perceptions of quality.

Among the full-service restaurants in my sample, the use of plastic
on table menus played a significant role in connoting quality. Plastic, of
course, is often a practical and necessary material choice: unprotected
paper menus quickly deteriorate with daily handling by customers. The
presence of plastic on a menu often signals a restaurateur's intent on a
menu's longevity; a menu with items that change daily may not require
such protection. But within the broad category of plastic, a restaurateur
has several choices to make.

Arguably the most ubiquitous protective plastics are laminate coatings on papers. These may be thin or thick, allowing for a wide range
in shininess and stiffness. Note that paper with laminate is distinct

from glossy paper, which may or may not be coated with a polymer and doesn't feel stiff unless the paper is heavy. In some instances, a very thick laminate completely seals a page on both sides. This gets the shiniest and stiffest results, making paper unbendable.

Also plentiful are plastic sleeves for sliding paper into. The thicker they are and the more loosely bound the papers in them, the more traction the sleeves gain on our fingers, making the menu feel sticky. The opposite occurs when clear sheets of plastic film are laid over menu pages. Because films tip in to the four corners of a menu-cover interior, they don't require diners to feel the slickness or tackiness of the plastic.

According to my research, the more a place identifies with fine dining (formal service and high prices) or gourmet cuisine (innovative dishes or special ingredients), the less likely it is to use plastic, even if its menu doesn't frequently change.

Many less-elite, yet still restaurant-class-aspiring restaurants, use plastic, but demonstrate a bias against the inherently synthetic quality of the material. The more natural—in other words, the less like plastic— the plastic feels, the greater the restaurant's status ambition.

The chain restaurants in my sample made this tendency most evident. Those making no claim to gourmet or fine-dining status used plastic that was slicker, stiffer, or stickier. For its multipage main menu, Rainforest Café chose the thickest of plastic sleeves on the market. The main-menu book at Claim Jumper was equally plastic. Hard laminate sealed every spiral-bound page. Because the spirals pierced the pages along a transparent edge of laminate, the laminate appeared as a margin along each page—and thus very prominent. The Dave & Buster's menu was perhaps the shiniest of the menus I studied. Designer Shannon Phillips told me that this effect derived not only from the combination of black paper and theatrical lighting in the restaurant but also from the coating of pages with laminate, most heavily on the cover, where diners would notice it first.

Meanwhile, chain restaurants asserting more upscale identities used plastics in distinctive ways. One tactic was to adopt a plastic that felt more natural, like paper. The change at Applebee's to a lighter coating of laminate exemplified this approach. In a 2017 article in *Aol.*, entitled "Applebee's Is Ditching Millennials after They Forced Hundreds of

Restaurant Closures," reporter Kate Taylor affirms my notion that Applebee's intended the redesign, which included that of the menu, to lift the brand's status. She quoted John Cywinski, then the brand president of Applebee's, who admitted that, "Over the past few years, the brand's set out to reposition or reinvent Applebee's as a modern bar and grill in overt pursuit of a more youthful and affluent demographic with a more independent or even sophisticated dining mindset." As the article title suggests, however, the efforts failed.

In other cases, restaurants wanting to set themselves apart used a heavy laminate, but gave their menus novel shapes. In keeping with their higher aspirations, The Stinking Rose (a garlic-themed restaurant) and California Pizza Kitchen did this by giving their menus atypical proportions. The Stinking Rose, the restaurant in this category most identified with special occasions, had the most outlandish menu shape, tall and narrow in the extreme. (Of course, that restaurant's attempt to create a strongly themed environment for entertainment purposes also explains its choice of a noticeably theatrical menu form.)

Better-burger chain The Counter claimed its superiority among burger places by using materials, including plastic, in a most unusual way. Plastic was just part of the main menu's assemblage, and not one that we touched first. The printed menu came in two parts, both attached to a first point of contact, a clipboard in the natural material of cork. Its metal clip grabbed a top layer of disposable paper on which we marked choices of meats, buns, and toppings with pencils provided on the table. Lifting it revealed the more permanent printed menu in the form of a stiff, vinyl slab with a granular texture. I'd never felt anything like it for a restaurant menu.

The Cheesecake Factory had the closest thing to a plastic-laden book. In this case, however, the choice was understandable. Considering the extreme length (over 250 items) and relative permanence of the restaurant's menu, increasing its lifespan with laminate made sense. Even so, it's noteworthy that, in stark contrast to Claim Jumper's laminated book, which displayed its laminate prominently, The Cheesecake Factory made an effort to minimize the appearance of plastic. While every page was coated, the laminate cleanly adhered to the edges of the pages. No edges stuck out, so the plastic was less noticeable as I turned the pages.

Generally speaking, while the chain restaurants parse the nuances of plastic, the gourmet and fine-dining restaurants avoid it. The materials they choose, however, correspond to the notions of quality that prevail in those niches.

The restaurants I visited with set tasting menus—whether their atmosphere and service were formal, like Nozawa Bar, or more relaxed, like the pop-up restaurant Amalur Project—were the only ones to offer no physical menu at all. The choice of nonmateriality in places of this sort had a clear logic. As journalist Sumathi Reddy points out in her 2011 *Washington Post* article "Less Is More on This Menu," a commentary on a trend in minimalistic, sometimes physically nonexistent menus, diners who go to these restaurants choose to put the fate of their meal in the chef's hands. The nonmaterial menu signifies acquiescence to that master.

This total trust gives the chefs the tremendous advantage of maximum flexibility. Having no physical menu allows them to change their plan of courses or the composition of dishes at any time if choice ingredients become unavailable or they feel spontaneous. The chefs have no obligation to justify or explain a modification.

With no menu to refer to, what customer would even notice one? The only reason I knew that chefs Sergio Lujan Perera and Jacob Kear had tinkered with the menu I had at Amalur Project was that I subsequently emailed Perera for a list of the courses, and what I got back differed from my experience. When I inquired about this, he confided that he and Kear had rethought the concept. Instead of the usual progression of vegetables before proteins, they decided it would be more interesting to separate the proteins. They would have vegetable-centered dishes lead up to each one, becoming heavier and more complex with each new sequence. I asked Perera when they had made this change. It was the night before.

The gourmet restaurants in my sample that did have physical menus took one of several main approaches to materials. One reflected, like the nonmaterial tasting menus, the supremacy of the chef. This tack involved the use of transient forms, easy to change on a daily or minute-by-minute basis. The copier paper on which all of the menus were printed at A.O.C. Wine Bar & Restaurant in West Hollywood may have looked flimsy compared with the restaurant's setting, which evoked a grand house in the wine country, but that's because it asserted the nobler value of responsiveness to nature. Chef Suzanne Goin was known for following the vagaries of the farmers' market.

Salt's Cure, another place with its ear to the earth, handwrote the daily main menu on a chalkboard. This made it easy to change not only day to day but in the same day. That happened, in fact, on the occasion Jamisin and I dined there. When we arrived, the kitchen had already substituted one of the proteins in a dish. The chalkboard menu at the restaurant differed from the one the staff had photographed and posted to the restaurant's Facebook page hours before.

Other restaurants in the gourmet vanguard used materials to define quality as intimacy with nature or as creative uniqueness. Both characteristics emanated from the use of unbound textured papers. I felt nothing slick or sticky. I mostly encountered papers in various states of fiber or grain. Two of the most ambitious menus in this category were also the most texturally complex. The papers at the experimental restaurant Ink. were pulpy. Maude, serving an inventive and strictly seasonal tasting menu, presented diners with stationery of whimsically ragged edge. Both irregular finishes call to mind not only an organic quality—suggesting that the restaurant uses superior ingredients (more "natural") as opposed to foods preprocessed by giant suppliers to hold over long distances (synthetic)—but also nonstandard production (i.e., original cuisine).

Except for vinyl covers convincingly aping leather, rarely did I find a gourmet menu with pages covered in plastic. When it occurred, the plastic was unusual and the restaurant was betwixt and between genres. A case in point was Mud Hen Tavern, a creative fusion of sports bar and gastropub. The food straddled the accessible (pizzas and burgers) and the playfully inventive (such as a spicy twist on deviled eggs with green-chile salsa called Green Eggs and Ham). The menu reflected this span. It arrived in a clear plastic sleeve, and it was uniquely long and narrow. It was also thin, unbordered, and finely tailored to the edges of the page, giving the impression of neatness and transparency. This then highlighted the organic qualities of the paper inside it, pale brown with visible grain. In other words, even Mud Hen Tavern, the most approachable of the gourmet restaurants in my sample, still managed to distinguish itself as a cut above the ordinary sports bar or pub through medium.

The most formal of the gourmet places in my sample that had physical menus took a slightly different approach. Commensurate with their greater pomp and price point, the menu materials of these restaurants expressed luxury. Their exposed white or off-white papers, maintained in pristine condition like the bed linens at five-star hotels, represented the meticulousness and extravagance of their operations.

Some of these dining rooms distinguished themselves further with uncommon materials. At Patina, the most formal of the restaurants in my sample, a crisp outer layer that General Manager Kevin Welby informed me was "architectural vellum"—a cotton designers use for drafting models that you'd never guess had a polymer stiffener—encased the orange paper of the menu cover. This hazy translucent sheath, severe yet dreamy, was what diners holding the menu touched first. It literally made the menu's first impression.

But, as with imagery, so with materials. Hierarchy isn't everything. In other pockets of the menu marketplace, snobbery over materials is immaterial. I found many instances, in fact, of full-service restaurants that were critically acclaimed and had plastic menus—some with the thickest, hardest, tackiest types.

Such places did, however, have something in common. They were trying to evoke, or actually belonged to, a traditionalist restaurant genre. A classic example is the bistro. A typical bistro menu consists of a page tucked inside a ribbon-bordered plastic sleeve. That's exactly what the reputable Bottega Louie, a stylish modern nod to the classic casual genre, used.

Some of LA's most revered historic restaurants have menus as plastic as anything I saw at midscale chains. Apple Pan in West LA, an institution respected for the burgers and pies it hasn't changed since 1947, presented one totally stiff laminated page. Canter's Deli, a fixture of Fairfax Avenue since 1931, had an eight-page menu no different in the plastic from Rainforest Café.

Also free from the prejudice against plastic were many of the single-ethnicity restaurants I studied—including Jitlada, Moun of Tunis, J&K Hong Kong Cuisine in Chinatown, NBC Seafood and Giang Nan in the San Gabriel Valley, and the ramen-focused Hana Ichimonme in Little Tokyo. Their menus exhibited stiff sealants, heavy coatings, and thick sleeves—every kind of plastic extreme.

The same logic that grants traditionalist restaurants carte blanche when it comes to plastic in menus may also explain why there's no shame—in fact, great pride—among restaurateurs who display replica foods, also made of plastic, in their shopfront windows. You'll find these menu augmenters at many Japanese restaurants in the United States and Japan. Hana Ichimonme, the place I observed, set out a profuse array, including models of ramen bowls, trays of faux full-meal ramen sets, and rows of dessert-ice illusions capped with heaps of fake fruits.

In Japan, these faux foods are a respected craft dating back to the 1920s, when they were made in wax. A connoisseur can tell the difference between the work of a master and that of a hack. The good work will cost you. According to recent reports, the prices for food replicas from the Gujo, the eye of the industry in Japan, can range from $70 for one *onigiri* rice ball to over $500 for a full main dish. A highly illusionistic crab might be closer to $1,000. No disrespect for plastic there—at least not among aficionados and for the best examples.

In the world of quick-service operations, menu mediums function differently. One reason may be that, since menus are typically signboards over ordering counters, the values they transmit don't pass through touch, and therefore don't depend on tactile properties for communication.

Also, the definition of quality differs from that of sit-down operations. Because queuing is customary and speed of service is king, menu mediums can enhance perceptions of quality to the extent that they relieve the pains of the queue. It's important that a board take a form that accommodates signage big enough, positioned strategically enough, to optimize legibility. The better we can read the menu, the faster we can make up our minds.

Many restaurateurs fall short of this mark. Although I personally experienced only one example of a signboard too small and inconveniently placed to read comfortably—the Washington Street location of the local chain King Taco comes to mind—there's some evidence that experiences like this are more common. In 2015, the market-research firm Datassential surveyed 1,500 consumers on their experiences and satisfaction with menu boards. One-third said that menu boards are usually too high up for them to easily read. Sixty percent noted that they look to menu boards in search of promotions and specials, but only 39 percent of them found that information easy to find.

If used wisely, digital signboards increase legibility. In recent years, a variety of quick-service restaurants, like the Burger King in Hollywood that we visited, have changed to this format. It's especially helpful in places, like Burger King, that regularly feature limited-time offers. By allotting them sufficient space, it can help solve the problem of hard-to-find promotions. The cold light that digital signs cast over a room may not be desirable in a romantic setting, but it is a fair trade-off in the spaces of fast food.

The best online ordering systems likewise alleviate the stress of waiting in the ordering queue. Like most, the Domino's ordering app saves your identifiers—address, credit-card details, and previous selections—to best expedite the process.

Consumer-survey research conducted by the National Restaurant Association (NRA) in 2016 revealed that adults of all ages, especially the young, had come to expect and appreciate the presence of digital ordering technologies such as smartphone apps, digital menu boards, tabletop tablets, and touch-screen kiosks—and that they like them especially for convenience and speed. Sixty-six percent of all adults and 76 percent of those eighteen to thirty-four who responded to the NRA's Technology Consumer Survey said they thought technology increased convenience. The belief that it increases speed was shared by 61 and 68 percent, respectively. As diners of all ages increasingly habituate to e-commerce, these percentages will only rise.

Although the definition of quality as a smooth-flowing queue is most germane to limited-service operations, the adoption of tabletop menu tablets at full-service chains that also thrive on sales volume suggests that this definition of quality doesn't apply only to the quick-service realm. At Applebee's in Azusa, for example, digital tablets expedited service and served as supplementary menus for appetizers and desserts.

Regardless of the model of service, however, restaurants of many kinds use menu mediums also to enhance entertainment. As Andrew P. Haley revealed in his history of the genre, the kid's menu has long been a special locus of creativity in this respect. Beginning in the 1930s and gathering force after World War II, as the restaurant industry saw the profit potential of appealing to families, the kid's menu emerged in novel interactive forms such as puzzles and cutout dolls. These were frequently complemented by other kid-friendly attractions in the restaurant itself.

I found a contemporary counterpart on the Applebee's tabletop tablet. It took advantage of the digital platform's unique ability to occupy children and profit from them at the same time. Between ads for appetizers and desserts, the screen continuously suggested games for $1.49 each.

But the entertainment value of menus isn't for children only. Menu mediums fulfill many an adult desire for novelty and theatrical immersion. In my survey, entertainment by menu took a startling range of forms. The Domino's online ordering app for iPad used the digital medium's capacity for motion graphics to spectacular effect. With each pizza topping I tapped on the menu screen, realistic images of that topping sprinkled onto a three-dimensionally rendered pie. At sit-down restaurants, I encountered everything from a shtick-y spoken menu— most notably at the historic The Gardens of Taxco, a Mexican restaurant in West Hollywood where the waiters recited the entire list in dramatic song—to the steakhouse theater of Wolfgang Puck's CUT in Beverly Hills, where in addition to a printed menu, the server brought us another in the form of a platter of raw meats. As he pointed out the merits of fat marbling on each one, the heavy red slabs were neatly swaddled, like precious infants, each in its own white or black cloth.

The display of real food, in fact—whether as a main menu or an auxiliary—was the most common medium I encountered for menus as entertainment. At the same time, real food was the most category-defying of all menu mediums in my study. It crossed upscale-downscale lines as well as genre categories.

Perhaps this is so because displays of real food are so rhetorically versatile. They can provide spectacle, testify to food quality, enhance ethnic authenticity, and arouse appetite. As such, they serve the messaging needs of many types of restaurants. It's no wonder, then, that I found them at the elegant fine-dining Patina, in the form of coffee, tea, and cheese carts; at the Brazilian *churrascaría* Fogo de Chão, in the gauchos' parade of grilled meats; and at Hama Sushi in Little Tokyo, in its wraparound shelf of refrigerated fish. It's also why I found them at so many fast-casual restaurants that boasted of top-notch ingredients—the likes of 800 Degrees, Lemonade, and Chipotle. These places glide patrons along their cafeteria-style assembly lines not just to get a closer look at the signboard menus on high, but also, and more importantly, to catch the multisensory sales pitches emanating from their ample trays.

Sharp restaurateurs stay attuned to how customers perceive mediums, and factor that into their designs. Yet they also make decisions according to mediums' cost-effectiveness and marketing capabilities.

Budget has some impact. Not everyone can afford the start-up and monthly costs of a digital system and technical support, which bigger chain restaurants like Applebee's, Burger King, and Domino's have incurred. Nor can all operators handle the high maintenance of immaculate fine papers, as Patina and Maude have demonstrated they can.

A host of other practical considerations not directly related to budget may also determine a choice of medium. Is a menu going to prioritize image or text? Text prints more cleanly on dull or textured paper. Photos are more luminous on a glossy surface.

How the menus will be used and how often they will be used can factor into an operator's choice of medium. The investment in a costlier medium could save the operator money in the long run. Lamination, for example, is approximately twice as expensive as glossy paper. But the cost may be well worth it for a busy place with a relatively stable menu, like The Cheesecake Factory, or a menu with extravagant photo layouts to protect, like Dave & Buster's.

Context ought to determine every decision about medium. For decades, the authors of menu-design manuals have wisely acknowledged this and advised would-be restaurateurs to choose materials that are durable where permanence is a priority and flexible where frequent changes to the menu are required.

Restaurateurs should get the durability-to-flexibility ratio right because it affects their menus' potential for cleanliness. If there's one material sign of quality that's universal among restaurants, it's an unsoiled menu. A thick, creamy card stock might look rich, but it is a poor choice if children persist in putting their sticky fingers on the diminishing copies.

At Connie & Ted's, the informal seafood-centric spot spearheaded by Providence restaurant chef Michael Cimarusti, the menu covers served practical as well as entertainment functions. Douglas Riccardi, the menu's designer, told me how well those "dopy, puffy vinyl" things, into which the papers of their menus inserted, contributed to the restaurant's branding. Their emulation of vintage menus evoked Cimarusti's childhood memories of the New England seashore. Riccardi also mentioned that he chose the covers because they were nearly "indestructible." "You can Windex them," he enthused.

Medium decisions also depend on restaurant architecture. Some restaurateurs take good advantage of the shape and size of their dining rooms. The chalkboard menu at Salt's Cure, for example, was a fine idea for a space consisting of one small room.

But not every place responds effectively to its spatial circumstances. Even though the shape of the building necessitated that the menu of the King Taco on Washington Street fit into its narrowest side, the signboards were still about a quarter smaller than they had to be. This problem was probably negligible for regulars who'd memorized the menu, but it certainly slowed me, a new customer, down. Since I was unable to read the menu during the time I stood in the long line, my decisions about what to order took unnecessarily long. In a fast-food operation like King Taco, seconds of stalling can amount, at the end of the day, to a lot of money missed.

A restaurant's model of service most certainly affects the choice of menu medium, too. At least it should. Having servers recite the evening's specials, appetizers, or desserts might be a good idea if the chef makes frequent changes to these parts of the menu. But only if the pace of dining at that establishment is leisurely enough to dedicate servers' time to this task and the prices are high enough to justify it.

Salt's Cure, the place with the ingeniously designed chalkboard main menu, performed less effectively when it came to the servers' recital of the dessert menu. Because it was impossible in the small space with crowded tables not to overhear other parties getting the spiel about dessert, it was noticeable when our server omitted it in an effort to hurry us out. Evidently compensating for the overbooking of tables that happened that night, our server came to us after our main course with hints that we should leave. She parked the big bag of our leftovers on the table and urged, "Will that be all?"

We looked at her in barely veiled disbelief. Jamisin broke the silence: "*Is* there anything else?" That's when, knowing she'd slighted us under the pressure, the server meekly caved and asked if we'd like dessert.

Finally, some decisions regarding medium are based on the marketing possibilities they create. The investment in digital systems, for instance, may allow restaurateurs to present limited-time offers without crowding their menu boards. If used smartly, they might also allow restaurateurs to respond nimbly to trends in data. They could feature or emphasize offerings on a variable basis, depending on the region, daypart, weather, or popularity of particular items.

Reports on digital technology for restaurants have suggested that the future of digital systems for restaurants lies in "surge pricing," also known as "variable pricing." This involves the fluctuation of menu prices based on real-time trends in item demand. In 2014, Justin Massa, CEO and cofounder of Food Genius, a food-service data provider, published a three-part article in *QSR Magazine* entitled "The Cost of Outdated Pricing Strategies" in which he advocated, clearly in his own interests, that restaurants start doing what other companies, including airlines and Amazon, have been doing successfully for years: they should be using customer data related to region, daypart, and past individual and aggregate purchasing behavior to push differing prices, depending on the menu type, to individuals or consumer groups.

The same year, Hudson Riehle, senior vice president of research for the National Restaurant Association, told *Nation's Restaurant News* reporter Ron Ruggless that NRA research showed potential for success in variable pricing. Seventy-two percent of restaurant customers the NRA surveyed said they'd dine out more if prices at restaurants were lowered at off-peak times. NRA research from 2016 raised that percentage to 75.

The enormous range of menu mediums makes untangling their patterns of occurrence a challenge. But I did find consistencies. As they do in the case of imagery, menu mediums follow a hierarchical order to a point. At the same time, they're strongly subject to differences in genre and dining occasion as well as the various pragmatic obstacles and opportunities relating to money, space, and time that restaurant operators face.

The examples of success and failure in my study show that the capacity of menu mediums to broker the interests of restaurateurs and diners hinges on two forms of agreement. The restaurant must fulfill the promises the mediums make, and the mediums must amplify the value of what the restaurant delivers.

CHAPTER 8

Choice Words

IN DEVELOPING HER MENU, KASJA (PRONOUNCED "SASHA") ALGER, chef and co-owner of the Melrose Avenue–adjacent Mud Hen Tavern, faced a dilemma. She told me it needed to be "interesting"—deserving of association, I figured, with famed-chef co-owner Susan Feniger—yet all the while "accessible," "neighborhood" style. She didn't want to alienate the diner "who just wants a cheeseburger and a beer." Accordingly, the menu couldn't seem "too foreign."

The duality Alger spoke of was hardwired into the restaurant. It even defined the architecture. True to the word *tavern* in the restaurant's name, the bar at the back wall anchored the inside dining space. As soon as we walked in, it captured my attention. Four tall chalkboard menus above the bar—decorated by artist Arlene Golant with wine, beer, and cocktail names in colorful scripts—gave the bar dramatic height. A TV mounted in the bar corner, showing a game, made the space sporty, as did the seating, a mixture of booths and communal tables with stools. The outdoor space shifted the mood in a more contemplative, perhaps romantic direction. Glass-walled off from TV and bar, it was all patio tables and potted plants lit by a suspended lattice of bulbs in the irregular pattern of starlight. A sophisticated cuisine could take center stage there.

To strike the balance between familiarity and novelty, Alger experimented not simply with concepts for dishes, as chefs do. She also tinkered with their names and descriptions, then watched how they affected sales. One item she'd listed as "Vietnamese Corn" wasn't selling very well, so she renamed it "Wheat Harvest Corn" and, so people would know there was Asian flavor, put "lemongrass" in the line below. It sold better, but Alger saw room for improvement. Taking advantage of the approaching season, she changed the name again to "Summertime Corn." Instantly, the dish became a bestseller.

Scientists have tested the strength of menu writing like Alger's. A study in 2001, for example, revealed the power of what its authors called "descriptive labels." After reviewing the sales records at a University of Illinois cafeteria, they selected six items in a range of food types that were popular enough to be offered twice a week. For Tuesday and Friday lunch periods for each of six weeks, the investigators used basic labels, such as "Grilled Chicken," for two items and descriptive labels for another two. They identified four types of the latter: geographic ("Iowa Pork Chops"), affective ("Grandma's Zucchini Cookies"), sensory ("Tender Chicken Parmesan"), and brand-related ("Jack Daniels® BBQ Ribs"). For the next two weeks, they rotated items and conditions until all six dishes had appeared in all conditions. Starting the fourth week, to control for event-related variables, they repeated the entire rotation.

In the end, they found that descriptive labels increased sales by as much as 27 percent. Furthermore, questionnaires completed by 98 percent of the 140 diners who had chosen one of the target items showed that descriptive labels also corresponded to higher satisfaction, perceptions of food quality, and intent to buy those items again.

The authors of the study and Alger demonstrated that evocative and emotionally resonant words persuade. But do they do so everywhere and all the time? That "Wheat Harvest Corn" fared better than "Vietnamese Corn" at Mud Hen Tavern shows Alger's good gauge of her guests, but "Vietnamese Corn" might have won out somewhere else. The greater appeal of "Summertime Corn" shows the power of occasion. The name would be much less alluring on any menu in winter. The contexts of language must count for a lot.

The language of menus has only one universal rule: descriptions must be accurate. If carrots are called "roasted," they can't be merely boiled. If the beef is labeled "Niman Ranch," it can't come from another source. If the menu states "butter," the chef must use the real thing.

Accuracy is essential for customer trust. It's also the law. With the understanding that restaurant menus are a form of advertising, the United States government adopted a truth-in-menu law in 1923. It has evolved in the decades since.

In 1977, the National Restaurant Association published and adopted an "Accuracy in Menu" position paper. It defined honesty in eleven different forms. It covered verbal and visual representations and specified truth in matters of quantity, quality, price, brand names, product identifications, food origins, merchandising terms (e.g., "fresh"), preservation methods (e.g., "frozen"), preparation methods (e.g., "broiled"), and dietary and nutritional claims.

The turn of the millennium brought more activity. In 1997, the Food and Drug Administration (FDA) required that all nutrient and health claims on menus be scientifically backed. With the popularization of organic foods, in 2000, the US Department of Agriculture spelled out, among other things, the proper use of the word *organic* (no less than 95 percent of the product) and distinguished it from *made with organic ingredients* (no less than 70 percent). The Food Allergen Labeling and Consumer Protection Act, instituted in 2006, obligated all food manufacturers to identify the presence of egg, fish, milk, peanuts, shellfish, soy, tree nuts, and wheat—the eight major allergens specified by the FDA.

Most recently, in 2010, the Obama administration passed a law as part of the Patient Protection and Affordable Healthcare Act that charged chains of at least twenty units selling restaurant-style food to post calorie and nutrition information for each item. The deadline for compliance moved several times during the writing of this book; at last, to May 2018.

While not illegal, less tangible statements of a misleading nature also pose problems. With good reason, menu consultants have warned for decades of the disappointment that follows overhype. One consultant, in 1939, advised not using too many adjectives when describing a dish. She said that would arouse distrust. Menu-design manuals I found from 1985, 1996, and 2009 all cautioned against the use of superlatives like "majestic" and "to perfection," especially if lacking in food-related specificity.

For the most part, this advice makes sense. But menu-design experts have tended to miss the nuances of language or context that make compelling exceptions. Take the name of a fried-chicken sandwich I found at Barrel & Ashes, a barbeque restaurant in Studio City we visited in 2016. Though not part of my study sample, I mention it because it makes the point better than any example in recent memory.

Strictly by the menu-design books, "The Best Damn Chick'n Sandwich Y'Ever Had" is a no-no. But I would suggest to all a grain of salt. The claim is so extreme and impossible to prove that it becomes ironic. Diners aware of the chefs' reputations might expect the sandwich to be good, and then order it out of curiosity—exactly what I did, so the ploy worked—all the while recognizing that the name, in drawl as tall as the claim, is a form of entertainment.

Apart from calls for accuracy, the rules of menu language diverge widely. Consider the terminology for describing dishes. My sample showed that the more uncommon and undefined the words on a menu are, the more a restaurant is distinctively gourmet—that is, high in food rarity, quality, or originality. Most nonnative speakers probably don't know the meaning of *charmoula*, *soubise*, or *vacherin*—some of the many untranslated words I found at A.O.C. Wine Bar & Restaurant—or what kind of glaze *gochujang* referred to on my slightly more accessible menu at The Church Key.

I'm not the first to notice the link between elite restaurants and esoteric terms. Dan Jurafsky, in his book *The Language of Food*, drew a similar conclusion from a far larger set of data. Computationally sorting 650,000 listings of dishes on 6,500 contemporary menus from seven of the largest and most culturally diverse cites in the United States, he and a team of fellow linguists calculated that longer words are rare. Also, they cluster around the more expensive restaurants. To be precise: "Every increase of one letter in the average length of words describing a dish is associated with an increase of 18 cents in the price of that dish!" In my survey, the priciest restaurants are also gourmet.

In addition, gourmet status corresponds with less explanation of how the components of dishes are prepared and plated. Take a look at these listings from some of the most experimental restaurants I visited:

Ink.: "**pork shoulder**, onion caramel, lardo, fermented apple"
Maude: "Hearts of Palm/avocado, raspberries, togarashi"
Providence: "**a5 wagyu**/daikon, peas, yuzu kosho"

From these lines, can you guess the cooking methods or the arrangements of ingredients? Only at the most vanguard places, which these represent, did I find descriptions totally devoid of this information, including for dishes unique enough to warrant an explanation.

When cooking methods are cited in these contexts, it's usually to describe one part of a dish, such as the "roasted cauliflower" in Ink.'s listing of "**branzino**, roasted cauliflower, caper, fermented grape." It isn't to reveal its relation to the whole. The pattern follows a certain logic. Telling us how a dish will look and taste is a form of handholding.

A restaurateur who knows that her diners are adventurous, food knowing, or trusting of the kitchen—which gastronomes visiting their temples are the most apt to be—can afford to do less, if any, of that. At the most vanguard places, in fact, mystery adds value. Hiding the form of a dish is key to the surprise for which diners go.

Contrast that with the listing of an appetizer I saw on the menu at the casual-dining chain BJ's Restaurant & Brewhouse. It read, "**MINI-BRUSCHETTA**/Grilled focaccia bread, topped with sun-dried tomatoes, onions, basil and fire-roasted red bell peppers." BJ's explained not only how it prepared key ingredients ("grilled," "fire-roasted") but also how it assembled them ("bread, topped with . . . ").

The difference in descriptions isn't just a matter of information quantity. It can't be, because nongourmet eateries in my sample had some of the shortest listings, and their brevity had little to do with creating mystique. Some descriptions were brief because other devices, such as displays of real food, did the handholding instead. Others were short because the foods they referred to were so familiar and generic—cheeseburgers, pizza, tacos—that no one needed an explanation. Many of the latter also maintained a speed of service that lengthy labels would have slowed.

Gourmet dish descriptions set themselves apart by the type of information they disclose and withhold. In 2006, sociolinguist Robin T. Lakoff made this point convincingly in a close examination of Chez Panisse and the Oriental Restaurant—two restaurants across the street from each other in Berkeley, California, yet miles apart in their menus' language. She noticed that the menu at Chez Panisse, a restaurant with a formative influence on contemporary gourmet menu writing, listed names of dishes and ingredients in their native Italian, French, and Spanish languages without explanation—a practice that assumed expansive cultural knowledge on the part of the diner. Terms she cited—including the French *noyau* (a type of brandy), the Italian *torta pasqualina* (a savory Italian Easter pie featuring a whole egg baked inside), and the Spanish *migas* (meaning either crumbs or a Tex-Mex dish with regional variations)—required familiarity with obscure items and would mystify most people. (I suppose even a *migas* expert would be left to wonder what version of the dish Chez Panisse had in store.) Meanwhile, in other listings on the same menu, such as "Grilled Paine Farm Squab with Green Olives, Leeks, and Wild Mushrooms," Lakoff noted that the information about food origin and fruit or fungus type was much more detailed than the vague designation "Mixed Vegetables" that she found on the menu of Oriental Restaurant.

Explaining the disparity, Lakoff recognized that the Chinese restaurant, while omitting certain details, wasn't doing so to mystify in the gourmet sense. She saw, in fact, that the Chinese menu elsewhere sought to inform the diner specifically about the appearance of available dishes. The menu cover stated, "There are pictures displayed in our store to make your selection easier." Thus, rather than obfuscating with its "Mixed Vegetables" label, Oriental Restaurant was just showing less regard than Chez Panisse for the diner's culinary knowledge and interest.

Overall, gourmet restaurants use language to differentiate the cognoscenti from the rest. They might do it by lacing their listings with details that only those in the know would appreciate, or they might do it through minimalism and obscurantism.

The use of menu language for social distinction is nothing new. As Rebecca L. Spang recounted in *The Invention of the Restaurant*, the earliest French menus to survive, from the early nineteenth century, were farcically cryptic. What she called "Menu French" was then fast becoming its own peculiar dialect, which even a native French speaker might not understand. As Spang elaborated:

> A "crapaud" was a toad and a "crapaudine" was a disease of
> sheep, so what did that make "pigeon a la crapaudine"? An

"epigramme" was a witticism, but what was an "epigramme d'agneau"? "Financier" had the same meaning in English and French, but in the latter language it was also the name of one of the most common sauces on an early 19th century menu.

Subsequent episodes of resistance to these barriers of language only show how much they endured. In the United States, backlashes of nationalism and anti-elitism tell the story. In his history of American elite restaurants, *Turning the Tables: Restaurants and the Rise of the American Middle Class, 1880–1920,* Andrew P. Haley shows that economic and cultural pressures from a rising middle class led many restaurateurs to relax their menus' use of untranslated French.

The Art of Naming Dishes on Bills of Fare by L. Schumacher, the earliest book on menu design that I could find (having been published in 1920), was symptomatic of that effort. This expert advised substituting English for foreign words whenever possible and using brief translations in the absence of adequate substitutes. "Fish Soup, *Chevreuse*," Schumacher urged; never just *"Chevreuse."*

Of course, the gratuitous use of French surfaced again. In 1981, *New York Times* restaurant critic Mimi Sheraton made the point in her famous rant, "Taking the Obfuscation out of Restaurant Menus." She decried the frequent and undeserved references she saw to the likes of *choucroute garnie* and *croque monsieur.*

Today's gourmet menus are no less fond of foreign terms. Yet, in keeping with gastronomic globalization, they've expanded their pool of languages well beyond French. Now, gourmets regularly read untranslated terms for ingredients and dishes in Italian, Spanish, Chinese, Thai, and more.

The menus have also gained a new tool for generating mystique. As Charles Spence and Betina Piqueras-Fiszman point out in *The Perfect Meal: The Multisensory Science of Food and Dining,* "modernist" cuisine of the 1990s and the first decade of the 2000s introduced "sensory incongruity"—the frisson of a pleasant discrepancy between a dish and its appellation—to the art of menu writing. The authors cite British chef Heston Blumenthal's "Meat Fruit," the surrealistic name for a chicken-liver parfait in the guise of a mandarin orange, to show how far chefs now go to make their menus thrillingly abstruse.

Also changed is what terms we deem exotic. Just twenty years ago, we didn't see *bruschetta,* which I saw on the menu at BJ's Restaurant & Brewhouse, on any menu likewise aiming for mass appeal. Terms like *sriracha* and *aioli,* now on the menus of the largest fast-food chains, were unheard of, too.

Still, even gourmet restaurants, in most incarnations, can't afford to be obscurantist all the time. While executive chef at Patina, one of my city's most refined and pricey restaurants, Charles Olalia explained to me that, while he used some French terms and mysterious labels for dishes on the menu, as a whole the document had multiple targets. It spoke to guests who know food, or want surprise, but also to those less informed, or who want to know what they're getting. For every *crépinette* or other term that Olalia said he used as "a power word," he made sure there was a *green salad* to counterbalance. Also, "vague" menu listings—by which he meant brief lists of ingredients that hint at flavor profile only—really made up only half of Patina's menu. After reviewing the copy the restaurant gave me, I realized he was right.

Except when restaurants rely on devices other than menu language to define themselves or their offerings, or when speed of service is the highest priority, menus are apt to do what designers call "romancing." To romance the menu is to describe dishes beyond the basics in order to make items attractive. Romancing is essentially the "descriptive labeling" that scientists have found so persuasive.

Romancing takes multiple forms and has various functions. It can appeal to the senses, cue quality, convey authenticity, or entertain. It can even signal health. Assuming the words are accurate, and therefore credible, success in romancing depends, like any ad, on sensuous and emotionally resonant language, and on making correct assumptions about patrons' notions of quality and occasion-based desires.

Throughout their history, even before any science supported their claims, menu-design consultants have advocated mouth-watering descriptions. In her 1940 book *Restaurant Menu Planning,* Ann Hoke suggested that *puffy* or *golden* would modify *omelette* better than *plain.* In a more elaborate tutorial on sensory labeling of 2013, entitled *How to Write Great Restaurant Menu Descriptions,* Steve Bareham claimed that menu listings should appeal to all five senses. A hypothetical description for "Grilled Pancetta Prawns" that he made up to demonstrate his ideal conveyed not just cues for taste—as in (italics mine) "wrapped in *robust* pancetta"—but also smell—by adding "*aromatic* basil and sage leaves"—touch—with the mention of "grilled to a delectable *crispy* finish"—and, finally, sight—by conjuring the image of prawns "threaded delicately on bamboo skewers."

These pieces of advice are in line with the science that says descriptive labels persuade. But I find them too universalizing with respect to style. Bareham's description of "Grilled Pancetta Prawns," for instance, is almost a paragraph long. Not every place or occasion demands such a heavy hand. Indeed, few menu consultants—or even scientists who study the impact of menu descriptions—have seriously considered that what titillates depends, to some degree, on the diner type and situation.

In my survey of menus, I found two distinct styles of sensuous description, which correspond to discrete diner profiles and occasions. The first uses evocative words in a way that's handholding, previewing details of the eating experience. The most extreme exemplars were the full-service casual-dining chains. Just look at these lines advertising the "Triple Chocolate Meltdown®," which I read at Applebee's in Alhambra: "A magnificently moist chocolate cake. Its fudge-filled center will erupt upon first bite! Served with vanilla ice cream and hot fudge." Or, contemplate the graphic exposition of a "Lemon Meringue Cheesecake," which I encountered on the back of the menu for The Cheesecake Factory: "Lemon Cream Cheesecake Swirled with Lemon, Topped with Layers of Lemon Mascarpone Mousse and Housemade Meringue on a Vanilla Crumb Crust." Surely, you'll see that the following description for an appetizer called "Bagna Calda," on my menu at the garlic-themed restaurant The Stinking Rose, is a master class in the effusively concrete. This description of the dish accompanied its fanciful illustration of a hot tub full of wine-toasting garlic-clove buddies: "Garlic cloves, oven-roasted in extra virgin olive oil & butter with a hint of anchovy, a wonderful treat for spreading on our house-baked focaccia bread, served at your table in an iron skillet."

This language has the paradoxical ability to stir up fantasy while leaving little to the imagination. All three examples represent the verbal equivalent of food porn.

Manuals on menu design have overwhelmingly adopted this mode as their model without acknowledging its niche character. Most have also failed to notice the very different appeal to the senses I discovered on the most vanguard of gourmet menus. Their language may be more implicit than explicit, more minimalistic than gushing, but they're still vividly sensuous: this description of a dessert—"**mountain yam**, caramelized white chocolate, popcorn, coconut"—from the menu I saw at Ink., as well as "Earl Grey Lemon Vacherin/Szechuan Pepper, Honey Chantilly" from Providence, have a poetic economy that's as stimulating as any adjective-laden caption. The lines of text arouse interest because their juxtaposition of ingredients is so unexpected.

The contrast between these two styles is a lot like the difference between abstract and realistic painting. Neither is more sensuous. But they attract differing tastes. Those tastes can have a hierarchical aspect.

From his statistical analysis of menu language, Jurafsky confirmed the stratified pattern of sensory descriptions: "Each appealing adjective like *rich*, *chunky*, or *zesty*," he concluded, "is associated with a price that is two percent lower." Moreover:

> Long, wordy menus with lots of filler words occur in the middle-priced restaurants—chains like Ruby Tuesday, T.G.I. Friday's, Cheesecake Factory, California Pizza Kitchen, etc.... Descriptive adjectives like *fresh*, *rich*, *spicy*, *crispy*, *crunchy*, *tangy*, *juicy*, *zesty*, *chunky*, *smoky*, *salty*, *cheesy*, *fluffy*, *flaky*, and *buttery* appear significantly more often in menus from these middle-priced restaurants.

The category of restaurants Jurafsky referred to actually covers a range in price points that many diners might find meaningful. Our bill for a meal for two that included every course and drinks was approximately $60 at Applebee's in Alhambra, $100 at The Cheesecake Factory in Glendale, and almost $140 at The Stinking Rose in Beverly Hills.

Nevertheless, that spread is still significantly lower than the equivalent meals we had at gourmet places also representing a full price range. At Mud Hen Tavern, among the least expensive of the gourmet restaurants in my sample, our bill came to roughly $150. At Ink., just over $200. A parallel indulgence at the formal-service Providence, one of the most expensive on my list, cost almost $500.

Although the hierarchical pattern is real, it's far from a full explanation of sensory menu descriptions. Most diners who go to places like Providence don't go only to those. While the minimalistic appeal may find its fans among gourmet diners alone, the same diners might, on other occasions, be tempted by more detailed descriptions.

My sample suggested as much. More explicit sensory appeals appeared at a wide variety of single-ethnicity and traditionalist restaurants also beloved by food aficionados.

But it might be true only to a point. The sensory descriptions I found at those places were indeed detailed; however, they were still markedly less elaborate than those at Applebee's, The Cheesecake Factory, and The Stinking Rose. For example, the Thai restaurant Jitlada called one dish "Savory White Tofu Dip" and described it as "crunchy fried tofu in choo chi curry dip." Here, *savory* and *crunchy* are sensory descriptors, but the listing, as a whole, isn't exactly lavish. Likewise, the brasserie-style Bottega Louie described the components of a "Porchetta" sandwich as "slow roasted pork, caramelized sweet onions, Peppadew peppers, arugula & brined caper aioli." The phrases *slow roasted*, *caramelized sweet*, and *brined caper* are full of sensuous specifics; however, the description is still relatively restrained. In the realm of sensory descriptions, the casual-dining chains remain in a class by themselves.

An especially stratified aspect of language on menus is cues for food quality. The pattern I saw is precisely parallel to one I discussed in the chapter on menu mediums. Like textures of plastic, certain markers of food quality reliably measure gourmet status.

Restaurant chains in my sample with no gourmet aspiration were inclined to use the word *fresh* to qualify everything from guacamole to lemonade. They were also prone to a variety of phrases beginning with *hand*. They used it for blanket references to an entire fabrication process, such as "handmade" for shakes at the dining-and-gaming chain Dave & Buster's, or to designate handiwork of low-level skill: "hand-spun" for the milkshakes and "hand-breaded" for the fried chicken at Chick-fil-A; "hand-scooped" for the ice-cream shakes and malts at Carl's Jr.

The same types of restaurants tended to describe an ingredient as "fine"—as in "a dusting of fine cocoa" for the listing of the "Triple Layer

Chocolate Cake" at Dave & Buster's and the description "a variety of only the finest, plump and luscious ripe berries" for the "Berry" pie at the midscale chain Marie Callender's. In these places, I also found—as in the line "Gourmet Mac and Cheese" at BJ's—the word *gourmet.*

Places with critical acclaim or top chefs have no rhetorical use for such terms, since their patrons assume the ingredients are fresh, that care is taken and skill goes into their preparation, and that the products are gourmet.

The gourmet restaurants in my sample either didn't boast at all about quality or they advertised a rarified quality. For example, the term *Atlantic* may have distinguished the cod at Carl's Jr. and the salmon at Claim Jumper and Marie Callender's, but it would have meant little at Connie & Ted's, the casual outpost of renowned chef Michael Cimarusti. There, the owners preferred to stress the eco-friendliness of their ingredients. Printed under the listings for "Catch of the Day," I read, "Our fish are wild caught and sustainable."

Other evidence of hierarchy in this regard is the aspirational behavior of quick- and full-service chains that advertise a higher standard than normal for their genre. These chains often ape the quality cues of the gourmet set. I found a message on the menu of the local burger chain Farmer Boys, for instance, that declared its ingredients were "locally sourced whenever possible." The header of the paper menu of the better-burger chain The Counter stated not simply that its beef was "fresh" but also that it was "100% Natural Angus Beef Hormone and Antibiotic Free." What's more, a message in a blue border next to that assured us that the meat was "Humanely Raised + Handled."

As we might expect from its effort to distinguish itself from other casual-dining chains, a point I discussed in chapter 4, The Cheesecake Factory made the most elaborate effort to assert its distinctiveness from other chains in food quality. The "Welcome" page of the menu I sampled professed:

> We prepare our food fresh each day in our own kitchens using the highest quality ingredients available. We use all-natural chicken with no added hormones, premium Certified Angus Beef®, American Style Kobe or U.S.D.A. Choice, fresh fish that is either Longline or Hook & Line caught

whenever possible . . . and much of our produce is sourced
direct from premium growers . . . .

The part about the fish is impressive by gourmet standards. Yet the
statement that fresh food is prepared daily in house, which would be
a given in truly gourmet restaurants, was mainly there to distance the
brand from the casual-dining chains with which it might be confused.
You know. The ones that truck in foods from giant suppliers who deliver
them prepared, frozen, and ready to throw in a microwave.

If they want to be held in higher esteem, gourmet and gourmet-
aspiring brands might soon have to find more distinctive language. In
the course of writing this book, I've heard with increasing frequency
the words *sustainable* and *cage-free* coming from TV ads for McDonald's.

In any case, if they want to romance quality, restaurateurs have another option. They can drop brand names. References to known trade-
marks on the menu can help build customer trust or restaurant prestige.

These distinctions have a hierarchical order. The more gourmet or
gourmet-aspiring a restaurant, the more likely it is to list brands of a relatively rarified kind. Conversely, the less gourmet or gourmet-aspiring a
restaurant, the more likely it is to identify with more accessible brands.
The largest fast-food chains tend to drop the most ubiquitous, and
therefore not especially distinguished, names. In my sample, I noted
the partnership with Oreo in Carl's Jr.'s "Oreo Cookie Shake or Malt" and
Taco Bell's declaration of allegiance with Doritos in the "Doritos® Locos
Tacos" on its menu. Because such brands derive their credibility from
sheer scale and mainline recognition, the value of cobranding in these
instances is simply to establish trust, a basic quality assurance.

The full-service casual-dining chains are more inclined to cite trade-
marks for distinction. The chocolate brand Ghirardelli cropped up repeatedly in these contexts in my sample, representing what counted for
quality in this echelon of the restaurant industry. In an italicized line
underneath the name and description of a dessert at Romano's Macaroni Grill, "**Homemade Chocolate Cake**/warm ganache, chocolate toffee,
whipped cream," I read, "*Made with Ghirardelli® Chocolate.*"

BJ's was even prouder of its link to the chocolatier. It mentioned its
name no less than four times in the listing of a dessert that also featured the restaurant's own trademarked item, the Pizookie. It appeared

once in the title, "**Triple Chocolate Pizookie® Made with Ghirardelli®**," and three times in the description: "A rich chocolate cookie made with chunks of Ghirardelli chocolate. Topped with two scoops of Ghirardelli double chocolate chip ice cream and a Ghirardelli SQUARES® dark chocolate." Like Oreo and Doritos, Ghirardelli is a widely known and available brand, but the general public views it as a bit more select.

Meanwhile, in gourmet places at all price points, menus consistently name-drop brands that connote greater discrimination in quality, and that are scarcer in stores. At Mud Hen Tavern, the beef for the "Classic Cheeseburger" was described as coming from "Lindy & Grundy," a butcher selling only organic and pasture-raised meat. The Church Key specified Benton's, a specialty purveyor from Tennessee, as its brand of country ham. Ink. cited a different, though still boutique, source of porcine product in the listing, "**la quercia ham**, chewy beets, pears, yogurt, nutmeg oil." The menu at Providence mentioned that the duck breast on offer was from "liberty farms." At this writing, I don't find any of these brands in a large chain supermarket. Ghirardelli, on the other hand, I can buy at my local Ralph's.

Only on one occasion did I notice the same brand named across restaurant classes. Reference to Nueske's bacon appeared on the menus of casual gourmet eateries Mud Hen Tavern and Connie & Ted's, in their descriptions of burgers; but it also came up at the chain California Pizza Kitchen, in a line about their "California Club Sandwich."

The overlap, however, still reflects a ranking order. Keep in mind that CPK is one of the aspirational casual-dining chains, like The Cheesecake Factory, trying to set itself apart. When I encountered these menus, Nueske's bacon was just where the line between gourmet and gourmet-aspiring blurred.

Elsewhere, the CPK menu showed its ordinary side. Its reference to "Häagen Dazs" as the ice cream to go with the "Butter Cake" would have sounded much less impressive at Mud Hen Tavern or Connie & Ted's. Respectable, but not rarified, that brand is equivalent to Ghirardelli.

The art of romancing may also take forms that don't relate to rank. Among these is the effort to convey authenticity.

Restaurants featuring food of a single ethnicity might demonstrate their bona fides in that cuisine by using the ethnic language. In my sample, Osteria Mozza, a celebrated destination for Italian food, strictly adhered to Italian terminology for courses of a meal—"Antipasti," "Primi," "Secondi," "Contorni," "Dolci"—on menu headings, and consistently used Italian terms in dish descriptions. Among the pastas, a tomato purée was "passata di pomodoro"; a sauce of butter and sage, "burro e salvia."

The menu of Romano's Macaroni Grill did just as well in upholding the chain's Italian-American theme. On a supplementary menu promoting new items with the English name "Braisers," the heading "introduzione dei nuovi" gave them an Italian accent. The dish names listed there—"Cremini Pork Shank," "Chicken Cacciatore," and "Classic Italian Bake"—had points of reference just Italian enough. Like Italian American culture, the foreign parts were half assimilated.

Sometimes menus assert their ethnicity through what designers call "merchandising copy"—the text on the menu that sells things other than the food and drink. These may include the restaurant itself, by way of an origin story, or services like takeout and catering. At the bottom of the menu at Moun of Tunis, a bit of merchandising copy read: "We are happy to bring you the rare treat of authentic cuisine and ambience from Tunisia and Morocco. Each dish is carefully prepared for you by our chef, a native Tunisian." This conveys an ethnic authenticity that the list of dishes alone can't.

Merchandising copy can also demonstrate fidelity to cultural traditions. At both sites of the Chinese dumpling specialist Din Tai Fung, I read a declaration of that sort. Under the heading "About Din Tai Fung," the company announced this reverence for dumpling craft: "A group of Din Tai Fung's steamed dumpling chefs summed it up best: 'Creating steamed dumpling is not just a technique, but an art.'"

Likewise, restaurants with a genre character might claim it in the merchandising text. Below the listing of desserts on the menu of Canter's Deli, I read a paragraph devoted to the "Canter's Story," which included the proclamation that "Canter's is . . . known for . . . a perfect blend of contemporary comfort with the nostalgic charm of some of its 1950s décor." At Applebee's in Alhambra, the menu evoked the familiar hospitality of the local bar and grill. "You're cordially invited to have a good time in the neighborhood," began the inscription on the first page. Meanwhile, California Pizza Kitchen put diners in a "California state of mind," a genre that, it claimed on the back of the main menu, was all about "originality, creativity, fresh and natural ingredients, and the often daring fusion of different ideas."

Many restaurateurs use merchandising text to craft a more personal brand. One way is to tell a family story. Apple Pan, a historic place to get burgers and pies, used the back of its menu to credit six "Original Family Recipes." It listed the name of the item, the family member responsible for the recipe, and the date and city of its birth. Reading that the "Apple Pie" hailed from "Roma Grover Baker" of "Gallipolis, Ohio," in 1881 made me think about the restaurant in terms of enterprising individuality and continuity with the past.

The back page of the Connie & Ted's menu took a more scenic approach. About the grandfather of the chef, the Ted in Connie & Ted's, the menu said:

> In 1947, Ted built a summer cottage in Matunuck, Rhode Island, where he enjoyed many years of fishing. That love of fishing was passed on to his grandson Michael . . . in spite of the fact that Ted made Michael clean and fillet the day's catch.

The loving tribute plants the restaurant's nostalgic root.

In romancing language, entertainment intertwines with branding. Both help define a restaurant's concept. Both may be dramaturgical, supplying the restaurant's scene with character and backstory.

But not all brand-building language is entertaining. Apple Pan's list of recipe credits, for example, wasn't especially so. Entertaining requires rousing novelty, prompting laughter or surprise, or engaging the diner in a participatory script. The Stinking Rose's creative names for steaks, including "Dracula's Porterhouse," and its punning captions, such as "we are (premium) stake driven," were examples I found of branding that were also entertaining. These descriptions add a playful dash of humor to the restaurant's garlic theme.

The bottom of the food menu at A-Frame, chef Roy Choi's boisterous restaurant in Culver City, entertained by inviting diners to take part in a stimulating party. There, a quotation from a persona of the chef named "Papi Chulo" created an atmosphere of casual conviviality that included the diner: "A-Frame is home. It's how I'd cook for you if this was a house party. No ridiculous pretentiousness, no hors d'oeuvres.

Straight macking, lip smacking, and big belly laughs." The restaurant's shared-plates format and ambience—especially the loud hip-hop, the large and vibrant bar zone, and the picnic-table seating—supported this lure to relax and let loose.

Of all the messages in my survey of romancing, the least pervasive was healthfulness. The scarcity could be due, in part, to the presence of related claims. Maybe references to "organic," "fresh," or "natural" ingredients are meant to imply healthfulness. If so, the preference for those other terms just begs the question.

Perhaps the omission stems from the belief that calling items healthful makes diners think they taste bad. Consumer research has shown that this notion, at least with regard to US consumers, is justified. Americans in particular have equated healthful with not tasty.

A 2016 study at the Stanford University cafeteria affirmed the power of what the researchers called "indulgent" descriptions over two types of health-oriented ones. For each weekday in an entire academic quarter (amounting to forty-six days), one vegetable received one of four types of descriptive labels: basic ("beets"), healthy restrictive ("lighter-choice beets with no added sugar"), healthy positive ("high-antioxidant beets"), and indulgent ("dynamite chili and tangy lime-seasoned beets"). The 8,279 diners who chose the vegetable selected it under the indulgent label 25 percent more than under the basic, 41 percent more than under the healthy restrictive, and 35 percent more than under the healthy positive. No significant increase in selection occurred in response to the other label types. Meanwhile, the researchers found that the quantity of vegetables the diners consumed was also greater in the indulgent case. They enjoyed the vegetables more.

What, then, explains the concentration of cues for healthfulness that I found on menus in one particular niche? Casual-dining chains with long and varied menus featured entire sections with boldly health-oriented labels. The menu at BJ's had one heading entitled, "BJ's Enlightened Entrées," and a claim beside it that all items in that section were no more than 575 calories. The menu at Applebee's in Alhambra announced its diet-conscious section with the heading "Under 550 Calories." Several listings in it were also tagged with a Weight Watchers logo that a menu key elsewhere defined as a sign of endorsement. Similarly, The Cheesecake Factory presented an entire supplementary menu, noticeably tall and slim, of low-calorie foods. This menu, tucked inside the main menu, bore the proud title *Skinnylicious*.

Why would these restaurants do what the science contraindicates? My suspicion is that restaurants in this category try to cover their bases. Of all restaurant types, they're the most eager to appeal to as diverse a range of cravings and dietary requirements as possible. These restaurants compete in an especially crowded market niche, where much of their clientele visits on impulse. So, it's imperative for them to satisfy the proverbial veto vote. In spite of the other differences they may have with each other, the likes of Applebee's, BJ's, and The Cheesecake Factory have done their best to win it.

My close look at the low-calorie sections of their menus also reveals that these restaurants, in an effort to lure every possible diner, actually hedge their bets. The health-oriented headings for some menu items risk repelling some, but they make it easier for the truly diet conscious to find them. At the same time, the descriptions of dishes labeled healthful were written to sound as indulgent as possible.

Behold this explication of the Barbeque Bison Burger, an item from the "BJ's Enlightened Entrées" section that the menu said was just 560 calories:

> An American original! Lean, ground buffalo boldly seasoned then grilled to order. Topped with chipotle BBQ sauce, a seared green chili and pico de gallo and served on a toasted bun with tangy slaw tossed with Baja vinaigrette and topped with green onions.

This has nearly all the features scientists have proclaimed an attractive label should. With phrases such as "boldly seasoned" and "tangy slaw," it appeals to the senses. By reference to the dish as "an American original," it acquires geographic and nostalgic character.

Normally, I avoid dishes labeled "low-calorie." But even I didn't mind ordering this one. In this case the words were persuasive, at least to me. But so was the situation. I was in a fitting place at the right time with an agreeable spirit. That the burger turned out to be decent also didn't ruin the wile.

CHAPTER 9

Write Prices

Two days before starting this chapter, I received a news alert that was very apropos. A photo of a Beijing restaurant menu had gone viral due to the menu's bizarre listing of prices. A 2016 *Daily Mail Australia* article entitled "Chinese Restaurant in Beijing Makes Customers Solve Equations to Tell How Much Dishes Cost," showed the image, first posted by a diner on Chinese social media, which affirmed its claim that the menu had, in lieu of prices, problems of complex math. Since the strings of symbols were longer and taller than the lines describing food, their visual weight was overwhelming. The sight was so amusing I had to share the item myself.

The meaning of that story for a chapter on menu prices became clear to me at once. The novelty put the norm in high relief. The Beijing restaurant penned its prices for entertainment—that and publicity for the brand. In most cases, the goal of writing prices on menus is completely different: to make us forget about price or think that the items for sale are good deals.

Not least because some of us are more apt to shop by price than others, either effort is complicated. Yet restaurateurs can improve their odds. They can deepen their grasp of the rhetorical anatomy of prices and what affects their power to persuade.

———————

Choices of price "format"—the manner of display—matter.

When discussing menus in print, authors of menu-design manuals tend to agree that it's a bad idea to align prices in a column or put leader dots (.........) between dish descriptions and prices. These maneuvers, they say, draw attention to price at the expense of the product and encourage comparison shopping by price.

That claim about focus is based soundly in the gestalt principle of visual communication. Less well founded is their implication that operators want always to downplay price. Not when their deals are competitive!

Even the tonier places sometimes want—or at least don't mind—the spotlight on price. The savvy Kasja Alger of the gastropub Mud Hen Tavern varies her tack. Most of the time, she told me, she wants her guests to focus on the food. So, she writes prices in subtle script and tucks them at the end of item descriptions. But for a special promotion—say, in honor of the Super Bowl—she wants the price of an offer to stand out. Then she'll make it as eye-catching as possible, even placing it first in a line.

Douglas Riccardi, designer of the menu I saw at Connie & Ted's, admitted to me that it's definitely "price forward" to put that restaurant's prices on a center line below item descriptions. But he wasn't afraid to do it because the prices were reasonable. Besides, he wanted the design to look like a throwback to menus from the forties. Connie & Ted's is, after all, a nostalgic brand.

What's the smartest way to spell prices out? Some studies show that people looking at menus choose items with prices ending in .99 or .95 more often than those with prices ending in .50 or .00. Possibly, we associate prices just under a dollar amount with discounting and thus good value. There's also evidence that menu prices expressed only in numerals induce greater spending than prices with monetary cues added, such as the $ symbol or the word *dollar*. Probably, the latter inhibit spending because they draw attention to price.

How, then, should we evaluate the technique of the Ethiopian restaurant in my study, Meals by Genet? The word *dollar* wasn't on the menu I saw, but there was something similar. The prices appeared in words. The "Mamoshye's Special Kitfo" was labeled "Fourteen"; the "Trout" as "Twenty-One."

We could say that writing prices in words puts stress on price because words take up so much space. To get people to ignore price, restaurateurs should avoid that. But it's also plausible that prices in words are so seldom seen that they have an estranging effect, similar to a disguise. If so, the use of words could be clever.

This menu was the only one in my survey to format prices this way. I wasn't sure what to make of it at the restaurant, and I haven't gained clarity since. I'm more confident saying that the same menu's alignment of those prices in a column, its printing of those prices in bold, and its use of leader dots between them and the dishes' descriptions made price a focal point. How desirable that was for the restaurant is to me unclear, since the prices struck me as neither low nor high.

Existing studies of price formats don't help in assessing this case. Not only have they tested too few variations. They haven't paid sufficient attention to the effect of context on perceptions of price format.

Other research indicates that the contextual factors of restaurant genre and price point are decisive. Surveys of diners and restaurateurs indicate that both populations view prices ending in .99 as advertisements of value and associate them most with quick-service eateries, where prices are low. Both also see prices ending in .00 as signs of quality. We identify these more with fine dining, for which prices are high.

It's hard to know how much the connotative power of these formats is due to their inherent features. Specifying cents does imply more concern for pennies than leaving the reference out. To what extent could the practice today be a response to industry habit? At least in the United States, the writing of price endings is strongly segmented.

In one study of the phenomenon, published in 2002, Sandra Naipaul collected 112 surveys from quick-service and fine-dining restaurants throughout the country. They revealed that prices ending in .99 concentrated in the quick-service sector and those ending in .00 aligned with fine dining.

A 2004 report on 450 menus in a collection corroborated her work. After dividing the menus into three piles—fine dining (with entrées of circa $20), casual dining ($10), and quick service ($4)—H. G. Parsa and David Njite found that fine-dining menus visually deemphasized prices, quick-service ones highlighted them, and casual-dining menus represented both methods.

Three years later, Naipaul teamed up with Parsa for a survey of fine-dining restaurants (those with tablecloths and items of $25 and up) and quick-service restaurants (with prices of $5 and down). From both surveys they registered the same division Naipaul found earlier.

In their report, they also presented a revealing review of marketing literature. It suggested that the tendency of low-end businesses to write cents ending in 9 and upscale outfits to favor the 0 has persisted, since the 1950s, in and beyond the realm of restaurants. Think of the difference between a discount clothing store, like TJ Maxx, where you might find a price tag for jeans that says "$68.99," and an upscale boutique, like Diesel, where, as I write this, a price tag for one midrange pair of jeans on the store website says "$278.00."

My own sample of menus followed a similar pattern of stratification. Yet the split between prices with cents and prices without was even starker than the segregation of odd from even cents. With few exceptions, cents-conscious pricing appeared in quick-service eateries, full-service casual-dining chains, and single-ethnicity restaurants. Meanwhile, the gourmet and most expensive omitted cents entirely.

I also found occasional departures from hierarchy and the advice of scientists, suggesting the need for more nuanced assessments of restaurateurs' behavior and the rhetorical impact of certain formats.

The most curious pattern I found was the use of dollar signs across restaurant strata. For example, they appeared at fast-food chains Burger King and Carl's Jr., but also at the gourmet brasserie-style Bottega Louie and one of the most expensive restaurants in my sample, the fine-dining Providence.

Were the designers of these menus unaware of the science saying that dollar signs suppress spending? Were the elite ones not worried about looking déclassé? The answers may lie in the dollar sign's use.

The symbol at the fast-food chains and Bottega Louie was printed in smaller font than the numerals. This implied a conscious effort to deemphasize monetary cues while answering a graphic need to separate prices from descriptions. Perhaps controlling for the size of the dollar sign would alter the scientific finding that the symbol is price forward.

At Providence, the dollar signs were just as tall as the numerals. But the contents of the menu challenged the notion that dollar signs always steer focus to price. Because the menu consisted of tasting menus only, dollar signs seldom appeared throughout the document. This alone de-emphasized price. When they did appear, as in "$210/$305 with wine pairing," they were at the bottom of each list of multiple courses. In that case, the dollar signs gave prices just enough visibility to serve as a courtesy to guests.

That the numbers next to the symbols were extremely high wouldn't have shocked most diners at Providence, anyway. On the contrary, the prices might have highlighted the restaurant's exceptional status.

Not everything about price formatting adheres to restaurant genre or expense. In my survey of menus, I found that the method of ordering prices in a list was the same everywhere. By accident or design, every menu I encountered with at least three items followed the unanimous advice of menu-design experts: Don't list prices in ascending or descending order. Stagger the amounts.

The point is well founded. Pattern recognition is inherent to cognition. To list prices in numerical order would encourage shopping by price as much as the graphic gestalts produced by the alignment of prices in columns, bold fonts, and leader dots.

Shannon Phillips, designer of the menu I saw at Dave & Buster's, told me that she mixed the order of numbers on purpose. She also never put the most expensive items at the end of a list. She explained that a restaurant might have something like a first item at $8.99 and a last item at $10.99, and then the $13.99 item might be inside of those two somewhere. She was convinced that doing anything other than placing the highest-priced item in the middle or near the beginning of a list would make it seem too expensive.

We can't know how many restaurateurs think likewise and how many are blindly imitating the others. Regardless, they do the same thing.

The rhetorical aspect of prices also extends to pricing. Prices must at least be acceptable. They can, however, be downright impressive.

"Concentrate on value and not price," Jack E. Miller and David V. Pavesic told would-be restaurateurs in their 1996 manual on menu pricing. They tried to dispel the notion that prices should be based on production costs alone. They didn't say that price is unimportant; rather, what matters is the customer's perception. No price yields a profit if no one is willing to pay it.

A great deal of research supports their claim and seeks to uncover the factors shaping perceptions of price and value. Menu engineering, a scientific subfield of menu design, specializes in devising ways for restaurateurs to use their own data on sales—a measure of perception—in addition to costs to decide the right pricing for them. Work in other fields—hospitality management, marketing, behavioral economics, and consumer psychology—focuses on learning the psychological dynamics and market forces that influence perceptions of value and responses to price.

A 2014 review of previous market research indicated that prices themselves can command perceptions of value. But what determines our perceptions of price? Since the 1950s, scholars have discovered myriad ways that price perception is irrational and context dependent.

In a 1966 article, André Gabor and C.W.J. Granger cited a recent break with the rationalist "demand theory," which asserted that people base assessments of price on dynamics of supply and demand. They also contributed their own landmark study opposing the rationalist idea. They asked consumers to choose "Buy," "No, too expensive," or "No, too cheap" as their response to prices for particular items. The authors revealed that people have an upper and lower limit in mind when determining the credibility and desirability of a price. Moreover, these don't correspond to objective schedules of demand.

Restaurants have applied similar surveys to great success. The way Taco Bell introduced its value menu in 1988 is notorious. In the research phase, the company asked likely customers: If you were to purchase this product at Taco Bell, at what price would you think it was too cheap, what would be too expensive, and what price would you expect to pay? Based on the answers, Taco Bell reverse engineered the products to be profitable in the desired price ranges. While the overall market was flat or in decline between 1988 and 1991, Taco Bell expanded its sales by 60 percent and increased its profits by more than 25. The company proved that customers' willingness to pay, not markups on costs, should be marketers' main pricing guide.

But what makes us think that one price is too low and another too high? The short—and, admittedly, circular—answer is perception of value.

So, what affects that? Value is, by definition, comparative. Thus, perception of value must derive from whatever calibrates our sense of relative worth.

Some scholars conclude that people's expectations of price vary with environmental cues, such as the type of table decorations, style of menu language, and style of service. That implies that restaurant genre is a factor in ranking value.

Others recognize that our perceptions of value involve not just appraisal of what charge is normal for a similar thing but also a subjective calculation of nonmonetary sacrifices—the cost of information search, physical cost, and time cost—we incur in a transaction.

The menu itself can also greatly affect judgments of value. A key factor is the mix of prices. In a 1990 study at a restaurant on the Cornell University campus, JoAnn Carmin and Gregory X. Norkus manipulated and monitored the price of one menu item over a six-week period. After three weeks of keeping prices as usual, the price of one item, a *pasta puttanesca*, was reduced for the remainder of the trial from $5.00 to $4.95. It was in a category of three pastas that originally ranged from $5.00 to $7.00. By the end, the sales of pasta overall had decreased markedly as a percentage of total sales, from 11 to 4 percent. At the same time, sales of the target item had increased from 24 to 33 percent of the pasta sales, and sales of the total menu's lower-priced items, meaning $7.00 and under, had gained 3 percent in the total sales. These results suggest that lowering a price in one category can lower the perceived value of an entire menu.

If this is the case, how should we assess the value menus we so often see at large fast-food chains? It would seem that restaurateurs should avoid them, but the reality isn't so simple. Tom Kelly, chairman and chief executive at the consulting firm Revenue Management Solutions, pointed out to one industry journalist that, if the restaurant markets premium items wisely, encouraging value items as add-ons, the value menu can pull the average check up.

Value menus also serve other purposes. Many fast-food chains today want a wide variety of customers. Value menus capture the vital slice of the market that's price sensitive. These businesses thrive on volume. If they sell enough value items, those items are probably worth having.

Evidently, for restaurateurs, getting prices right the first time is no easy task. They must consider so many variables. It's much simpler to tell if prices they've already set are right for their market. To do this, they can monitor sales vis-à-vis the price mix.

Most menus have a range of prices. The menu is well balanced in its pricing if the most popular items fall in the middle of the range. If they fall on the cheap end, the menu doesn't have enough perceived value or the prices are too high. If they fall on the expensive side, the items are too cheap.

This rule of thumb is helpful, but it doesn't solve the problem of how to spread prices in the mix. Does the distance between one price and another affect our estimation of each one? A principle of pricing psychology called "coherent arbitrariness" says yes.

Since the 1950s, researchers have demonstrated how consumer choices and estimations of value depend less on objective or preexisting knowledge of markets than on how choices at the point of sale are framed. The concept of coherent arbitrariness is one product of that research. It refers to the way our judgments of prices vary in accordance with a price suggested.

In 2003, Dan Ariely, George Loewenstein, and Drazen Prelec demonstrated this. They showed fifty-five students six items representing a range of product categories: computer accessories, wine bottles, luxury chocolates, and books. They briefly described each item to the students without mentioning their market prices. Following the introductions, they suggested to each student a price for each good that was equal to the last two digits of her social security number—in other words, an arbitrary price. For each product, each student was then asked to accept or reject the price and to state what price she was willing to pay. To make the situation as realistic as possible, the investigators allowed each student to purchase one item. The experiment revealed that, for every product category, the suggested price had significant influence on what each was willing to pay. The students with social security numbers above the median offered prices between 57 and 107 percent greater than the students with social security numbers below it.

This finding could mean that "anchor" pricing—the practice of putting one item on the menu with a price that's extremely high compared with the others—is persuasive. Even if the lower prices are high by some point of reference outside the menu, the anchor on the menu will make them seem reasonable.

I felt the pull of the anchor myself when visiting the Beverly Hills steakhouse CUT. In a bordered box down the list of steaks, the menu read: **"True Japanese 100% Wagyu Beef From Miyazaki Prefecture, Kyushu**/Rib Eye $155 8 oz. ($45 each additional 2 ounces)/New York $135 6 oz. ($45 each additional 2 ounces)." The prices for the cuts of Wagyu made the 14-ounce "New York Sirloin" on the same page look like a bargain at $57.

That doesn't mean that the "New York Sirloin" will always be more attractive than the "100% Wagyu Beef." For some diners in some situations, the anchor will be a draw. In that case, the high price is what menu designers call a "prestige price." In other instances, however, diners may avoid price extremes. Which tendency wins out depends, of course, on our knowledge of the products, the steadfastness of our preferences, and personal motives. When we're uncertain of the market valuations of products, don't have well-established preferences in the product category, and aren't trying to make a point by spending a lot or as little as possible, our choice of items is the most susceptible to the choice frame.

In 1992, Itamar Simonson and Amos Tversky were among the first to demonstrate tendencies related to frames of choice that can account for avoidance of price extremes in some situations and attraction to high price in others. In one test, they asked groups of students to choose on a questionnaire between two differently priced models of Minolta cameras. In another experiment with different students, they added a third, more expensive option. All cameras were represented with photos and descriptions from a sales catalog. To make the scenarios as realistic as possible, the investigators offered the items for sale. When there were two choices only, both models were equally popular. When the third was added, subjects strongly favored the middle-priced camera. The authors called this the "compromise effect." (This has since been tested and confirmed in a real restaurant context.)

In a further study with otherwise similar conditions, the investigators presented students with a trade-off between quality and price. In this case, the high-quality, high-price model in a series of choices was the favorite and the low-quality, low-price choice was the least. The researchers named this trend "polarization."

Apparently, anchor pricing in either choice frame—with or without a trade-off between quality and price—can influence our perceptions of value and purchasing behavior. But restaurant-industry experts debate anchoring's overall benefit to the profit-making cause.

I was fortunate to speak to two menu engineers with extraordinary experience, people who'd been designing quick-service, casual-dining, and fine-dining restaurant menus since the 1980s. Each one had put his stamp on hundreds of menus. But while Mark Laux, cofounder of the menu-engineering firm Hot Operator, expressed a big belief in anchor pricing, even for quick-service chains with mostly low prices, Bill Paul, founder of the menu engineering company The Menu Advantage, was unequivocally against it.

Both made worthy points. Laux insisted that an anchor never hurts. If people buy the item—what should be in low supply, anyway—that's a bonus. If not, the restaurant will do well on the other items. In contrast, Paul claimed that, if the anchor doesn't sell, it's wasting valuable space on the menu. Paul said he'd rather focus on the restaurant concept and design the route to profit most suitable for it. He gave the example of a pizza place. He doesn't want a high-priced $25 pizza if he can sell slices of it for a lower price at a higher margin.

To alter perceptions of value, restaurateurs have yet another pricing option. They can "bundle." This means offering a set of items for a single price.

Bundles come in many forms. The combo meals advertised by fast-food chains may be the most familiar. Think of Burger King's 2016 rollout of the "2 for $10" deal—two quarter-pound Whopper burgers, two small fries, and two small drinks for $10.

The power of the bundled price lies in how difficult it is to compare with other promotions. BurgerBusiness.com astutely pointed this out in its 2016 article "BK's 2 for $10; The Counter's New Menu." The site's anonymous "administrator" also put the Burger King deal in its proper market context. Burger King was responding to two other recent offers: the "McPick 2 for $5" from McDonald's and Burger King's own "5 for $4" deal. In relation to either, a diner would be hard pressed to compare the value of the "2 for $10." The author explained one cause for confusion:

> That previous [Burger King] deal was a Bacon Cheeseburger, four crispy chicken nuggets, chocolate chip cookie, small fries and a small drink for $4. So consumers are still getting

small drinks and fries with the "2 for $10" but a Whopper is a bigger burger. There's no cookie, though, if that matters to you. You need a scorecard to keep the deals straight.

A no-less ingenious style of bundling was the fast-casual Qdoba's turn in 2014 toward all-inclusive pricing. The chain announced that it would henceforth be offering all entrées at $7.80 or $8.40, depending on the protein, but that customers could get unlimited toppings, including guacamole and choices of cheese, for no additional charge. The new scheme brilliantly distracted from a price increase on the entrées by raising perceived value. It also lessened the presence of prices throughout the store, thus taking the focus off price. One industry report noted that the new pricing was followed by a first-quarter increase in same-store sales of 14 percent and a rise in the average check of 9.8 percent.

My own survey of restaurants found more bundling types. I was impressed by the novel packaging of wine at Osteria Mozza and Romano's Macaroni Grill. They offered wine not "by the glass" but by "*quartino*," a carafe equivalent to one-third of a bottle of wine. This demonstrates bundling by upping the usual portion of an item. By creating an atypical portion-price equation, the item becomes harder to compare to other offers of wine by price. It's also a great way to upsell wine.

The tasting menus I sampled, up to nine courses for a single price, epitomized bundling's rhetorical prowess. The large number of items included in menus like these decommoditizes their value more than any other bundling type. By presenting the entire meal as a unique experience, tasting menus suppress our impulse to itemize. At the same time, these menus retain all of bundling's normal profit-making advantages. Whatever they include in the bundle with a low profit margin they can balance with items at a high margin. At a place like Providence, a dessert made mostly from sugar and egg probably compensates for the cost of wild king salmon.

Clearly, pricing structures on menus sway perceptions of value. But they don't do all of the menu's work in this regard. Descriptions of items play a critical role, too. Consider my encounter with "Roasted Duck": It was easy for me to think that a dish so labeled on the menu at J&K Hong Kong Cuisine was worth the mere "$7.50" listed there. There was no explanation of the dish and the name had minimal descriptive appeal. I could also see why Meizhou Dongpo was asking "$68.00" for a whole and "$38.00" for a half of its version of that dish, the "Meizhou Roast Duck," on account of this description:

> Dongpo-style roasted duck bears the characteristics of Peking duck and incorporates the strengths of others. Meizhou Dongpo selects the highest quality Confucian Style ducks and roasts them whole with superb technique in a pure Jujube wood-burning oven. It becomes Dongpo-style roasted duck with the characteristics of tender and mild meat with crispy skin without a greasy taste.

> There are three ways to enjoy the flavors of Meizhou Roasted Duck. The first method is to dust the golden crispy slices of skin with white sugar, which imparts a luscious and crispy taste. The second method is to wrap the sliced duck meat and scallions in special pancake [sic], which enhances the rich, fruity aroma of duck meat. The third method is to wrap the duck meat in a pancake and add the Meizhou duck sauce, which creates a unique Sichuan flavor and a complex taste.

Not all menus must go this far to make a high price look right. What's more, as I argued in the previous chapter, the style of the description ought to account for the restaurant genre, clientele, and occasion. Nevertheless, the point that descriptions can add value stands—and not just on the basis of my example. Multiple studies comparing the effects of complex versus minimal menu descriptions on diner perceptions of quality, price, and purchase intention have led to the same conclusion.

Restaurateurs can also raise our perceptions of value by making their items unique. They shouldn't settle for what consultant Ronald F. Bryant justifiably disparaged in his book, *On the Menu: The Art and Science of Profit*, as the "me too burger." An item too easily compared to others on the market puts our focus on the price. That makes it more likely we'll judge it on price rather than product attributes.

Instead of a "me too burger," they can offer something as incomparable as the "Counter Burger." By giving it a unique build—"1/3 lb Beef, Provolone, Crispy Onion Strings, Lettuce Blend, Sautéed Mushrooms,

Tomato & Sun-Dried Tomato Vinaigrette"—the burger chain The Counter made that item's price of $10.95 harder for me to gauge against the deal at the chain down the street.

If they stay in business long enough, restaurateurs will face a common pricing conundrum: How do I to raise prices without alienating regular customers?

Menu-design consultants have put forth many options. The most convincing follow from the same proven principles of price formatting and pricing I cited above.

Some reasonably advise minimizing the visibility of a change: First, they should avoid a price rise all together. They should bargain with suppliers for better deals or consider making changes to the dishes themselves. They could reduce the portion in a subtle way or substitute one component for another that costs less. A further alternative to raising prices is to work on boosting sales in other areas of the business, such as the bar.

If price rises are inevitable, they should avoid changing all prices on the menu at once. Also, they should watch the timing. They might try what a representative of Captain D's Seafood, speaking on a conference panel in 2014, claimed Captain D's did with much success. The company refrained from raising prices during times of the year, such as right before school starts, when families were likely to be especially burdened and thus more sensitive to price.

If their menus spell prices in cents, restaurateurs ought to resist the impulse to price items as low as possible under the dollar amount. For example, even if items are profitable with prices ending in .25, they should start out instead with prices ending in .99 or .95. If the studies showing preference for the latter are any indication, the just-under prices will be at least as compelling as the ones ending in .25 and the few cents more in profit will delay the need for a price rise.

For items with volatile costs that must change price often, restaurateurs are better off advertising them in less permanent forms. A specials list on cheap paper, a server's recital, or a "market price" designation, as we sometimes find in listings of lobster, might do. If the main menu is expensive to produce, printing new ones every time the fluctuating item prompts a hike in price will waste money.

Other clever price-raising tactics involve distracting people from increases by formulating new offers hard to compare with the old. For this, bundling comes in handy. A new combination of items for a new price is difficult for us to compare to a different set for another price. Another way to discourage price comparisons is to change the individual items on the menu. At least, they could change parts of the items and alter the descriptions to reflect that.

Which tactics work best for restaurateurs depends on the restaurant genre and price point, their diners' sensitivity to price, and their perceptions of value. The practice of covering old prices with new ones on stickers, however, is never a good idea. When I encountered this at ramen specialist Hana Ichimonme in Little Tokyo, I thought the stickers were the visual version of screaming that prices had changed. And, since the stickers were the only obvious amendment to the menu—no changes to the items themselves were apparent—they implied a decrease in the menu's value. Most unfortunate for the restaurant, a customer unfamiliar with the previous prices wouldn't be able to tell if the overlaid numbers were rises or discounts. Would anyone have assumed the latter? I didn't.

Then again, I must admit that the prices on stickers at Hana Ichimonme didn't bother me as much as my logic says they should. Upon reflection, I realize why: First of all, I wasn't particularly sensitive to the prices. They seemed reasonable. Moreover, my perception of the items' value was in sync with the stickered prices. That my expectations of quality and my desires for the meal were affirmed by my ramen experience also worked in the restaurant's favor. I was satisfied.

In the end, it may be wise to temper our judgments of rhetorical devices by recognizing the power of context to shape their effects. Even the worst way to write prices doesn't always have to hurt a menu's success.

CHAPTER 10

Selective Selling

WE'VE SEEN MANY WAYS THAT RESTAURATEURS CAN MAKE ITEMS ON A menu more desirable. They can calculate the right amount of choice and make wily use of imagery, materials, language, and price. But how can they increase the chances we'll notice? And, if there are items they want to sell most, can they get us to focus on those?

I've yet to read a guide to menu design that doesn't advise restaurateurs on how to steer attention to high-margin items, or say that doing so will increase sales. Most of these claims, I believe, are suspect. They're insufficiently grounded or more limited in scope than they pretend to be. But because capturing attention is part of the art of persuasion, I took up the challenge of distinguishing the viable from the bogus ideas.

When I started my field research, a lot of what I knew about menu design came from the guides. Since most presumed that all restaurateurs have, or should have, some items they want to sell more than others, so did I.

That thinking drove me straight into a cognitive-dissonance ditch. In one of my first interviews, I kept asking Kevin Welby, the general manager of the fine-dining restaurant Patina, about methods for selective selling, the practice of nudging diners to buy certain items over others on the same menu, normally those with the highest profit margins.

He responded in ways that didn't compute. Welby was patiently trying to tell me that Patina's menu had a different logic all together.

Initially, I thought he was being evasive. But, after studying the menu I collected from the restaurant more closely, I found that what he said made sense. By no graphic means did particular items or sections on a page disproportionately stand out. Moreover, the dishes in each category, such as appetizers and main courses, were consistently listed from heavy to light. Their order was culinary.

As my research evolved, I saw that Welby wasn't just deflecting when he said that he aimed for a balance in the sales mix. I realized that the way the Patina menu orchestrated the total guest experience—optimally, as a multicourse extravagance enhanced by consultations with the sommelier—made pushing one dish over another beside the point.

That approach to selling contrasts completely with the midscale casual-dining chains I visited. One look at their menus divulged a multitiered pecking order of appeals. Applebee's in Alhambra used a wide range of photo sizes. Some dishes got nearly full-page pictorials, suggesting that Applebee's wanted you to pay the most attention to those. The chain also used typographic devices in the margins or top lines of listings. By contrasting size, color, and shape, Applebee's created a hierarchy of text and symbols. You could say that some were there simply to help diners in search of special features, such as low-calorie dishes, to quickly find the relevant items. Graphic symbols—such as a little green apple with the number "550" in it, printed to the left of listings under 550 calories—certainly did that. But even among items within one menu category, there was a hierarchy. The little green apples, for example, were less pronounced than the Weight Watchers logos (in bands of dark blue) in the top lines of items approved by that organization. Their prominence was on a par with the tags in the margins of other items saying "New" in a distractingly loopy green cursive. The restaurant clearly wanted diners to notice the newest items on the menu just as much and to notice both new and Weight Watchers items more than just anything tagged with a little green apple.

The menu graphics further suggested that Applebee's had even higher sales priorities than the Weight Watchers or new items. To indicate the greater importance of "Applebee's Riblets," a signature dish, a red ribbonlike strip even thicker and longer than the blue Weight

Watchers bands highlighted that. It encompassed a message in all-caps that screamed "GREAT NEW TASTE." Elsewhere, and even more prominently, a paragraph-size red outline of a circle with the words "Add to your meal" inside it highlighted an item stressed further by indentation. In case one missed the message, the circled words recurred in the item description: "Add to your meal: Toasted garlic breadstick basket...." A menu this fragmented in categories and crowded with options used redundancy as another way to break through the clutter. (Never mind that, by proliferating and diversifying attention-grabbing devices, clutter only increases—a classic advertising dilemma.)

Most of the menu-design experts I'd read had prepared me to interpret menus in the style of Applebee's, but not Patina. Realizing this, I doubted the consultants' universalizing claims and wondered if they were even right about menus that *do* try to selectively sell.

Some ways the experts recommended selective selling have a basis in a tried-and-true cognitive principle: we notice deviations from pattern. When they suggested the use of boxes around items, bolder or larger or differently colored fonts, larger images if there are images, unusual alignments in a graphic layout, or protruding materials such as clip-ons and oddly shaped inserts, they were pointing out that contrast draws attention. When they advised using table tents or banners to promote certain items from the main menu, they were indicating that repetition strengthens a pitch. If they'd acknowledged the existence of spoken menus, they might have listed vocal repetition and emphasis—changing up volume, pace, or rhythm—as parallel techniques. The idea that repetition and contrast make items stand out struck me as defensible.

Granted, we may not always notice what designers emphasize. The knowledge, agendas, and moods we bring to any menu-apprehending situation might incline us to process information in ways that designers can't totally control. But it's still plausible that information communicated by repetition and contrast has a better chance of disrupting our walls of distraction, habits of scanning, and other predilections than information not so organized.

From the start, however, I resisted the experts' claim that pulling attention to an item leads to sales of that item. Noticing something and resolving to buy it are distinct processes. Therefore, every time I visited a restaurant for this book, I made a point of testing it myself. I ordered

whatever, by redundancy or aesthetic contrast, a menu was clearly trying to emphasize. Then I made a note of whether or not I would have
ordered the item otherwise. Unless it was already a personal favorite,
my recurring answer was no. I wasn't even tempted.

Reports of empirical experiments have only encouraged my skep-
ticism. I found two promising studies of the impact of drawing boxes
around certain menu items—a common menu tactic. Both did a good job
of isolating the effects of boxing from other merchandising wiles. One
showed a significant positive correlation between boxing and item selection. The other showed none. Since it was the only one to take place in a
real restaurant setting, I give the edge to the study that showed no effect.

And yet, menu-design consultants have claimed much more than
the selling power of aesthetic emphasis. In fact, the majority of their
assertions about diners' patterns of fixation on menus, and their belief
that luring attention can direct choice, hinge on what they call "sweet
spots" or "prime spaces." These are zones on menus where they say diners automatically focus and, therefore, order from the most. Experts regularly advise putting high-margin items there.

Since I couldn't determine what the highest-margin items were on the
menus I sampled, and I didn't have records of sales, I couldn't tell from
my own survey of restaurants if sweet spots were used or effective there.
Thankfully, I found other ways to scrutinize the menu experts' claims.

Most expert ideas about sweet spots refer solely to the printed menus
we're handed in a sit-down restaurant. But there's little consensus. I identified more than twenty-five distinct assertions by menu consultants
about the most powerful place to advertise items on these menus.

Some of the propositions concern ideal positions on a menu-category
list. Claiming items are most heeded and memorable there, some experts say restaurateurs should list the item they most want to sell first in
a line. Others advise putting it either first or last. Still others say the first,
middle, and last spots are best. But I also read that the most valuable
positions are the first and last two. At least regarding a list of five items,
they can't all be right.

The other group of claims addresses best zones in a page layout.
Strangely, some authors don't specify how many panels a menu must

have or what configurations they should take for their advice to apply. Others give specific—and differing—advice for single-panel, two-panel, three-panel, and book-style menus. Most argue that restaurateurs should put the items they most want to sell where the diner looks first. Some say instead that the sweet spot is where the diner looks the most times while scanning a menu. Others propose that where we look first and last are the prime selling spaces.

Experts then differ widely on where those spaces are. In the case of single-panel menus, some assert that the more persuasive position is the top. Others say it's the upper left. Some point to the center. A different group insists on the upper right. Dissenters don't think we scan a menu in a fixed order. They say our eyes bounce around, landing on the parts that demand attention by contrasting color, size, bold font, and other tools of graphic emphasis. To sell items, make them stand out regardless of location.

What menu consultants say about the sweet spots on two-panel, three-panel, and book-style menus is just as diverse and irreconcilable. I'll spare you the full, dizzying spectrum of eye-scan paths and declarations of sweet spots that they've collectively put forth. But, so you can appreciate just how elaborate their theories of our gaze patterns on menus have become, note this proposition about a three-panel menu with a vertical fold by consultant Ronald F. Bryant: In a 2014 book on menu design, he claimed that our gaze begins in the middle of the center panel, then moves diagonally up to the center of the top of the right panel. We subsequently drift over to the center of the top of the left panel, drop down to the middle of the bottom of the same panel, then dart across the menu to the middle of the center of the right panel. After that, we take a diagonal jag down to the bottom of that same panel and terminate our gaze after flitting to the right side of the center of the right panel. With equal confidence and what I assume is no irony, Bryant claimed that the best position for sales is the first or second site of attention.

Theories about sweet spots on menus we don't hold in our hands are much sparser. Those I discovered concern the signboards above counters or along drive-thrus at limited-service restaurants. One says that, since customers entering from either side of the store won't get a good look at the items on the opposite end, the middle of the signboard above the counter is the optimal selling position. Another simply states that the right side of a menu board is always most compelling. A less blanketing claim is that the upper right zone of a menu board is prime in a store with a right-side entry aisle. A fourth view, which encompasses all signboard types and architectures, is that we scan a menu board quickly and superficially until we find what we're looking for. Positions on the board are less important than keeping the messages there brief.

When trying to gauge the validity of sweet-spot theories, it's easy to get frustrated. Menu-design consultants are incomprehensive and inconsistent in how they address the many menu formats in use. Some of their claims are incompatible with others in the same publications. Most assertions come with no argumentation or reference to evidence. Only a few authors point to anecdotal evidence or scientific studies. The anecdotes largely go unspecified and are, therefore, unverifiable. But, if we want to find the valid ideas, we need to suss out the relevant studies.

Of the claims about menu signboards, I know of only two that stand on scientific grounds. The idea that we favor items in the upper right over those in the lower left in stores with right-side entry aisles derives from a four-week experiment conducted at ten fast-food restaurants belonging to Bonanza International, Inc., in 1980, then one of the top fifteen fast-food franchises in the country. Having two horizontal rows, with six entrée positions in each row, and a right aisle for customer entrance, all ten signboards had comparable viewing conditions. The investigators were permitted to give two items—the fourth and fifth most popular in each case—two different positions: the lower left and the upper right. On weeks one and three, they appeared in one. On weeks two and four, they showed up in the other. After statistical maneuvering to make the sales records comparable, researchers Marion G. Sobol and Thomas E. Barry found that, in all permutations of positions and stores but three, the same items sold significantly better in the upper-right spot.

The authors admitted that the experiment was narrow in scope and the results had limited applicability. They tested only two item positions and stores with right-side entryways. But the well-controlled and real-world conditions gave their conclusions some credibility.

The most broadly applicable perspective on the signboard scenario, in my view, comes from Paco Underhill. Since he founded the market research firm Envirosell in 1987, Underhill and his team have honed a methodology that involves countless hours of meticulous fieldwork. Among other things, they observe how we navigate retail environments. They note how we move about a store, where we look for information, and how long we look. From this, they advise on the design of a store's pathways and signage. For *Why We Buy: The Science of Shopping*, the landmark book in which he advocated that fast-food menu boards be brief, Underhill drew on decades of company research, including studies he did for fast-food juggernauts McDonald's and Starbucks.

What he said there isn't just backed by exhaustive observation of diner behavior. It's well reasoned. His fundamental point is that we look for and are willing to pay attention to differing kinds and amounts of information in varying parts of a store. Messages should be briefest in zones where time pressures are greatest, such as the space before the ordering counter from which we, especially as new customers, scan the menu board.

Also, messages should take advantage of the phases of our movement before and after. There's no point, he said, in putting ads for burgers near the condiments, where we go after picking up our order. But that's a fine place to suggest dessert.

Reading on, I find that Underhill's consideration of what signage gets the most attention where and when accounted for the specific restaurant type as well. He stated that the deeper we go, spatially and temporally, into a fast-food dining experience, the longer the messages we're willing to absorb. In the following passage, Underhill not only explained his basis for that claim but also why this behavior is distinctive to the fast-food space:

> We tested table tents in two types of restaurant—the "family" restaurant and the fast-food establishment. In the family place, the table tents were read by 2 percent of diners. At the fast-food joints, 25 percent of diners read them. The reason for that dramatic difference was simple: At family restaurants, people usually eat in twos, threes or fours (or families!). They're too busy talking to notice the signs. But

the typical fast-food customer is eating alone. He's dying for
some distraction. Give him a tray liner with lots of print and
he'll read that.

Many of the fast-food restaurants I sampled for this book—including Burger King, Chipotle, Chick-fil-A, Farmer Boys, and Taco Bell—followed Underhill's model. They took advantage of posters in windows,
tray linings, food wrappers, boxes, or bags for messages about various
menu items or the restaurant itself. So, within the limits of my own experience, I was able to see the impact of Underhill's advice.

The most impressive messages I documented for the post-ordering
phase were by Farmer Boys and Chipotle. Both seized the basket liner as
the propaganda opportunity it is. At Farmer Boys, anything served in a
basket sat atop this full-page statement about a signature burger: "Farmer's Burger 100% pure beef, ground fresh, award-winning cheese, fresh
produce served within days of harvest, hand-smashed chunky Hass avocado, all on a locally-baked bun. Whoa. That's a Mouthful." While too
long for the menu board, it was perfectly pitched for the dining room.
There, I had as much time to absorb the message as the message had to
absorb my crumbs and excess sauce.

Chipotle had a mosaic of phrases and sentences in differing scripts
and sizes that covered every centimeter of its basket liner. There was
so much to read that it could withstand repeat visits without exhaus-
tion. The seemingly endless maze of varied messages made the paper
engrossing and thus well suited to the dining situation. A few of the
messages, such as "I think about a grilled chicken burrito," involved direct item advertising; while most—including "one delicious bite" and
"responsibly raised, pasture raised"—functioned exclusively as branding. The glut of messages on the liner contrasted starkly with the same
eatery's menu board, whose one-word listings, in sync with Underhill's
advice, couldn't have been more minimal.

The windows and entryways of the fast-food chains I sampled followed Underhill's program for those, too. Most advertised combo deals
or signature items in posters with large photos and very few words.
According to Underhill, messages in windows or just inside doorways
should be legible in the two or three seconds it normally takes to walk
past them.

Though it often promotes several items at once or the restaurant as a whole, as opposed to one specific dish, I find scent an even more arresting and fast-acting way to get customers' attention and tempt them at the same time. The thick, smoky wafts of slow-cooked brisket and ribs were so captivating as I walked up to the ordering counter at Bludso's BBQ in Compton that I thought I'd be a fool to leave with just the collards and cake.

It also occurred to me that what Underhill said about the entryways of fast-food restaurants could apply to other types of places, too. Even if we take his point that the motions we go through after we enter fast-food restaurants differ from those at sit-down places, the act of walking through an entrance is fairly universal.

In my survey, full-service places had distinct ways of making the décor sell the menu before the menu got the chance. Several places in my sample featured a wall of wine bottles visible from the entrance. This was a stunning and instantaneous cue that those places were prime for ordering wine.

I can't be sure what the impact of these environmental prompts is on sales, but I appreciate Underhill's and these restaurants' sensitivity to the power of contextual factors—especially the restaurant space and our movements through it—to affect our attention to menu items. The theories I read about how we pay attention to handheld menus in sit-down restaurants were sorely lacking in that respect. Instead, most relied on rigid ideas about patterns of scanning and fixation. Without regard to the dining situation, they asserted that there are certain parts of the menu that we always see first or first and last.

The menu consultants didn't specify why some of them emphasized what we see first while others declared last and first positions as sweet spots and another insisted on the area scanned the most. Occasional statements to the effect that certain positions are most memorable, and uses of the terms *primacy* and *recency* to make the point, suggest that many experts' ideas derived from a body of memory theory. *Primacy* means that we remember best what we see first. *Recency* is the idea that the last thing we see is most memorable.

The relevant research began in the late nineteenth century, when American physicist Francis Nipher (1847-1926) first conducted experiments in memorizing lists of numbers. He described a U-shaped pattern on a chart of accurate responses he called the "serial position curve." Subjects consistently recalled the first and last few numbers on a list the best.

The psychological phenomenon now referred to as the "serial position effect" has been elaborated and modified in the many decades since Nipher first described it. The entire discourse, however, deals with dynamics of memorization, not reading a menu.

To the situation of restaurant dining, these just don't apply. At no point has it been customary for a restaurant to demand that we memorize listings. Typically, we refer back to the menu as many times as it takes to make a decision.

The only exception I can imagine is the case of a menu delivered only in speech. The Gardens of Taxco, a Mexican restaurant in my sample, gave me experience with one of these. When our waiter recited each option within a course category, of course memorizing was relevant. Knowing that the menu would be communicated this way, I made sure to pay close attention to how I listened to the choices. Would the menu experts' ideas of primacy and recency hold up?

The main pattern I recognized was that, for each menu category, I listened for an item that appealed to me, committed that to memory, and, in the process of trying to memorize it, listened less closely to the remaining choices. I tried to keep an ear open for something I liked better but was challenged by trying to recall the first appealing dish. I didn't want the waiter to have to repeat his spiel.

Since my "experiment" was so limited in sample size (one), I won't claim that what happened in my case applies to anyone else. At the very least, the number of items on a list, the differing capacities of people's memories, and their willingness to tax the patience of the server would vary the results. Too bad those menu consultants who invoked primacy and recency in their theories of sweet spots didn't test the one scenario to which they apply.

Sales of menu items on graphic menus may not depend on us memorizing them, but memory does play some role in our selection of items on a graphic menu. A 2015 study in a Taiwanese restaurant demonstrated that exposure to the name of a menu item before viewing the menu can make us more likely to choose it. For two weeks at a time, on Wednesdays and Fridays for a total of eight weeks, the researchers featured one in a series of four regular and popular menu items on a blackboard stationed at the restaurant's entrance. They tested representations of just the item name as well as the name with a sentence of description. When prior exposure occurred, there was a 35 percent rise in the sales of those items. Presentations of the item name alone fared better than names with descriptions, but only slightly.

Because memory, but not memorizing, is decisive when we view graphic menus, a more plausible basis for judging the validity of position effects on graphic menus is to test the sales results of a variety of ordering schemes for menu items presented simultaneously, not one at a time as for a spoken menu. Recognizing that, researchers Eran Dayan and Maya Bar-Hillel developed two studies—one in a lab, another in a real restaurant—to test the effect of manipulating positions on a menu-category list.

The lab study tested the most positions of the two studies. For it, 240 Hebrew University students in Tel Aviv were shown one of four different versions of a menu, differing only in the order of items within a menu's listings of four appetizers, ten entrées, six soft drinks, and eight desserts. While not all positions of all items were tested, all of the last-versus-middle options on a list were.

The experiment was thoughtfully designed not only in the controls but also to be as realistic as possible. The students were promised that one of them, chosen by lottery, would get to have a real meal comprising his or her choices at the pizzeria from which the menu names and descriptions had been borrowed.

The second study, at a Tel Aviv café, had the advantage of actual restaurant conditions, but fewer menu variations could be tested. The waitstaff recorded sales of items ordered from two different versions of the menu for fifteen days each in an alternating pattern that ensured each version was tried on the same days of the week. The two menus were the restaurant's usual and one that differed only in the order of items from the list of coffees with alcohol (four items), the list of soft drinks (six), and, finally, the desserts (ten).

Both studies produced similar results. Items at the beginning or end of their category list increased in popularity by approximately 20 percent. The results had no correlation to the item type or the size of the list. We shouldn't ignore the researchers' findings, but they leave us to wonder why the pattern occurred.

The reasons become even harder to interpret against the background of other scientific literature on "simultaneous position effects" that the authors reviewed in their article. Although previous investigators didn't test restaurant menus, the results of their studies involving people selecting items from a "simultaneous choice set"—a presentation of all options at once—were mixed. Some studies showed strong preferences for the middle position, while others revealed a marked gravitation to the edges.

Various empirical studies have tested the relationship between location of items on a menu's graphic layout and item selection. It's remarkable that none have supported any of the menu consultants' claims about prime spaces. But we shouldn't take that as a final word on the matter. The experiments themselves have been problematic.

In spite—and sometimes because—of their flaws, however, collectively and individually they offer valuable insights. It's instructive, for example, that, of the experiments whose methods and results were published by this writing, spanning from 1987 to 2014, fewer than half were conducted under real restaurant-dining conditions. Studies from 1987 and 2012 outfitted subjects with infrared eye trackers and video recording devices, then asked them to read and select an item or meal from a menu in a lab. One from 2014 made up several menu designs and had students choose items in a schoolroom. In all cases, the subjects weren't personally invested in their choices, didn't expect a meal to result, and didn't experience any of the contextual pressures—distractions or social cues—that we normally find in a restaurant.

A study from 2010 took place in multiple restaurants, but ironically, created the least realistic conditions of all. The participants had to choose a dish from a menu in fifteen seconds and immediately report their selection and their sequence of gazes on a questionnaire.

At least some experiments on menu-page sweet spots—those reported in 1995, 2003, and 2004—occurred under real restaurant-dining conditions. Of these, only a 2003 study by Clark Kincaid and David Corsun is somewhat useful for understanding the impact of prime spaces. It alone controlled specifically for menu-item placement, isolating it from other means of graphic emphasis, such as drawing borders around items. Like the other real-restaurant studies, however, Kincaid and Corsun's didn't support the prime-space theory it was testing. Sales for items that changed location on the menu over the course of the experiment didn't change the sales mix at all.

It's possible, however, that this result is due to a flaw in the study. The restaurant chosen for the experiment had a static menu and very localized clientele. Perhaps the dominance of regular customers made them impervious to changes in item position. The regulars might have hunted down their favorite dishes no matter where their listings moved. A restaurant whose clientele or menu changed often might make a better testing ground.

Every one of the studies is flawed, but not all is lost. The findings of one stand out for their validity and significance. In 1995, John Bowen and Anne Morris set out to test whether or not redesigning the restaurant menu at Eric's—a 106-seat restaurant in the University Hilton Hotel on the campus of the University of Houston, Texas—could improve sales of the salad bar. None of the multiple profound changes to the graphic design and placement of the salad-bar listing increased the (indexed) sales of salad.

By accident, however, in what was supposed to be a control week of the experiment, the restaurant introduced an unforeseen variable that happened to yield a well-controlled positive result. Forgetting the agreement to withhold new promotions during the five-week experiment, the restaurant management introduced specials in week four. In spite of the salad-bar listing's prime location and visual emphasis, it was the specials, not the salads, which spiked in sales. Notably, the specials weren't promoted by the menu's graphic design, but rather by the server. Because they didn't plan for this variable, Bowen and Morris didn't specify what the server did that was so persuasive. We know only that he or she was. This accidental finding points to the potential for social suggestion or pressure to direct attention and choice.

In practice, restaurateurs deploy a variety of social signals to steer us. In some settings, the goal might be to sell one item more than another. In others, it might be to lure us into having one more course or an after-dinner drink.

Among these devices, servers have rhetorical advantages. They can make their pitch at the crucial moment of decision, and norms of sociality require us to listen and respond. So, we're apt to pay attention when servers make recommendations ("My favorite is the cherry cobbler") and when they try to upsell ("Would you like ice cream with your pie for only $2 more?").

Once they have our attention, servers can make creative pitches. The casual-dining chain Romano's Macaroni Grill used servers to try to sell us more wine in an ingenious way. Calling it the "honors system," they packaged the upsell in a social bond of trust. This involved a scripted routine. Our server brought over a bottle of wine that we never asked for. With a purple crayon, he drew a stick-figure diagram of a glass on our white-paper tablecloth cover to show us how to keep track of the number of wine glasses we were welcome to pour from a large bottle he would leave on our table. Each stroke of the crayon in the curve of the glass was to signify one imbibed.

Whether or not one resists the bottle's convenient proximity from that point on depends on the diner and the moment. But only a server could have made it a prop in a performative pitch.

The server's power to grab our attention and motivate purchases also has to do, I imagine, with the social cost they raise in turning them down. It may be a minor matter. But you still have to disappoint a person and face them as you do.

When they take the trouble to roll out dessert or cheese carts, as at a fine-dining restaurant, we might feel obligated to ponder the offer. As servers direct our attention to the offerings, the carts pick up the pitch from there, making their temptations palpable.

With good reason, many menu consultants advise that servers at sit-down restaurants bring out dessert menus automatically after clearing the main course. It's vital to time a presentation of dessert before we have a chance to decline. Dessert is tough to sell to the satiated but golden for raising checks.

With some justification, we can say that servers help direct attention and sales. But experiments conducted under real restaurant conditions offer mixed support for that conclusion.

A 1990 report on a controlled study of the impact of suggestive selling on sales at a family-style casual-dining restaurant in the United States strongly affirmed the power of the server to increase sales. The investigators conducted the study over fifteen weeks. To establish a baseline, they recorded sales under normal conditions for the first three weeks. In separate blocks of subsequent weeks, the servers used techniques for suggestive selling of appetizers, cocktails, and then desserts for which the servers were trained and rewarded. The rise in sales differed dramatically across the menu categories—by 8 percent for cocktails, 27 percent for appetizers, and 100 percent for desserts—yet all showed the significant positive influence of servers.

An experiment Underhill conducted for one of his fast-food restaurant clients pointed in the same direction. According to him, having a clerk ask customers if they wanted to "supersize" their drinks succeeded a remarkable 47 percent of the time.

A field study at a self-service restaurant in the Netherlands between March and June 2013 likewise affirmed the effectiveness of server nudging. During the testing period—on weekdays, while the restaurant offered a fixed-price breakfast—cashiers asked visitors, "Would you like to add orange juice for 50 cents?" during weeks 11 through 19 and 23; "Would you like to add a fruit salad for 75 cents?" in week 20; "Would you like to add pancakes for 50 cents?" in week 21; and, changing the script a little, "Do you want to have a fruit salad or pancakes with your breakfast?" in week 22. Cash-register receipts showed that sales of orange juice increased significantly—accounting for 35 to 42 percent of breakfast sales compared with a baseline of 20 percent, established weeks 1 through 10. Sales of fruit salad and pancakes jumped less dramatically, but still meaningfully, regardless of the cashier's change in script. Sales of fruit salad went from 3 to 9 percent. Pancakes rose from 1 to 3 percent.

A 2005 study of server nudging in a full-service context, however, told a less buoyant story. At a fine-dining restaurant in Britain, researchers tested the impact of positive, neutral, and negative server comments. Positive were mentions that the dish in question was popular. Neutral were no or noncommittal comments. Negative were statements that the dish was less popular than the other dishes. A server's positive statement about a menu item had very little influence on sales of that item. Diners chose the positively recommended dishes 41 percent of the time, while diners chose dishes sold in the neutral condition 40 percent of the time. Hardly an impressive showing for the positive recommendations. The impact of negative comments, in contrast, was significant. In that case, diners chose the item 19 percent of the time.

Perhaps it makes a difference whether the situation is self-, limited-, or full-service. Or, maybe what kind of comment a server makes has an effect. Would the results have been otherwise if the server had said a dish was a personal favorite? What would have happened if, as in the first three experiments I mentioned, the server simply asked if the diner would like a particular item?

The 2005 study's recording of how much diners liked the targeted dish offered even less robust support for the server's influence in the post-purchase phase. The average level of enjoyment (on a nine-point scale) of that dish was the same in all three cases. This finding suggests that, even if diners were influenced to purchase something recommended by a server, their satisfaction with the dish—and, by extension, the chances they'd order it again—wouldn't fall under the server's spell.

To be sure, any claim about servers' power to direct our attention and choice must also consider our cultural backgrounds. Several cross-cultural studies of restaurant patrons' beliefs about quality service have indicated that people hold contrasting ideas of welcome behavior. One study showed that Hong Kong diners wanted the server to assist them in selecting dishes, while Midwestern Americans placed greater value on servers' knowledge about menu items, ingredients, and specials. Another revealed that Americans liked more personalized service than people from the Republic of Korea. Koreans preferred shows of concern and deference.

Given the right conditions, servers might capture our attention and, with it, our purse. But other forms of nudging may also work.

In the effort to sell wines by the glass, the practice of recommending food-and-wine pairings on a menu has proof of success. In 2016, Lohyd Terrier and Anne-Laure Jaquinet made this conclusion from their experiment with a daily set menu in a Swiss restaurant. For a first, control, week, there were no wine-pairing suggestions on the menu. But, in a second week, customers received the daily set menu with two possible wine-by-the-glass pairings for the main course, chosen by the sommelier. Out of the seventy-seven set menus ordered during the control week, customers ordered only five of the cheaper and fourteen of the more expensive wines by the glass. But, out of the eighty-two set menus ordered the week the pairing suggestions appeared, customers ordered twenty-six of the cheaper and thirty-five of the more expensive glasses of wine. That's a remarkable increase.

I was reminded of this experiment recently, when, just before this book went to press, the restaurant Maude, which I discussed in chapter 1, changed its concept from a tasting menu that revolved around one seasonal ingredient a month to a quarterly changing tasting menu designed to complement a single region of wine. The newer menu went well beyond the occasional suggestion of wine pairing undertaken by the aforementioned experiment. Of course, the new Maude menu entailed a trade-off of narrower appeal—not everyone wants to drink wine or make it their meal's central theme—but anyone willing to go to the redesigned Maude would be well primed by the advertised concept to buy not just one glass but a series to complement the numerous courses. Maude's new menu tied the suggestive selling of wine to the restaurant's very identity, thus suffusing the entire menu with the suggestive selling of wine.

The silver-cart service at Lawry's The Prime Rib that we experienced exemplified a further selective-selling technique, known as conspicuous consumption. If we ordered a prime-rib dinner, we would be entitled to the limousine spectacle of a silver cart parking at our table. Only then would a costumed carver dazzle the dining room by cutting our choices of spotlighted steaks and sides.

The silver carts did lure the attention of diners. But did they stoke even a mild envy for what, functionally speaking, is nothing more than a warming station? That probably depended on the diner. I ordered the prime-rib dinner for research but would have otherwise chosen my preference of rib-eye steak. No cart.

Unfortunately, I didn't find relevant research on the impact of conspicuous consumption on sales to compare with my own experience. There's more to say, however, about sales prompts of the online kind.

With the rise of marketing by email, text messaging, and smartphone-app notifications, the suggestive selling once confined to the scene of the dining room has vastly extended its reach. Unlike traditional-media advertising, these means of communication have the server's more personalized touch.

The technology making them possible has also brought new forms of intelligence to the process. Industry reporters have written for years about the potential for restaurateurs, especially with mobile ordering apps, to harness electronic data about us. The idea is that, if restaurateurs can make their promotions especially relevant to us as individuals, taking our moment-by-moment situations into account, we'll be more inclined to pay attention.

For this purpose, industry experts have posited honing their pitches not only from "big data"—meaning, patterns in aggregate sales, traffic, the weather, etc.—but also from "little data," the past behavior of individual customers. Digital marketer Noah Glass suggested one model use of the latter: "[A] chief marketing officer can view mobile ordering records, find customers who have never visited one of their stores during the breakfast daypart and send them a coupon for a free breakfast sandwich, without throwing away marketing dollars on existing breakfast customers."

A related form of contextual marketing for digital ordering systems is "predictive ordering." According to the National Restaurant Association website, the restaurateur assigns a SKU number to each item on the menu. When a customer orders an item, the appropriate software will save identifiers of the individual, the item, the time of day, and the customer's location. Over time, the system will recognize patterns of behavior. If it learns that we like milkshakes, it will suggest one when we next select a cheeseburger.

Online ordering service and menu aggregator GrubHub, owner of the Seamless app that I surveyed, offers participating restaurateurs a range of insights about its customers that could help them craft more relevant messages. This includes enabling restaurateurs to fluctuate the contents of their online menus.

In 2014, the editors of *Restaurant Hospitality* reported that Grub-Hub's analysis of the previous year's pickup and delivery orders from its nationwide network of restaurants gave restaurateurs actionable insights like this:

> If your restaurant stays open late at night, be aware that men
> are nearly 55 percent more likely to order takeout in the 10
> p.m.-2 a.m. period. You'd probably want to slant your menu
> toward male-heavy food preferences then. Or if you get a lot

of takeout business from nearby office workers, be aware that women are nearly 30 percent more likely to order food at work than men. If that's the case for your operation, adding more healthful-type items to your menu could boost business.

GrubHub said women strongly preferred more healthful items than men. While men preferred bacon, poutine, sriracha, biscuits, and fried chicken much more than women, women were far more interested than men in chia seeds, cupcakes, frozen yogurt, and beets. Armed with knowledge of who wants what when, restaurateurs can brighten their chances of catching the attention of the right diners at the right time with the relevant content.

Mobile technologies also give restaurateurs the ability to send notifications to customers (who sign up for offers) at opportune places and times. I have yet to find published studies of restaurant messaging that indicate the most profitable places and times, but a well-designed experiment with offers of discounted movie tickets provides useful insights.

The researchers created a smartphone app that dangled discounted movie tickets in front of 12,265 randomly chosen mobile users. They text-messaged them with the offer for a movie to start on the last Saturday in August (2012) at 4:00 p.m. No user received more than one message and each received the message at one of three times. Some got one at 2:00 p.m., which was two hours prior to the event. Another group received a notification one day before the show time. The rest got a message two days ahead. The experiment also controlled for the users' distances from the movie theater. The closest were up to 200 meters away. Those in the medium range were between 200 and 500 meters. The farthest away were between 500 meters and 2 kilometers.

As you might expect, by far the most sales occurred when there was greatest proximity in time and place. Urgency combined with convenience of the opportunity could explain this. (The researchers who surveyed the subjects' motives after the experiment posited that the subjects closest in time and place were able to conjure a more concrete mental picture of the offer, and that helped to motivate them.) Also, not surprisingly, the combination of proximate time and farthest location had the poorest results. Perhaps the urgency existed, but so did far less opportunity. In addition, the investigators found that a too-long lead (two days) at any distance was bad for sales. It was worst of all when the distance was greatest. Again, it's easy to see why. Where's the urgency?

The only finding that might not be intuitive is that messages sent to users farthest away but only one day ahead generated almost as many sales (a 71 percent increase in the probability of a sale) as those sent to people the same day and closest to the theater (a 76 percent rise).

The follow-up survey of the users eliminated many alternative explanations for taking or declining the offer—including price sensitivity, impulsiveness, concerns about the intrusiveness of the message, age, gender, education, experience with mobile technology, taste in movies, and frequency of movie watching. In the end, we learn that variables of proximity, in time and space, were decisive. The most opportune point for marketers to send notifications of special offers for things like movie tickets, at least by text message, is on the same day to proximate users or one day ahead to users far away.

Because the event of watching a movie is comparable in time commitment to going out to eat, the results of this study could well apply to the restaurant context. Of course, nothing is sure. And, even if a marketing tool guaranteed success, restaurateurs might not use it as prescribed.

Some deviations will result from ignorance about marketing or technology or lack of consistent effort. Others will be justifiable, reflecting differences in the character of brands.

To understand the latter, I observed the practices of the restaurants in my sample. Between March 26, 2014, and February 24, 2015, I signed up for notifications from every one of the restaurants and menu aggregators in my survey in whatever form they offered them. (I provide a log of what I signed up for and when in Appendix A.) I kept track of their notification activity for roughly a year and a half.

In the process, I noticed how very differently the brands wielded the digital nudge. Most of the restaurants didn't offer email or text notifications or they rarely or never contacted me—perhaps underutilizing the resource. Of those that did, the vehicle, frequency, content, and timing of their messages varied notably according to restaurant genre and marketing strategy.

Most of the fast-food chains used text messaging at least as much as email; whereas sit-down restaurants of all stripes, from Applebee's to Patina, overwhelmingly used email.

My observation of the contents of their messages suggested a reason why. Texting fits a more casual and brief messaging approach. Email can be more formal and lengthy.

It can also be more lavishly pictorial, which explains why plenty of full-service casual-dining chains, like Applebee's and Romano's Macaroni Grill, as well as fast-food chains, like Domino's and Farmer Boys, used email, when they did so, to send poster-style ads starring vivid close-ups of food and beverages. These pictorials were consistent with their food-porn approach to imagery on menus or menu supplements.

Domino's offered notifications by email or text. Since I signed up for both, I could see how the company capitalized on the mode of address most suitable to each platform. By contrast to the all-image ads that Domino's sent by email, the company's texts were mainly two-liners that economized on language as much as possible. Many text messages beaded together a short string of emoji-laden phrases.

Choices of message frequency and content were intertwined. Whether quick service or sit-down, places with an aggressively price-forward style of marketing not only made their notifications consistently about specially priced deals, but messaged often. The full-service casual-dining chain Romano's Macaroni Grill normally emailed me between three and five times a week, and almost all of their content was discount related. While most of the discount offers I received from restaurants made their appeals in response to special events, like the Fourth of July or the Super Bowl, Romano's would use any frivolous excuse. On August 5, 2016, I received an email with the subject line, "Happy Weekend! Take 20% Off!" Three days later, another one read, "Kids eat free every Mon & Tues!"

Except when offering limited-time deals for ordering online or by carryout—such as, "Carry out Lrg 3-top pizzas for $7.99 all week long!" on July 22, 2016—text messages from Domino's didn't hype the fact of the discount quite as much. Domino's spent more time pushing offers without explicitly stating they were discounts—for example, "Domino's Alert: We're adding new salads to our Choose Any 2 or More for $5.99 Each deal" from August 1, 2015. Still, Domino's messages tended to highlight price and come often. The texts were occasionally staggered and unpredictable but very often appeared three days per week.

Restaurants that advertised less by price and more to remind you of their holiday or seasonal specialties, including the availability of gift cards, or to simply share developments at the restaurant, didn't contact me as often, sometimes not for a month or more. Fine-dining restaurants like Patina (under the umbrella of the Patina Restaurant Group, which also shared news of its other properties) and Nozawa Bar were inclined toward this approach.

Tam O'Shanter, a Scottish-themed white-tablecloth restaurant owned by the Lawry's The Prime Rib chain, exemplified a middle ground. They used the occasions of prix fixe dinners celebrating a particular theme in wine to email me approximately once a week.

The difference between the frequent, price-forward messaging and the more occasional notices of special news or events suggests not only a contrast in marketing strategy but also a difference in restaurant type. The former aligns with the genres most likely to get visits on impulse and often. The latter corresponds to places you plan to go to in advance, perhaps make a reservation for, and visit occasionally.

The timing of messages likewise relates to their content and reveals significant differences in marketing strategy and restaurant type. I'm not surprised that the more reliant a restaurant was on impulse visits or marketing by limited-time offers, the more consistent and strategic they were in the times of day they messaged me.

Romano's and Domino's, two especially frequent, price-forward messengers, sent their promotions at particular times of day. Most of the Domino's texts arrived between noon and 1:00 p.m. These might catch a late lunch taker at the crucial point of decision or plant an idea for dinner that night. Romano's smartly sent its emails of discounts that could be used at lunchtime in the morning. Friday afternoons were typical for messages of the chain's all-weekend deals.

Tam O'Shanter consistently messaged about its wine-themed menus in the morning, although the time of day wasn't as significant as the pattern of days it messaged me before its advertised events. The restaurant was fairly consistent in how far ahead it messaged me for the last time about an event, and there were usually two reminders of it spaced several days apart. For a prix-fixe menu featuring wines from the Halter Ranch Winery on July 13, 2016, I received an email promoting the menu (for $75 per person) on July 1 and again on July 7. For the "La Vie en Rose" menu with French summer wines (at $65 a head) taking place August 10, 2016, the restaurant emailed me on August 2 and again on

August 6. Considering that participation in these specially priced offers requires making a reservation, and the events are ephemeral, emailing multiple notices several days in advance made sense.

Meanwhile, the more elite restaurants in my sample, which rarely offered discounts or specially priced menus and many diners would consider "special-occasion" destinations, typically meted out their emails throughout the year. Some anticipated holiday seasons, taking advantage of these to remind recipients of gift cards. Others were periodic newsletters with varied content, from additions to the menus to news of other ventures helmed by the chef or restaurant group.

Because Maude's nine-course tasting menus (until 2018) were designed around a different ingredient each month, it made sense that Maude sent advance monthly emails announcing the availability of reservations and enclosing educational paragraphs about the featured ingredient.

The tasting menu at Nozawa Bar didn't demand such an approach, yet I still received similarly educational messages. Occasional emails from the restaurant were just to explain the intricacies of a certain ingredient and the quality and care involved in its sourcing and use by the chef. Over the course of my study, I received literature on nori, rice, fluke, uni, and toro. On June 9, 2015, for example, Nozawa Bar wrote that "*Hirame*, the Japanese name for fluke, makes great sushi, with its sweet, subtle flavor. In contrast, Pacific halibut, the fish that you would likely eat if you ordered a cooked halibut steak in a California restaurant, is not a good fish for making sushi." The restaurant, it seemed, wanted to prime me to appreciate the art of sushi. Within the same email, the statement, "We source our fluke/halibut from the east coast of the United States," justified the menu's high price.

You can see from the content of these messages that precise timing in hours or even days isn't the most important thing for the more elite restaurants. As long as they send relevant branding content of interest to their clientele, without too long a lag and more often during holiday seasons, their timing fits their purpose.

Regardless of fitness and stylistic approach, getting our attention remains tricky for restaurateurs. It becomes even more of a challenge as competition for it intensifies and our time gets ever more taxed. Marketers have long spoken of how difficult it is to resound above the noise of other marketing messages and the irony that every success only raises the level of din.

In this respect, restaurateurs face the same challenge as other marketers. But the uniqueness of the menu as a tool for drawing attention—its situation between the diner and a meal—brings special rhetorical opportunities. And, as I found so many times in my study of menus, context is key. Not only does the charm of a menu depend on its fitness to the restaurant genre, the occasion, and our inclinations as diners—whether we notice does, too.

When the restaurateur enlists the help of menu "wingmen"—table tents, banners, tray liners and burger wrappers, servers, scripted opportunities for conspicuous consumption in the dining room, or digital notifications—even more situational factors come into play. Then it matters also what restaurateurs can find out about our preferences and habits, and whether or not they can send us menu-related messages that pique our interest at compelling times and places.

CONCLUSION

Now, after surveying so many styles and components of restaurant menu design, noting the range of factors affecting a menu's power to persuade, and seeing how much the scrutiny of these unearthed caveats and exceptions, your head may be spinning. Take heart. There's order in the apparent mess. The multitude of ways that menus present their offerings, what I think of as their styles of choice, spring from a common set of drivers. In addition, all convincing menus, no matter the style, have the same fundamental traits.

At base, menus are the responses of restaurateurs to their market situation. This includes the restaurant's niche or genre as defined by cuisine type, service style, daypart, and targeted diners. (Are restaurateurs crafting a menu for a vanguard gourmet place that serves just eighteen adventurous diners at one seating per night, or for a quick-service chain looking to build 2,000 units and win the veto vote?) It also encompasses operational constraints, such as available resources for market research and for food production and service. How restaurateurs respond to their market situation, of course, depends greatly on their ideas about business effectiveness and their own priorities.

Some restaurateurs design menus in a deliberate fashion, as Dave & Buster's did by strategically staggering menu prices and laying out images. Others just imitate the conscious actors. But their imitation doesn't change the basic logic by which both groups of restaurateurs design menus. In my survey of menus and discussions with restaurateurs, I observed wide variances in restaurateurs' awareness of menu-design principles, and yet some expert-recommended practices, such as staggering menu prices, appeared consistently across my sample. What forges a menu with intention in the first instance molds it unconsciously in the second.

Conformity to the conventions and traditions of restaurant niche or genre affects every aspect of menu design. It dictates the amount of choice; the way the menu structures a meal; if and how the menu regiments the ordering process; how secret menus get composed, initiated, and communicated; the menu's language, imagery, materials, and price writing; and, finally, the content, vehicle, frequency, and timing of supplemental alerts.

Restaurant niche determines so much because it encompasses so many aspects of an operation. Consider the cuisine. Ethnic tradition can decide whether or not the menu has a temporal structure. Novelty can determine how much instruction the menu, or its "wingmen," must give. Is the cuisine defined by the creativity and renown of a chef? If so, the chance that the menu has little or no choice goes up.

Price point and gourmet identification distinguish a menu. Both establish the price format, such as whether a menu says "20" or "$19.99." Gourmet identification has a bearing on language, imagery, and materials.

Daypart governs some aspects of design. If the menu has photos, the lighting of items for breakfast might be softer than those for viewing bar-side at night.

Much about a menu depends on mode of service. Is there elegant tableside attendance by a battery of servers, or do customers queue behind a counter to order their meals? All restaurateurs face a trade-off between volume and price. Their choice corresponds to speed of service. For places to be profitable, slower tables must compensate with higher checks. Conversely, restaurants requiring high volume and quick service need lower prices.

What does this mean for menus? Where restaurants fall on the volume-price spectrum doesn't affect only price format and pricing. Because it takes time for diners to read and understand menu descriptions, their length can be cut or kept according to the desired speed of customer decisions. Sometimes, restaurateurs use pictures to hasten the pace. How much servers bolster the menu with tailored, expert advice is also a consequence of desired service speed. Their guidance takes time.

Service style has been the primary force behind secret menus. Whether it's personalizing, as at many table-service restaurants, or standardizing, the type we normally find at fast-food chains, makes much of the difference in their design, initiation, and promotion. Look out for changes in practice, however, as personalizing restaurants increasingly adopt the customs of standardizing places.

Service and daypart are sometimes intertwined. So are their effects on the menu. If tables must turn briskly then, weekday lunch will likely demand a shorter list. (In this case, a long list is advisable only if it's full of familiar items.)

Some aspects of market niche aren't readily apparent to us diners, yet contribute to the menu's style of choice all the same. The more establishments cater to impulse visits, vie for the widest slice of the local market, and aspire to the largest scale possible in numbers of units, the more likely they are to have long and varied menus. More than other places, they need to win the veto vote.

When producing menus, restaurateurs make assumptions about targeted diners. What restaurateurs think they know about our adventurousness or knowledge of cuisine conditions what their menus withhold and disclose about items in pictures and words.

Of course, resources weigh heavily on menu design. Budgets and architectural constraints can nail down menu materials. The space and shape of dining rooms, kitchens, and storage facilities; the extent of kitchen equipment; the reliability of ingredient costs and supply; production efficiencies; and the skills of staff all cap the menu's contents and range. So does the publicity restaurants get—sought or accidental— for phased-out or off-menu items. If it leads to a barrage of customer requests, restaurateurs may be tempted to keep secret lists.

The extent and sophistication of market research can inform every part of a menu. Depending on how much information restaurateurs get about our eating schedules, meal-structure habits, and past purchases, or about market and environmental conditions, they can tailor menu content to us as individuals or groups. With some digital forms, they can fluctuate menu contents and engage in strategic suggestive selling in real time throughout the day.

The true impact of resources on menu design, however, rests on their use. Restaurateurs can install digital systems that mine loads of data, and then do little to analyze or apply the intelligence. Having content-management capability doesn't guarantee, either, that restaurateurs will use it to highlight the items we're most likely to buy on certain occasions or to make high-margin items and promotions more noticeable. The possibilities hinge on operators' understanding of data, application of data insights to menu design, and follow-through.

To a great degree, menus are also the result of marketing and management philosophies. As we learned from the clash of titans at T.G.I. Friday's in chapter 4, restaurateurs, even in the same market niche, can take equally sophisticated yet totally opposing approaches to menu design. Still others don't believe in the merchandising power of the menu at all and will allocate resources anywhere but. In rare cases, restaurateurs don't care if they make the most in profits. Whatever the priorities of the restaurateur, they're bound to make their mark on the menu.

Largely, the persuasiveness of menus depends on how well they meet or exceed our expectations of restaurant genre, appeal to our notions of quality and value, and suit our fluctuating, occasion-based interests and constraints—even our individual cognitive styles. To fulfill this tall order, restaurateurs need skill, of course, but luck just as much.

Rarely is the same advice warranted for all menus in all situations. It is, however, for achieving a credible menu. Always, menu descriptions must be accurate, the menu must be physically clean, and the restaurant must deliver what the menu promises. This last can decide whether or not we return.

Every other rhetorical technique comes with qualifications. The best way to fulfill even the most basic requirement—that a menu be legible, audible, or otherwise perceptible—depends on the diner, place, and time. We'll heed the messages of a menu or a menu augmenter, such as a text message from Domino's promoting a pizza deal, only if it is relevant to us, issued in the times and places we're likely to take interest, and of a length we can digest while there.

The size and scope of menus matter a lot. Menus should be long or varied enough to maintain our interest, but brief enough to make profit-making items easy to find. Our judgments of sufficient length and variety, however, are subjective and situational.

If the content is unfamiliar to us diners and we don't have all day to peruse, a list that would otherwise feel excitingly abundant might seem stressfully long. By the same token, the amount of choice on an objectively enormous menu will feel manageable if it follows the conventions of a well-known restaurant genre. Because we know how to navigate it, a familiar menu format can make us less anxious. If the menu describes contents in a way that's typical for the genre, all the better. For example, traditional American diner menus tend to be sprawling documents, but if the menu has standard menu headings—like "Eggs" and "Pancakes, Waffles & French Toast," two examples from the Canter's Deli I visited—and then describes those items in familiar ways, as Canter's did, the total length of the menu will feel less daunting.

Restaurant genre can also establish the amount of choice we think we ought to have. A gourmet menu, especially from an acclaimed kitchen, can count on diners' adventurousness and willingness to submit to the will of the chef. A menu that looks, sounds, and feels like a gourmet menu has a good chance of attracting diners willing to relinquish the agency they might not want to give up at a traditional diner or deli.

The right amount of choice is also a function of the local marketplace. For example, Hanbat Shul-Lung Tang's ability to thrive with only two dishes on the menu owes something to its Koreatown neighborhood, brimming with Korean-dining alternatives. There, a specialized two-item menu doesn't constrain.

While our ideas of sufficient choice on a menu are subject to personal predilections and circumstances of restaurant genre, history, and the local marketplace, menu design can also influence how we perceive menu length and variety and how we respond to them. Restaurateurs can improve the chances that the amount of choice on a menu is agreeable and noticeable. They can even alter how much variety we think a menu has.

Whether content is agreeable and noticeable depends in part on menu navigability and legibility. To make information easy to find on a graphic menu, restaurateurs can give menu contents clear visual hierarchy. On a long menu, that makes variety less daunting and more apparent. Where it's advantageous for restaurateurs to maximize the appearance of a limited number of choices, they can employ illusion-making tools. They can use the same stock of ingredients in multiple ways or turn to a customizable format. Either way, a minimal number of ingredients can seem to diners like infinite possibilities.

In the case of a long menu, there's a danger we won't notice its variety unless its categories are optimally labeled and laid out. One way restaurateurs can ensure that we notice a menu's breadth is to separate long lists of items and give the parts discrete presentations (in the case of printed menus, over multiple pages). When a menu must fit on a single page, labels for menu categories should be of the sort that readily break down logically into further subcategories. As we saw in chapter 4, attribute-based categories (black tea, green tea) increase perceptions of variety in a single-page presentation better than benefit-based ones (energy boost, stress relief).

The way restaurateurs divide their menus by category can also affect how much we seek variety in the menu and how much we buy to fulfill that desire. As long as food categories aren't very familiar—if they are, they probably won't shake deep-seated preferences—cutting down the number of subdivisions on a menu can enhance our perception of variety and stimulate us to buy more and in a wider range.

When it comes to maximizing the desirability of what a restaurant is selling, including the total restaurant experience, operators have many tools at their disposal. Having secret menus is one route to seduction. But to be effective promotions, secret menus must maintain a paradoxical state of mystery and rampant rumor regarding their contents. They must also stoke our desire to feel special. That means there has to be a risk—even if only for other people—of not getting an off-menu item. So, restaurateurs need to perpetuate uncertainty about available goods.

Regular menus—as opposed to the secret kind—seduce by the art of describing. In all but the places with the speediest service and most familiar items, emotionally resonant or sensuous menu descriptors are a must. Evocative words, images, or displays of food can entice us by stimulating appetite, cueing quality or healthfulness, and offering entertainment.

The materials and forms of a menu primarily shape our impressions of quality. They can assert quality as a claim to status, identifying a restaurant as upscale or elite, if they follow the medium conventions of gourmet or fine-dining restaurants. They can also communicate and determine quality in the sense of brand integrity. For that, a restaurant's promise must align with its product.

The effectiveness of menu descriptors depends greatly on their fitness to the restaurant genre with which the place identifies. Does the menu address the standards of quality we expect from a restaurant of its type? If innovation is a hallmark, as it is in the vanguard-gourmet realm, diners there will welcome less explicit description. They'll want surprise. But the same gourmand visiting a restaurant to learn about the cuisine of a particular region might appreciate more handholding from descriptors there.

Restaurateurs must design menus that take targeted diners' comfort level with a menu form into account. The urgency, of course, is greatest when new forms, such as digital tablet menus or menus on mobile apps, require us to assimilate new experiences or adopt new behaviors. Still, restaurateurs must realize that comfort with forms evolves. For example, the young may expect and feel more at ease with digital menus than older people at the moment, but that's rapidly changing.

A key part of effective description is savvy writing of prices. A persuasive menu must distract us from the cost of the meal or convince us that it's worth the price. To make us forget how much we're paying, restaurateurs can downplay the physical presence of price. On a graphic menu, they can use lighter or smaller fonts, dispense with decimal points and cents, and tuck prices right next to item descriptions. They can also minimize the occurrence of price by bundling offers. If a deal is so swell that highlighting price is advisable, they can make numbers and other monetary cues like dollar signs bigger and bolder, and place them prominently—apart from or before the item descriptions.

Giving us the impression of a good value, however, may require tinkering with a host of factors. The relationship of prices within the menu itself is crucial to consider. The price mix and spread can affect how we perceive the value of the entire menu as well as the relative worth of each item. Behold the power of the choice frame.

The next level of value perception requires modifying our perception of the items' value vis-à-vis the marketplace at large. If restaurateurs want to avoid the race to the bottom that shopping by price can cause, they must get us to focus on value instead of price, then raise our estimation of value.

To do so, they must make those items or their pricing hard to compare with others in their vicinity, even the same restaurants' prior offers. Making the composition or description of items unique can do the trick. So can offering bundled deals. Environmental cues, such as tablecloths and flower arrangements, which connote restaurant genres high in price and quality, have also proven to raise perceptions of value. Caution, however: product execution must live up to the expectations that prompts like these create. Perceptions of brand integrity depend on it.

Menus can also manage the desirability of items by signaling scarcity. Conveyor-belt menus, which leave us never knowing when or if the items we want will come by, make a specialty of this. Other menu formats can signal scarcity with notices of limited-time offers. Whatever the case, scarcity messages induce "anticipatory regret," resulting in the urgency to buy more than we normally would of something we want. Precisely this overcame me on the outing for dim sum.

Limited-service and full-service casual-dining places with speedy-service models have a unique rhetorical challenge. They must lessen the pain of waiting in line. The queue could be physical, as at 800 Degrees, or virtual, as on a Domino's ordering app or a tabletop tablet at Applebee's.

With a well-designed assembly-line structure, a menu can relieve the lack of control we feel when we wait. It can choreograph the line so that it's user-friendly and our movements along it are smooth. All the better if it can make our procession entertaining, engaging, and a constant source of reassurance that the staff is trying to move us along. In these ways, an assembly-line menu can increase our satisfaction with the restaurant experience. At the same time, the format's unique ability to direct us through a sequence of messages and actions makes it ideal for suggestive selling. As long as we're in line, we're beholden to the flow.

If restaurateurs hope to increase the chances we'll buy a particular item by making it stand out above the rest, they should be wary of common misconceptions. They should question universalizing claims about how people scan information on a menu. Similarly, they should steer clear of the fallacy that noticing an item alone makes us more likely to buy it. Restaurateurs are better off making suggestions that are con-textually relevant. Those made in the restaurant—by servers, features of décor, or by the menu itself through recommendations of item pair-ings—have some proof of success. Beyond the restaurant's walls, digital notifications of menu promotions that we, specifically, would find com-pelling at the places and times we're likely to care can prompt us to buy.

Indeed, restaurateurs have many rhetorical tools. And yet, how swayable we are in any situation is ultimately an unknowable and moving target. The right amount of choice depends, to some extent, on conditions beyond restaurateurs' control. There's no way they can anticipate our OSLs—our optimal stimulation levels—inherent and purely personal needs for arousal by novelty or variety. Nor can they foresee our willingness to take risks. Then there's the matter of our information-processing styles. Are we visualizers or verbalizers? No restaurateur can know. There's no way, either, that they can plan for our personal habits of processing or scanning particular types or combinations of signifiers—verbal, visual, or otherwise—or the ur-gency we may feel in a moment to make a selection—all factors that affect whether we notice, ignore, or like particular items or sections of a menu.

What's more, restaurateurs will never be able to predict precisely how we, as individual diners, will judge the relative value of menu options. They can never presume our sensitivity to price or how, exactly, we might weigh, in any instance, the monetary or nonmonetary sacrifices in a transaction. Moreover, because we walk through their doors with unpredictable motives (do we want to show off or save money tonight?), they can't dictate which end of a choice set we'll gravitate toward. Will we choose the extremely high-priced "anchor," the Wagyu beef for $155, or will we set our sights on the $57 steak that the anchor made look like a bargain? All a restaurateur can do is increase the chance we choose one of the two.

Generally speaking, some of us are inherently more susceptible to pressure and suggestion than others. Also, depending on the menu, we may find ourselves subject to deeply entrenched preferences that no force can move. Always, the certainty we feel about our selections—which grows in line with the familiarity of items—determines our re-ceptiveness to any wile.

Nevertheless, I'm willing to speculate that, while restaurateurs can't foresee or control many aspects of our responses, they have one especially powerful inherent advantage. That is our desire to be persuaded.

Whenever we enter their restaurants hoping they'll serve our interests, we gain a motive to buy into their promises. Why would we want menus to contradict the notion that what they offer is what we want? That would only remind us of our dependency on vendors and marketplace conditions, that we don't control as much as we'd like. As long as we want our relationships with restaurateurs to work—and we do insofar as we go out to eat—we diners may be our own most potent persuaders.

ACKNOWLEDGMENTS

This book was brought to you in part by doggedness. It took consistent, incremental efforts over summer and holiday teaching breaks and nearly every Sunday for more than three years. I passed up swell opportunities that would have delayed the project. I had to say no to people I would have liked to oblige. There are no sabbaticals or other leaves of absence to credit for my getting it done, and there were no research grants to soak up the restaurant bills it took to make this study adequate. There are friends I haven't seen in so long; I hope they still remember me. This work took many tolls. My belief in the value of this project and the joy of writing kept me steadfast.

To those who made the venture more efficient, better informed, and more interesting: I'm ever grateful. Foremost among them are the chefs, restaurant owners and managers, and menu engineers and designers who took the time to be interviewed. I tried not to mangle the wisdom these generous folks gave: restaurant owners and managers Georgette Farkas, Daniel Scoggin, Sarintip Singsanong, Frank Steed, Allan Tam, Martin Riese, and Kevin Welby; executive chefs Kasja Alger, Charles Olalia, and the late Suthiporn Sungkamee; menu engineers Mark Laux and Bill Paul; menu designers Shannon Phillips, Woody Pirtle, and Douglas Riccardi; menu-app UI/UX designer Whitney Hess; and the Off the Menu app's executive team of Lawrence Longo, Arabella Roberts, and

Mike Stasyna. Although I didn't formally interview my Department of Art colleague, Raymond Kampf, our conversations over the years about his experience as an art director and menu designer for restaurants have enriched my understanding of the designer's perspective in intangible ways. Comparing our menu collections was as enlightening as it was amusing.

When researching a book, one always needs information on specialized topics and advice on the best ways to research them. For being so responsive and informative in these ways, many deserve my thanks. They include Julie Shen and Christy Stevens—librarians at the California State Polytechnic University, Pomona—for their advice on finding materials related to the ancient history of menus and trends in social media. Eric C. Rath was helpful on the subject of kaiseki. When I asked him if I was missing anything in my plans to address the subject, Andrew F. Smith shared his profound expertise on trends in snacking and fast food. James Robert Watson and Rush Bowman made the essential introductions to Daniel Scoggin and Frank Steed that so enriched this project. Andrew Coe clarified my understanding of early Chinese menus. Hofu Wu was invaluable for his translations of supplementary menus that the restaurant Giang Nan posted to its back wall only in Chinese. Klara Seddon gave me good leads for sources on Japanese food replicas. Nancy Kruse and David Sax shared their experience in contacting representatives of restaurant chains. I'm grateful to Lisa Timouk for helping me understand price elasticity on menus. I appreciate Rachel Salabes for her guidance regarding the National Restaurant Association's research on restaurant goers. Katie Cameron didn't have to bother with my unprofitable questions about Technomic, Inc.'s research on restaurant patrons. But she was kind enough to offer explanations and free resources.

I'm beyond fortunate to have the support and collaboration of my agent, Malaga Baldi, whose depth of expertise and resourcefulness continually amaze me. I thank her profusely in this instance for introducing me to Jessica Easto at Agate Publishing. I couldn't have asked for better judgment in an editor or a better writer-editor relationship. Jessica's suggestions were wise and helpful at every (page) turn. I'm convinced that no writing workshop anywhere would have raised my game as much as she has.

My final, and most personal, acknowledgment goes to Jamisin Matthews. He accompanied me on most of my restaurant visits for this book. I benefitted from his superior sense of direction, his professional photography tips, and his calling attention, on occasion, to something I didn't notice. His graciousness and good spirit throughout the nearly two years it took to visit all of the restaurants on my list made the largely solitary experience of producing a book feel in those times like a great, shared adventure.

APPENDIX A

Because the conclusions of this book rest heavily on my study of particular LA-area restaurants, and I'm committed to transparency, I want to reveal as much as possible about the data-gathering and sorting I did for this crucial component of my research. To this end, I offer Appendices A and B. They reveal the various classification schemes I used to constitute my restaurant sample and, in the case of menu descriptors like imagery, mediums, language, and price writing—too numerous to compare without drafting the chart in Appendix B—to make observations about that sample. The appendices also detail my schedule of restaurant visits, and when and what I signed up for with regard to menu-related notifications from restaurants. It's essential to disclose that data because restaurants close or change design frequently. What I observed at the times of my visits will probably have changed by the time you read this, yet may still be traceable if you research the time frames I provide here. Armed with this information, you can best judge the validity of my sample and categorization methods for yourself. Perhaps you'll also gain insights from the data that I missed.

Log of Physical and Virtual Restaurant Visits

Listings of restaurants that have more than one location, physical or virtual, indicate which site I visited. Also, even if I studied each one at the same restaurant location, I marked my experiences of drive-thru and interior menus as separate site visits.

Some restaurants on the list have since closed or changed location, concept, name, architecture, menu content, or aesthetic. Some began one or more such transformations as this book went to press. Since the restaurant business is dynamic, this is to be expected.

Restaurant	Location	Date(s) of Visit(s)
800 Degrees Neapolitan Pizzeria	90024	June 28, 2014
A-Frame	90066	February 8, 2014
A.O.C. Wine Bar & Restaurant	90048	June 7, 2014
Amalur Project	moving pop-up	November 22, 2013
Apple Pan	90064	October 12, 2013
Applebee's	91801	September 15, 2013
Applebee's	91702	July 9, 2015
BJ's Restaurant & Brewhouse	91502	August 3, 2013
Bludso's BBQ	90221	December 15, 2013
Bottega Louie	90017	August 10, 2013
Burger King	90028	September 13, 2014
Burger King	same location, drive-thru site	December 8 and 21, 2013
California Pizza Kitchen	91203	July 27, 2013
Canelé	90039	August 3, 2014
Canter's Deli	90036	August 1, 2013
Carl's Jr.	91604	April 1, 2014
Caviar	iPad app	December 5, 2014
Caviar	iPhone app	December 12, 2014
Caviar	TryCaviar.com	July 30, 2014 August 8, 2014
Chick-fil-A	90028, drive-thru site	October 12, 2013, December 21, 2013 January 16, 2014
Chipotle	90004	August 23, 2014
Claim Jumper	91505	September 8, 2013
Connie & Ted's	90046	October 5, 2013
CUT	90212	July 26, 2014

Restaurant	Location	Date(s) of Visit(s)
Dave & Buster's	91007	August 4, 2013
Din Tai Fung (store 1)	91007	September 28, 2013
Din Tai Fung	91210	December 28, 2013
Domino's	iPad app	May 4, 2014
Domino's	iPhone voice-ordering app	January 3, 2015 July 11, 2015
Domino's	Dominos.com	August 30, 2013 November 1, 2013
Farmer Boys	90021	May 10, 2014
Fogo de Chão	90211	August 25, 2013
Giang Nan	91754	March 8, 2014
Hama Sushi	90012	April 24, 2014
Hana Ichimonme	90013	March 1, 2014
Hanbat Shul-Lung Tang	90020	August 14, 2013
In-N-Out Burger	90028, drive-thru site	August 20, 2014
Ink.	90069	April 26, 2014
J&K Hong Kong Cuisine	90012	January 18, 2014
Jitlada	90027	July 12, 2014
King Taco	90015	December 24, 2013
Lawry's The Prime Rib	90211	September 7, 2013
Lemonade	91101	September 6, 2014
Marie Callender's	91403	December 21, 2013
Marouch	90029	November 2, 2013
Maude	90212	July 5, 2014
Meals by Genet	90019	January 14, 2014
Meizhou Dongpo	90067	March 15, 2014
Moun of Tunis	90046	August 18, 2013
Mud Hen Tavern	90038	June 15, 2014
NBC Seafood Restaurant	91754	August 17, 2014
Nozawa Bar	90210	August 29, 2013
Opaque: Dining in the Dark	90403	August 31, 2013
Osteria Mozza	90038	July 19, 2014
Patina	90012	March 29, 2014
Providence	90038	May 31, 2014
Rainforest Café	91764	August 16, 2013
Ray's and Stark Bar	90036	May 3, 2014

Log continues on next page

Restaurant	Location	Date(s) of Visit(s)
Rivera	90015	April 19, 2014
Romano's Macaroni Grill	91324	September 1, 2013
Salt's Cure	90046	April 12, 2014
Seamless	iPad app	July 30, 2014
Seamless	Seamless.com	August 26, 2013
Taco Bell	91205	May 11, 2014
Taco Bell	iPhone app	July 18, 2015
Tam O'Shanter	90039	August 11, 2013
The Cheesecake Factory	91210	April 11, 2015
The Church Key	90069	February 15, 2014
The Counter	90036	October 19, 2013
The Gardens of Taxco	90046	September 14, 2013
The Stinking Rose	90211	October 26, 2013

List of Restaurant Characteristics and Quantity of Sample Represented by Each

Restaurant Types: Assigned Numbers	Restaurant Type	Unique Locations	Visits
1	Full-service multi-unit restaurant concept	21	21
2	Full-service single-unit restaurant concept, not part of a restaurant group	16	16
3	Full-service single-unit restaurant concept, but part of a restaurant group	12	12
4	Pop-up/temporary restaurant	2	2
5	Fast food/quick-service local or regional chain at the time of visit	5	5
6	Fast food/quick-service national or international chain	12	15
7	Drive-thru experience	6	7
8	The only location of the restaurant that is quick-service	1	1
9	Fastaurant (partial service: table service of food, but no order taking or further attention by servers)	1	1
10	Restaurant with a theme (not simply that of a cuisine)	4	4
11	Focus is split between food and another sales opportunity (gaming, a bar, a shop, etc.)	3	3
12	Food-specialty menu (e.g.: a steakhouse, a barbecue spot, an all-dim-sum service, a specialist in fried-chicken sandwiches, an all-garlic menu, etc.)	14	15
13	Offering only fixed tasting menu(s)	5	5
14	Newly opened at the time of visit	8	8
15	Open for at least 5 years, but not yet historic (by reputation), at the time of visit	9	9
16	An LA institution at the time of visit (by reputation)	23	23
17	Smart casual (fit for gourmets, yet informal)	13	13
18	Fine dining (formal service or where the server plays a varied, extended, and highly ritualized, scripted role)	9	9
19	Gourmet-vanguardist dining (where servers are relatively informal, not especially ritualized or scripted beyond introductions to the restaurant concept)	6	6
20	Casual-dining chain	10	10
21	Brunch, breakfast, or lunch daypart visit	9	10
22	Dinner daypart visit	49	51
23	Serving ethnically, regionally, or culturally specialized foods in traditional forms (not massified foods or ethnic foods in brand-specific or innovative versions)	19	19

List continues on next page

Restaurant Types: Assigned Numbers	Restaurant Type	Unique Locations	Visits
24	Multicultural menu	20	20
25	Traditionalist in cuisine (need not do so exclusively)	55	58
26	Asserting originality in cuisine (need not do so exclusively)	41	41
27	Extremely short menu	4	4
28	Extremely long menu	10	10
29	Unusual menu formats or menu formats specific to a restaurant genre	19	19
30	Unusual menu text (language) for the genre	2	2
31	Web-based ordering system shared by more than one restaurant	4	4
32	Web-based ordering system exclusive to that restaurant	4	6
33	Tablet or touch-screen menu or digital menu board	2	2
34	Full-service restaurants especially accommodating to families with young children (with children's menu or entertainments; need not do that exclusively)	6	6
35	Noticeably accommodating to the elderly (advertised AARP discount; need not do that exclusively)	1	1
36	Nonsequential menu structures (not in courses, at full-service restaurants)	26	26
37	Sequential menu structures (in courses, at full-service restaurants)	18	18
38	All-you-can-eat formats (buffet-style or otherwise)	1	1
39	Cafeteria-style with diner decisions made by moving along assembly line	3	3
40	Dim-sum-style cart service (not all-included all-you-can-eat)	2	2

Field-Study Sample Indexed to Restaurant Characteristics
The numbers in the following table correspond to the characteristics described in the table on page 213. Restaurants with an asterisk indicate that I made two visits to that location under the same conditions. Multiple listings of the same restaurant indicate differing conditions. Differing conditions may be that the restaurant introduced a significant new menu format (which I included because it was not otherwise represented in the field study, such as a tabletop tablet) or that I made an additional visit to the same restaurant (at either the same or a different location) to experience a different menu format, such as a drive-thru menu, that the restaurant also offered). In cases of restaurants with more than one location, I indicated the specific locations I visited in parentheses. All visits were during the dinner daypart (evening) unless otherwise noted.

Restaurant Name	1	2	3	4	5	6	7	8	9	10	11	12	13	14	15
800 Degrees Neapolitan Pizzeria					•							•			•
A-Frame			•												•
A.O.C. Wine Bar & Restaurant			•												
Amalur Project				•									•	•	
Apple Pan		•										•			
Applebee's (91801)	•														
Applebee's (91702)	•														
BJ's Restaurant & Brewhouse	•														
Bludso's BBQ	•				•		•					•			
Bottega Louie		•													•
Burger King (drive-thru)						•	•								
Burger King (daytime, drive-thru)						•	•								
Burger King (in store)						•	•								
California Pizza Kitchen	•														
Canelé (brunch)		•													
Canter's Deli	•														
Carl's Jr.						•									
Caviar (iPad app)															
Caviar (iPhone app)															
Caviar (TryCaviar.com)															
*Chick-fil-A (daytime, drive-thru)						•	•				•				
Chick-fil-A (drive-thru)						•	•				•				
Chipotle						•									
Claim Jumper	•														
Connie & Ted's			•										•		
CUT	•											•			•
Dave & Buster's	•									•					
Din Tai Fung (91007)	•														
Din Tai Fung (91210)	•														
Domino's (iPad app)						•						•			
*Domino's (iPhone voice-ordering app)						•						•	•		
*Domino's (Dominos.com)						•						•			
Farmer Boys								•							
Fogo de Chão	•														
Giang Nan	•														
Hama Sushi		•										•			
Hana Ichimonme		•													
Hanbat Shul-Lung Tang		•													
In-N-Out Burger (drive-thru)					•		•								
Ink.		•													•
J&K Hong Kong Cuisine		•													

16	17	18	19	20	21	22	23	24	25	26	27	28	29	30	31	32	33	34	35	36	37	38	39	40
	•								•	•			•							•			•	
	•		•			•		•		•			•	•						•				
•			•				•		•												•			
	•		•			•		•		•			•								•			
•						•			•		•										•			
				•		•		•	•	•		•						•		•				
						•		•	•	•		•					•	•						
				•		•		•	•	•		•								•				
•					•		•		•															
	•				•		•		•	•										•				
						•			•	•														
					•				•	•														
					•				•	•							•							
				•		•		•	•	•		•								•				
•					•			•												•				
•						•	•		•			•					•			•				
									•	•														
						•									•									
						•									•									
						•									•									
					•				•															
						•			•															
									•	•	•													•
				•		•		•	•	•		•						•	•	•				
	•					•			•	•												•		
		•				•			•	•												•		
				•		•		•	•	•										•				
•						•	•		•				•							•				
•						•	•		•	•			•							•				
						•			•							•								
						•			•							•								
						•			•							•								
									•	•														
						•	•		•				•									•	•	
•							•		•			•								•				
•						•	•		•				•							•				
•						•	•		•				•											
•						•	•		•		•									•				
•				•					•															
	•	•				•		•		•										•				
•						•	•		•			•								•				

Table continues on next page

Restaurant Name	1	2	3	4	5	6	7	8	9	10	11	12	13	14	15
Jitlada		•													
King Taco					•										
Lawry's The Prime Rib	•											•			
Lemonade					•										
Marouch		•													
Marie Callender's	•														
Maude		•											•	•	
Meals by Genet		•													
Meizhou Dongpo			•										•		
Moun of Tunis		•													
Mud Hen Tavern			•										•		
NBC Seafood Restaurant (daytime, dim sum service)		•									•				
Nozawa Bar	•											•	•	•	
Opaque: Dining in the Dark				•						•	•	•			
Osteria Mozza			•												•
Patina			•												
Providence			•									•			
Rainforest Café	•									•	•				
Ray's and Stark Bar			•												•
Rivera			•												•
Romano's Macaroni Grill	•														
Salt's Cure		•											•		
Seamless (iPad app; ordered from Chi Dinasty, 90027)															
Taco Bell						•									
Taco Bell (iPhone app)						•									
Tam O'Shanter			•							•					
The Cheesecake Factory	•														
The Church Key		•											•		
The Counter	•														•
The Gardens of Taxco		•													
The Stinking Rose	•									•	•				

16	17	18	19	20	21	22	23	24	25	26	27	28	29	30	31	32	33	34	35	36	37	38	39	40
•						•		•	•		•									•				
•						•		•																
		•				•		•													•			
										•			•											•
•						•	•		•												•			
				•		•		•	•	•								•		•				
		•				•				•			•											
•						•	•		•				•								•			
						•	•		•															
•						•	•		•				•								•			
	•							•		•										•				
•					•		•		•				•							•				•
	•					•	•		•	•			•								•			
						•			•		•		•								•			
	•	•				•			•	•											•			
•	•					•		•	•												•			
•	•					•		•	•												•			
			•			•		•	•	•								•			•			
•				•				•		•			•							•				
•	•					•			•												•			
			•			•		•	•															
•		•				•			•	•			•							•				
						•								•										
								•	•	•														
						•		•	•	•							•							
•		•				•			•															
						•		•	•	•		•								•				
	•		•					•		•			•							•				•
	•					•			•	•			•							•				
•						•	•		•				•								•			
				•			•		•	•	•													

Log of Sign-Ups for Online Text (SMS) or Email Notifications from Sample Restaurants

On March 26, 2014 (unless otherwise noted), I signed up (via the restaurants' websites unless otherwise noted) for the following. Making this list helped me to spot patterns in the way restaurants of differing types notified—or didn't notify—me of menu-related offers or information. This research fed my conclusions about the use of digital notifications for selective selling in chapter 10.

Restaurant	Digital notifications sign-up
800 Degrees Neapolitan Pizzeria	None offered.
A-Frame	None offered.
A.O.C. Wine Bar & Restaurant	Subscribed to mailing list I first found on April 20, 2014.
Amalur Project	Newsletter subscription.
Apple Pan	None offered.
Applebee's	Newsletter and email club subscription.
BJ's Restaurant & Brewhouse	None offered.
Bludso's BBQ	None offered.
Bottega Louie	Newsletter subscription.
Burger King	BK Alerts. On August 27, 2014, I downloaded the Burger King app for iPhone, advertised to me via text message first the same day.
California Pizza Kitchen	None offered.
Canelé	None offered.
Canter's Deli	None offered.
Carl's Jr.	Signed up for exclusive offers and email deals.
Caviar	Began saving promotional emails automatically sent to my inbox on February 17, 2015.
Chick-fil-A	Signed up for Email Insiders.
Chipotle	Registered for an "account" on May 10, 2014.
Claim Jumper	Signed up for E-Club.
Connie & Ted's	None offered.
CUT	None offered.
Dave and Buster's	None offered.
Din Tai Fung, Arcadia "store 1" and Glendale locations	None offered.
Domino's	Signed up for email and text offers.
Farmer Boys	Signed up for E-Club.
Fogo de Chão	Signed up for E-Club.
Giang Nan	None offered.
Hama Sushi	None offered.
Hana Ichimonme	None offered.
Hanbat Shul-Lung Tang	None offered.

Restaurant	Digital notifications sign-up
In-N-Out Burger	None offered.
Ink.	None offered.
J&K Hong Kong Cuisine	None offered.
Jitlada	None offered.
King Taco	None offered.
Lawry's The Prime Rib	Joined E-List.
Lemonade	None offered.
Marouch	None offered.
Marie Callender's	Signed up for E-Club.
Maude	Signed up for the restaurant's email newsletter on May 5, 2014.
Meals by Genet	None offered.
Meizhou Dongpo	None offered.
Moun of Tunis	None offered.
Mud Hen Tavern	None offered.
NBC Seafood Restaurant	None offered.
Nozawa Bar	None offered on the website; however, a reservation required a credit card and input of contact information. The restaurant subsequently used that to send me a regular email newsletter, beginning April 3, 2014.
Opaque: Dining in the Dark	None offered.
Osteria Mozza	Subscribed to mailing list with interest in new menu items or menu changes.
Patina	None offered. Even though I didn't sign up for notifications, the Patina Restaurant Group sent me regular emails anyway, beginning June 7, 2014.
Providence	None offered.
Rainforest Café	Joined email club.
Ray's and Stark Bar	None offered. The restaurant was part of the Patina Restaurant Group. (See Patina entry above.)
Rivera	Subscribed to mailing list.
Romano's Macaroni Grill	Signed up for "Exclusive Offers" on website.
Salt's Cure	None offered.
Seamless.com	Began saving promotional emails automatically sent to my inbox as of February 24, 2015, even though I never had the opportunity to sign up for any such messaging.
Taco Bell	None offered.
Tam O'Shanter	Signed up for E-List.
The Cheesecake Factory	Signed up for email.
The Church Key	None offered.
The Counter	None offered.
The Gardens of Taxco	None offered.
The Stinking Rose	None offered.

APPENDIX B

Characteristics of Sample Restaurant Menus' Descriptive Features (Imagery, Materials, Language, and Price Writing)
Making the following table helped me make sense of the large amount of data I collected—including written notes, photographic documentation, and collection of actual menus—from my visits to the restaurants in my sample. The table made it easier for me to spot patterns of difference in how restaurants used a wide variety of menu descriptors. Chapters 6 through 9 show the results of this research. In the key below, you'll find a detailed description of each menu characteristic, which corresponds with the descriptions and numbers in the table. Each characteristic falls under one of four subcategories: language, language (writing prices), imagery, or materials. For occasional notes on a specific restaurant's characteristics, see the footnotes.

Menu Characteristics Key

Language

1. **Minimalistic vanguard:** lists components for unusual items only, no descriptions.
2a. **Branded terms, widely known:** uses very widely known branded terms (beyond restaurant's own terminology) in item names or descriptions (drinks don't count).
2b. **Branded terms, restaurant:** uses the restaurant's own branded terms in item names or descriptions.
2c. **Branded terms, quality:** uses branded terms to indicate quality or ethical sources of ingredients in item names or descriptions.
3. **Creative terminology:** regularly includes creative, esoteric, or exotic terminology. (Restaurants of single ethnicity don't count. Branded nomenclature doesn't count.)
4. **Minimal dish descriptions:** consistently uses no or minimal dish descriptions. (Descriptive names or names as lists of ingredients don't count.)
5a. **Romancing dish descriptors:** uses seductive descriptors in dish descriptions to titillate or to drop quality cues (not counting cocktail menus, which typically do so regardless of genre by naming liquor brand names).
5b. **Romancing merchandising copy:** uses seductive descriptors in merchandising copy on menus to signal brand identity and quality.
6. **Handholding:** uses informative item names or descriptions.
7. **Wingmen:** employs features of décor or servers to explain or romance items. This can mean using graphic design (still or motion graphics); prominent bar area or wine-rack wall or bucket of wine in décor; indirect graphics, such as cookbook display; generic illustration; cabinet displays of historical material relating to the food or menu; actual food or kitchen equipment; food replicas; open kitchens; using servers to explain or romance items, unprompted; and other.

Language (Writing Prices)

8. **Minimal presence of numbers:** infrequently represents prices or expresses them only in whole numerals (e.g., "10" as opposed to "$10" or "$10.00").
9. **Cents conscious:** uses cents-conscious pricing (e.g., " xx.95," "xx.99," "xx.50").
10. **Dollar signs:** uses dollar signs.

Imagery

11a. **Handholding, supplemental:** uses photos of dishes on supplemental menu(s) (not on the main menu).

11b. **Handholding, main:** uses photos of dishes on main menu.

12. **Illustrations, menu items:** uses illustrations to describe specific menu items.

13. **Illustrations, nonspecific:** uses illustrations (not necessarily of menu items) or nonfood photos for branding.

14. **No imagery:** uses neither photos nor illustrations on any menu.

15. **Web imagery, unnamed:** uses images of food on website only, but any dishes shown are not named (the food imagery is just for branding).

16. **Web imagery, named:** uses images of food on website only, but dishes shown are named.

Materials

17. **Signboard, digital:** uses a digital menu signboard.

18. **Table tablet:** uses a digital tabletop tablet for at least one menu.

19. **Real food:** uses prominent display of actual food as supplement to menu or as main menu.

20. **Model food:** uses model (plastic or wax) food as supplement to menu or as main menu.

21a. **Thick plastic:** has printed table menu that uses plastic unabashedly via lamination or plastic cover and feels stiff or tacky or like the plastic layer is thick.

21b. **Thinner plastic:** has printed table menu that uses plastic via lamination, but feels less plastic, more like paper.

21c. **Plastic sleeve:** has printed table menu that uses plastic to cover paper in a plastic sleeve or under a neat film (more elegant, as with single panel and ribbon border or in leather-like binding with tip-ins, etc.).

22. **Natural:** has printed table menu that uses materials with fine, clean, or "natural" associations (e.g., plain or textured paper, with leather-like covers).

23. **Immaterial:** provides list from a tasting menu only upon request (would otherwise not have been published).

24. **Signboard, food:** uses a nondigital menu signboard or chalkboard for food, including specials.

25. **Signboard, drinks:** uses a nondigital menu signboard or chalkboard for drinks/bar.

26. **Online:** provides a fully online ordering experience.

27a. **Spoken menu, main:** conveys the main in-restaurant menu via speech only.

27b. **Spoken menu, supplemental:** conveys at least one supplemental menu via speech only.

Restaurant	Minimalistic vanguard	Branded terms, widely known	Branded terms, restaurant	Branded terms, quality	Creative terminology	Minimal dish descriptions	Romancing dish descriptors	Romancing merchandising copy	Handholding	Wingmen	Minimal presence of numbers	Cents conscious	Dollar signs
	1	2a	2b	2c	3	4	5a	5b	6	7	8	9	10
800 Degrees Neapolitan Pizzeria							•	•	•	•		•	•
A-Frame				•			•		•	•	•		
A.O.C. Wine Bar & Restaurant [1]	•			•						•	•		
Amalur Project [2]	•			•									
Apple Pan [3]							•		•	•		•	
Applebee's (91801)		•		•			•	•	•	•		•	
Applebee's (91702) [4]		•		•			•		•	•		•	
BJ's Restaurant & Brewhouse		•	•	•			•	•	•	•			
Bludso's BBQ						•				•			
Bottega Louie [5]							•		•	•	•		•
Burger King (in store) [5]		•				•				•		•	•
Burger King (drive-thru) [5]		•				•				•		•	•
California Pizza Kitchen		•		•			•	•	•	•		•	
Canelé (brunch) [6]									•		•		
Canter's Deli							•	•	•			•	•
Carl's Jr. [5]		•	•	•			•	•		•		•	•
Chick-fil-A (drive-thru) [5]		•				•	•			•		•	
Chipotle						•				•		•	
Claim Jumper							•		•	•		•	
Connie & Ted's			•				•	•	•	•	•		
CUT	•				•					•	•		•
Dave & Buster's [7]		•		•			•	•	•	•			•
Din Tai Fung (91007) [8]						•		•		•		•	•
Din Tai Fung (91210) [9]						•		•		•	•		•
Domino's (iPad app) [5]		•				•						•	•
Farmer Boys [10]		•				•	•		•	•		•	•
Fogo de Chão [11]							•		•	•	•		
Giang Nan [12]						•						•	•
Hama Sushi [13]						•				•	•		
Hana Ichimonme [14]						•				•		•	•
Hanbat Shul-Lung Tang						•						•	•
In-N-Out Burger (drive-thru) [15]		•				•						•	•

	Handholding, supplemental	Handholding, main	Illustrations, menu items	Illustrations, nonspecific	No imagery	Web imagery, unnamed	Web imagery, named	Signboard, digital	Table tablet	Real food	Model food	Thick plastic	Thinner plastic	Plastic sleeve	Natural	Immaterial	Signboard, food	Signboard, drinks	Online	Spoken menu, main	Spoken menu, supplemental
	11a	11b	12	13	14	15	16	17	18	19	20	21a	21b	21c	22	23	24	25	26	27a	27b
					•		•			•					•		•	•			
					•	•									•						
				•			•								•						
																•					•
					•					•		•									
		•										•									
		•							•				•								
												•									
				•											•		•	•			
					•									•							
		•						•													
		•															•	•			
	•												•								
					•	•											•				
					•	•				•		•									
		•															•	•			
		•															•	•			
	•						•			•							•	•			
												•									
				•											•		•	•			
						•				•					•						
		•										•									
		•											•		•						
		•										•			•						
		•																	•		
		•															•	•			
	•									•				•							
					•									•			•				
	•									•							•				
		•									•										
					•												•				
		•															•	•			

Table continues on next page

Restaurant	Minimalistic vanguard	Branded terms, widely known	Branded terms, restaurant	Branded terms, quality	Creative terminology	Minimal dish descriptions	Romancing dish descriptors	Romancing merchandising copy	Handholding	Wingmen	Minimal presence of numbers	Cents conscious	Dollar signs
	1	2a	2b	2c	3	4	5a	5b	6	7	8	9	10
Ink.[1]	•			•	•					•	•		
J&K Hong Kong Cuisine						•				•		•	
Jitlada									•			•	
King Taco						•				•		•	•
Lawry's The Prime Rib		•	•	•			•			•	•		
Lemonade	•									•		•	•
Marie Callender's[16]			•				•		•	•		•	
Marouch									•			•	•
Maude[17]	•				•					•	•		
Meals by Genet								•					
Meizhou Dongpo							•	•	•	•		•	•
Moun of Tunis[18]						•		•				•	•
Mud Hen Tavern[1]			•		•		•		•	•	•		
NBC Seafood Restaurant (dim sum service)[19]						•				•		•	•
Nozawa Bar[20]											•		•
Opaque: Dining in the Dark							•		•		•		
Osteria Mozza					•					•			
Patina	•			•	•					•	•		
Providence	•			•	•					•	•		•
Rainforest Café			•				•		•		•		
Ray's and Stark Bar[21]	•				•		•	•	•	•	•		
Rivera[22]					•			•	•	•	•		
Romano's Macaroni Grill[23]		•		•			•		•	•	•		
Salt's Cure[24]	•			•				•		•	•		
Taco Bell		•	•	•		•				•		•	
Tam O'Shanter		•	•	•					•	•	•		
The Cheesecake Factory[25]		•		•			•	•	•	•		•	
The Church Key	•			•	•					•	•		•
The Counter		•		•		•			•			•	
The Gardens of Taxco							•		•	•	•		
The Stinking Rose[26]					•		•		•	•		•	

	11a	11b	12	13	14	15	16	17	18	19	20	21a	21b	21c	22	23	24	25	26	27a	27b
Handholding, supplemental																					

(Column headers, left to right: 11a Handholding, supplemental; 11b Handholding, main; 12 Illustrations, menu items; 13 Illustrations, nonspecific; 14 No imagery; 15 Web imagery, unnamed; 16 Web imagery, named; 17 Signboard, digital; 18 Table tablet; 19 Real food; 20 Model food; 21a Thick plastic; 21b Thinner plastic; 21c Plastic sleeve; 22 Natural; 23 Immaterial; 24 Signboard, food; 25 Signboard, drinks; 26 Online; 27a Spoken menu, main; 27b Spoken menu, supplemental)

11a	11b	12	13	14	15	16	17	18	19	20	21a	21b	21c	22	23	24	25	26	27a	27b
				•										•						
•											•									
	•										•					•				
				•		•										•	•			
				•		•			•					•						
				•	•				•			•				•	•			
	•								•		•	•				•				
				•									•							
				•	•									•						
				•	•									•						
	•													•						
	•										•			•						
				•	•									•			•			
•									•		•			•						
														•	•					
				•										•						
				•	•									•						
				•	•				•					•						
		•			•				•					•						
	•								•											
				•	•									•						
		•			•				•					•						
•														•		•	•			•
				•	•									•						•
		•														•	•			
			•											•						
			•						•		•									
		•			•				•					•						
•													•				•			
																			•	•
		•	•								•	•								

Table continues on next page

TABLE FOOTNOTES

1. Wingmen appeared only in the bar.

2. The spoken menu appeared only in an opening offer of champagne.

3. The romancing dish descriptors appeared only on the back of the menu.

4. I didn't observe romancing merchandising copy during this dining experience.

5. The dollar signs were small.

6. The signboard did not include the brunch menu.

7. There was minimal romancing merchandising copy.

8. Thinner plastic was used for a picture brochure while natural materials were used for the ordering menu.

9. There were dollar signs on the drink menu only. Thinner plastic was used for a picture brochure while natural materials were used for the ordering menu.

10. The dish descriptions were mostly minimal, with occasional romancing descriptors. Handholding was used only for items with unusual names.

11. Romancing descriptors were present on the cocktail menu only. Handholding was present on the cocktail and dessert menus only. Wingmen helped sell wine only, and only the dessert menu was cents conscious.

12. The signboard took the form of copier paper on the back wall that listed specials only in Chinese.

13. Handholding was evident, but only via a generic sushi list.

14. The model food did not represent the entire menu, and some models for dishes were not present on the menu.

15. Only three meals were illustrated with photographs (handholding).

16. Thinner plastic was present on the supplemental menu, while natural materials were used for the pie menu and placemat. The signboard was used for pies in the front bakery.

17. Wingmen helped sell wine only.

18. Natural materials were used for the wine book only.

19. Dollar signs appeared only in the menu price key and the signboard for just seafood. The handholding was present in the dim sum carts, the equivalent of the main menu. Thick plastic was used on the supplemental menu only, and a signboard was used only for the seafood list, not for dim sum service.

20. Minimalistic numerals, dollar signs, and natural materials were used on the drink cards only.

21. Romancing descriptors, romancing merchandising copy, and handholding were present on the water menu only.

22. The nonspecific illustrations were photos.

23. The spoken menu was used only to explain the honor-system wine.

24. The spoken menu was used only for dessert.

25. The widely known branded terms were used in the cheesecake list only.

26. Thick plastic was used on the supplemental menus only, and thinner plastic was used on the main menu.

NOTES

MANY OF THE INSIGHTS I GAINED ABOUT MENU DESIGN AND RESTAU-
rant operations came from interviewing a wide variety of restaurateurs,
designers, and industry consultants. A list of these generous people appears in my Acknowledgments. Unless otherwise stated, I conducted
the interviews by phone. All occurred between 2013 and 2015.

Throughout this book, I quote dish names and descriptions on
menus. Since the interpretation of menu layout and design is a goal of
this book, I felt it was important to replicate menu text as closely to the
original as possible. In quotations, I used bold font wherever there was
bold font in the source. I used a slash symbol (/) to indicate a line break
in the original layout. Any words capitalized or lowercase appeared as
such in the quoted menu as well. However, any passages I quoted from
a menu for which I didn't use slash symbols, including merchandising
copy and paragraphs-long dish descriptions, reflect the original layout
of the lines of text on the menu in the paragraph breaks only.

Frequently, I refer to menus or restaurants as *gourmet*. This means
that they offer experimental or premium-quality cuisine. I use the term
fine dining throughout the book to designate restaurants with formal
service and higher-than-average checks.

Introduction

About the origins of restaurants and menus: Steven J. R. Ellis carefully lays out the evidence for the various types of institutions we would call restaurants—places open to the public serving choices of food and drink to paying customers who may dine on the premises—in the ancient Greek and Roman worlds in the chapter "Eating and Drinking Out," in Paul Erdkamp, ed., *A Cultural History of Food in Antiquity*, Volume 1 (2012), 95–112. His citation of the bar with the wall-written menu, the first evidence of a menu, is on page 108. A good discussion of "viewing dishes," my example of an early alternative menu form, is in Stephen H. West, "Playing with Food: Performance, Food, and the Aesthetics of Artificiality in the Sung and Yuan," *Harvard Journal of Asiatic Studies* 57, no. 1 (June 1997): 94.

PART I: DIRECTING EVENTS

Chapter 1: The Privilege of Submission

Michelin's ratings for major US cities in their 2018 guides, published at the end of 2017, exemplify the tendency of their rating guides to give the ultimate recognitions to tasting-menu-only establishments. The 2018 guide for New York City gave four out of five of its three-star honors to restaurants that were tasting menu only. The fifth was tasting menu optional. At the same time, both of Chicago's and five of the six three-starred dining rooms in the San Francisco Bay Area and Wine Country offered tasting menus exclusively. If I count restaurants with à la carte in addition, the percentage of top tables with tasting menus on Michelin's and The World's Fifty Best Restaurants (TWFBR) lists for 2017 was 100. (The 2018 rankings for TWFBR were not yet published when this book went to press.)

The pattern of tasting-menu-only restaurants receiving top honors from TWFBR for 2016 and 2015 and from Michelin for 2017, 2016, and 2015—the previous years I checked—held with minor fluctuations. For example, in the case of TWFBR, tasting-menu-only places numbered eight of the top ten in 2016. In 2015, they amounted to seven. For Michelin, the case of New York City is typical. In the 2017 guide, four out of the six three-star restaurants were tasting menu only. In 2016, all six were. In 2015, five of the six were.

To get a brief overview of contemporary and historical kaiseki standards and how they may be varied, as well as the continued influence of kaiseki on international chefs today, see Yoshihiro Murata, trans. Masushi Kuma, *Kaiseki: The Exquisite Cuisine of Kyoto's Kikunoi Restaurant* (2012), 6–13. Sources that succinctly discuss variations on the order of dishes in a kaiseki menu include Murata, *Kaiseki: The Exquisite Cuisine of Kyoto's Kikunoi Restaurant*, 13; and Vaughan Tan, "Understanding Kaiseki," TheAtlantic.com, October 8, 2009. You can find a more in-depth and scholarly treatment of how kaiseki menus evolved since the seventeenth century in Eric C. Rath, "Reevaluating Rikyū: Kaiseki and the Origins of Japanese Cuisine," *The Journal of Japanese Studies* 39, no. 1 (Winter 2013): 67–96.

For an account of Western chefs' exposure to kaiseki in the 1960s, which served as a model for the tasting menus of nouvelle cuisine, see Charles Spence and Betina Piqueras-Fiszman, *The Perfect Meal: The Multisensory Science of Food and Dining* (2014), 3.

That chefs in the West didn't artfully compose dishes on individual diners' plates prior to nouvelle is the common thread of various sources, which otherwise give differing accounts of historical trends in Western dining service. For example, the account of table service in Europe by Jean-Louis Flandrin—in *Arranging the Meal: A History of Table Service in France* (2007)—differs greatly in the details from that of Stephen Mennell—in *All Manners Food: Eating and Taste in England and France from the Middle Ages to the Present*, second edition (1996)—and differs yet again from that of Margaret Visser—in *The Rituals of Dinner: The Origins, Evolution, Eccentricities, and Meanings of Table Manners* (1991)—on the matter of how precisely the medieval *service à la française* (dominant till the late nineteenth century) changed with the emergence of *service à la russe*, widely adopted by the end of the nineteenth century. Nevertheless, their accounts all agree that the chef didn't arrange food on individual diners' plates in either mode of service.

Ideal introductions to gastrophysics are Spence and Piqueras-Fiszman, *The Perfect Meal*, 2; and Spence, *Gastrophysics: The New Science of Eating* (2017), xvii. The following article puts the gastrophysical trend of chefs choreographing increasingly multidimensional, theatrical dining experiences into a larger historical perspective, tracing it from nouvelle through modernist cuisine: Joshua Abrams, "The Scenographic Imagination and the Contemporary Restaurant," *Performance Research: A Journal of the Performing Arts* 18, no. 3 (September 2013): 7–14.

I'm not the only one to point out the revelatory aspects of tasting menus. Jason Kessler summarizes this argument by various defenders of the form neatly in "Tasting Menus and the à la carte Internet," DailyDot.com, January 15, 2013.

On the existential, affective, and ethical perils of too much choice in many aspects of contemporary life, including consumer choice, Barry Schwartz's *The Paradox of Choice: Why More Is Less* (2004) is a classic.

Chapter 2: The Four Faces of Togetherness

A history of Chinese restaurants in the United States, which discusses their first arrival with the Gold Rush in the latter half of the nineteenth century, is detailed in Andrew Coe's book *Chop Suey: A Cultural History of Chinese Food in the United States* (2009).

Various sources indicate that the transition toward full acceptance and familiarity of the family-style Chinese menu in the Unites States has been ongoing, and increasing by degree, since the 1920s. A well-documented article that draws on Coe's account, and includes many reproductions of menus spanning the turn of the twentieth century through the 1920s, shows pictorial evidence of the emerging family-style format through the 1920s. The menus show that some Chinese restaurants designed for Americans were able to let go of the Western-style course structures and designed menus predominantly by food type. See menu historian Henry Voigt's "West Meets East: Chinese-American Restaurants 1896–1926," blog post, June 27, 2015, for TheAmericanMenu.com. You can also view the menus of Chinese-American restaurants from this period in the famously gigantic collection of these menus amassed by Harley Spiller, entitled "The Harley Spiller Chinese Menu Collection." It resides at CoolCulinaria.com.

The 1960s marked the next big turning point in the acceptance of family-style menus in American Chinese restaurants. According to Naomi Trostler and Liora Gvion's "Trends in Restaurant Menus: 1950–2000," *Nutrition Today* 42, no. 6 (2007): 255–62—a study of 1,000 menus from the 1960s through the 1990s in the collections of the New York Public Library; the Johnson & Wales College in Providence, Rhode Island; the University of Michigan in Ann Arbor; and Harvard's Schlesinger Library in Boston—many Chinese restaurant menus still tried to ingratiate themselves to American diners by giving a semblance of app-main-dessert structure. The authors note that this tendency lessened significantly after the 1960s as a result of greater ethnic assimilation, growing multiculturalism, and increased exposure to various ethnic traditions through more frequent dining out.

Regarding cross-cultural notions of what an ideal meal consists of, other sources besides Visser's may be of interest. I recommend the landmark work of Mary Douglas, "Deciphering a Meal," *Daedelus* 101 (Winter 1972): 61–81; and Paul Freedman's "Introduction" to his edited volume, *Food: The History of Taste*, no. 21 in the series *California Studies in Food and Culture*, edited by Darra Goldstein (2007), 16. Without saying so explicitly, these writers are describing what Massimo Montanari calls the "grammar of food." See Montanari, "The Grammar of Food," in *Food Is Culture* (2006), 99–103. This "grammar" consists, most basically, of a lexicon (available ingredients), a morphology (how the ingredients are prepared), a syntax (the order of dishes), and modifiers (for example, condiments). Together, these elements constitute rhetoric (the effect, or argument, the meal is designed to produce).

My use of the phrase *family-style menu* in this chapter refers to cases in which the menu proper communicates family-style service. Most full-service restaurants with family-style service communicate that style of service through the printed menu. But not all do. For example, at Meals by Genet, the Ethiopian restaurant we visited, the waitstaff introduced guests to the restaurant's manner of dining during the ordering process. The restaurant's printed menu, a brief list of individual dishes, gave no indication that the dishes would be served together on a single communal platter.

Jay Porter discusses the conflation of "shared plates" with "small plates" in "How Small Plates Have Conquered America's Menus," Quartz.com, April 12, 2014, but I date the origins of the phenomenon a bit earlier based on my research in *Smart Casual: The Transformation of Gourmet Style in America* (2013), especially 27–28.

The small-plates and shared-plates phenomenon was part of a larger arc of upsets to traditional menu course structures, tied to the rise of tasting menus as well. Both have in common the empowerment of the chef as creative individual. For a discussion of the rise of coursing upsets that offers some historical perspective and represents and chronicles an active moment in that very history, see William Grimes, "Menus Challenging the Old Order: Entrée? Appetizer? Three Courses or . . . ," *New York Times*, February 4, 1998, F1.

For a commentary on the demise of the *small plates* terminology, see Joe Satran in "Family-Style Dishes Thrive as Diners Experience Small Plate Fatigue," HuffingtonPost .com, March 5, 2013.

There's plenty of documentation of the trend toward flexible menus, including small plates, among chain restaurants. See Suzanne Kapner, "Food Panelists: Trends Promise to Keep Molding Menus," *Nation's Restaurant News* 30, no. 6, March 1996; Jacques Kochak, "Casual Theme Market Segment Report," *Restaurant Business*, November 20, 1991; and Dennis Lombardi, "Trends and Directions in the Chain-Restaurant Industry," *The Cornell Hotel and Restaurant Administration Quarterly* 37, no. 3 (June 1996).

The trend involves the incorporation of multiple meal structures in one menu, including prix fixe bundles. On that, see Mark Brandau, "Chains Balance Value, Price Hikes," *Nation's Restaurant News* 45, no. 14, July 11, 2011; and Erin Dostal, "Restaurants Bundle Up," *Nation's Restaurant News* 46, no. 20, October 1, 2012. Dostal attributes the increase of these offerings in part to the recession. But talk of creating prix fixe bundles preceded the recession. See Ron Ruggless, "Dishing Out Equal Helpings of Value and Choice," *Nation's Restaurant News* 39, no. 8, February 21, 2005.

Examples of the trend toward including small plates are legion: Sarah E. Lockyer, "1st Q Results Earn Industry's Optimism," *Nation's Restaurant News* 43, no. 15, May 4, 2009; Paula Forbes, "TGI Friday's Latches on to the Small Plates Menu Trend," Eater. com, April 24, 2013; Monica Watrous, "Slideshow: Small Plates, Big Trend," *Food Business News*, September 18, 2013; "Study Reveals Growth Trend for Starters, Small Plates, and Sides," Blogs.Technomic.com, September 16, 2013; Kelly Weikel, "Leveraging the Left Side of the Menu," Blogs.Technomic.com, September 25, 2013; Technomic, "Starters, Small Plates, and Sides Present New Growth Opportunity," Newswire.ca, March 6, 2014; Bret Thorn, "Famous Dave's Tests Shareable Menu Items," NRN.com, February 3, 2015; and Maeve Webster, "Sneak Peak: Appetizer Report Featuring Key Consumer Insights, Trends," Smartblogs.com for *Food & Beverage*, March 2, 2015.

For my discussion of trends in women's employment and nonstandard work schedules in the United States, which I suggest have impacted meal times and, therefore, structures, I relied on various sources. One was Harriet B. Presser, *Working in a 24/7 Economy: Challenges for American Families* (2003), 1, 3–5, and 15. As spurs to the growth of the service sector, Presser discusses the increase in women's employment, the tendency to delay marriage, and population aging. The globalization of corporations has also produced enabling trends, including advancements in telecommunications and overnight shipping. Presser also found, on pages 20–21, a correlation in the May 1997 CPS data between nonstandard schedules and service-sector occupations. The following sources were also helpful: Terence M. McMenamin, "A Time to Work: Recent Trends in Shift Work and Flexible Schedules," *Monthly Labor*

Review (December 2007): 3 and 11; US Department of Labor, "Contingent and Alternative Employment Arrangements, February 2005"—on page 1 of report USDL 05-
1433, a survey of 60,000 US households filed July 27, 2005 on BLS.gov—and Peter
J. Mateyka, Melanie A. Rapino, and Liana Christin Landivar, 70–132, "Home-Based
Workers in the United States: 2010," Current Population Reports, US Census Bureau,
Washington, DC, 2012, 2. The statistic I refer to comes from the Survey of Income
and Program Participation (SIPP), which surveyed 50,000 households. That report
is on Census.gov.

To measure the trend toward a "24-7 economy" in the United States, scholars
have relied mainly on data from the US Department of Labor's Current Population
Survey (CPS). To generate it, the Bureau of the Census surveys a representative sample of more than 50,000 US households for their employment status annually. Since
1973, the survey has also looked at patterns in work schedule.

The data for the latter are admittedly not ideal. The survey's methodology has
been inconsistent, and that makes comparisons over time difficult. Also, the survey
of work schedules has been sporadic. At this writing, the most recent CPS report
with comprehensive work-schedule data dates back to May 2004. The one before
that was for May 1997. Over email, survey director Lisa Clement revealed that there's
no funding yet in sight for another collection of work-schedule data, and that the
earliest that could be scheduled, if funding arrived, would be in 2020.

In spite of the intermittent government data, experts have been able to extract,
from these and other sources, sufficient evidence that, in the past several decades,
nonstandard work schedules have been fairly common. Referring to the CPS from
1997, Harriet B. Presser found that 40 percent of all full-time employees worked in
the evening, at night, on a rotating shift, or on the weekends. When Presser figured
in part-timers, the population of nonstandard workers became 45.6 percent. Consulting historical data and the CPS of May 2004, Terence M. McMenamin found that,
from approximately 1984 to 2004, the percentage of workers with nonstandard
schedules remained steady.

Supplemental studies from the US government offer more updated glimpses into
narrow slices of the workforce that might keep nonstandard hours. One from 2005
charted an increase in contingent workers (uncontracted temporary workers, such
as freelancers) from between 1.7 and 4 percent in 2001 to a range between 2.2 and
4.9 percent of the total employed population in 2005. It also reported a rise in independent contractors during the same period from 6.4 to 7.4 percent.

A report from the US Census Bureau in 2010 noted growth in the number of
those who worked from home. Whereas 7 percent of all the employed did so at least
one day a week in 1997, 9.5 percent did in 2010. In the same stretch, those who
worked exclusively from home went from 4.8 to 6.6 percent of the workforce.

Although slight in the extent it might hasten or delay mealtimes, the trend of em-
ployers offering flexible schedules—shifts that deviate from traditional start and end
times—adds demographic range to the potential demand for nontraditional mealtimes. Unlike others with nonstandard shifts, who skew toward service-sector and

lower-income employees and tend to have little choice in their schedules, flextime workers are more likely to be managerial or professional and opt for those hours.

Still, the marked trend toward flexibility in the workplace, which flextime experts Ellen E. Kossek and Jesse S. Michel tell us, in a contribution to the *Handbook of Industrial and Organizational Psychology* (2011), began in the 1980s, does add somewhat to the population who might want to eat earlier or later than the norm. It adds a lot when you consider the snapshot of flexible schedules from May 2004. One-third of all employed Americans fit in this category.

For historical perspectives on the behavior and reputation of snacking in the United States, see Abigail Carroll, *Three Squares: The Invention of the American Meal* (2013), especially 57–76. Regarding the stigmatizing of snacking during that period, refer to 159–66, and on the resuscitation of snacking's reputation, consult 183–206. Also see Rhonda S. Sebastian, MA; Cecilia Wilkinson Enns, MS, RD, LN; and Joseph D. Goldman, MA, "Snacking Patterns of U.S. Adults: What We Eat in America NHANES 2007-2008," *Food Surveys Research Group Dietary Data Brief* 4, June 2011, on ARS. USDA.gov; Marcia Mogelonsky, "Food on Demand," *American Demographics* 20, no. 1 (January 1998): 57–60; and Watrous, "Snacking Offers Ripe Opportunity for Restaurants," FoodBusinessNews.net, March 18, 2014.

A more global perspective that offers evidence that snacking has a centuries-old history worldwide is in Megan Elias, *Lunch: A History*, volume III of *The Meals Series*, edited by Ken Albala (2014), 10–2, 15, and 22.

Chapter 3: Assembly Lines and Conveyor Belts

For discussion of the Domino's "fail fast" strategy—trying many things and failing early to learn faster how to make better products in tech—and for a comprehensive narrative of the company's rise from near bankruptcy to leading e-commerce retailer, see Jonathan Maze, "How Domino's Became a Tech Company," NRN.com, March 28, 2016. Maze also refers to the company's development of a new way of ordering quickly by sending an emoji to the Domino's Twitter account. Also note Shareen Pathak, "Domino's Is Now an E-Commerce Company That Sells Pizza," Digiday.com, April 3, 2015.

The following reports give a sampling of Domino's various rollouts by the time of writing: Kari Jensen, "Domino's Pizza Expands Mobile Ordering to Car through Ford AppLink," MobileCommerceDaily.com, January 9, 2014, for ordering by Ford cars; Frederic Lardinois, "Domino's Launches Its Pizza Ordering App for iPad with 3D Custom Pizza Builder," Techcrunch.com, April 24, 2014, for the introduction of an iPad app with a custom pizza builder that shows vivid, perspectival views of your pizza and uses motion graphics to sprinkle on the toppings you choose; Maureen Morrison, "Forget Siri, Domino's Wants You to Meet Dom," AdAge.com, October 5, 2014, for the launch of the "Dom" voice-ordering service; Maze, "Domino's Debuts Smartwatch App," NRN.com, March 2, 2015, for the smart-watch app for Android; Dale Buss, "Domino's Lets Samsung Smart TV Watchers Order from Couch," Forbes.com, March 31, 2015, for ordering by Samsung Smart TV; and Bruce Horovitz, "Domino's to Roll Out Tweet-a-Pizza," USAToday.com, May 14, 2015, for ordering on Twitter.

Several industry reports identified tabletop tablets as a solution to the customer "pain point" of waiting for the check, chosen by Panera, which began installing them in 2012, and Applebee's, which started its rollout in 2014. These include Nicole Troxell, "Is Panera 2.0 Starting to Pay Off?" FastCasual.com, February 6, 2015; Ashley Lutz, "Applebee's Just Killed the Most Annoying Thing about Eating Out," BusinessInsider.com, December 10, 2013; and Lisa Jennings, "Applebee's Parent Sets Traffic-Driving Strategies," NRN.com, July 29, 2014.

David H. Maister archived his article, "The Psychology of Waiting Lines" (1985), foundational for so many scholars engaged in queue theory, on DavidMaister.com.

A recent scientific study that demonstrates and elaborates on Maister's maxim about "occupied time" is Gumkwang Bae and Dae-Young Kim, "The Effects of Offering Information on Perceived Waiting Time," *Journal of Hospitality Marketing & Management* 23 (2014): 746–67. The study had a small sample (twenty-two graduate students in South Korea), yet it took place in a real restaurant setting. The investigators control-tested the gap between perceived wait time and actual wait time in a waiting area of a sit-down restaurant in conditions of music, no distraction, and provision of menu information. The most striking positive results derived from the menu-information condition. While they found no significant effect of music (which could be due to a number of factors, including the musical tastes of the students), the provision of menu information prompted 81.3 percent of the subjects to estimate shorter wait times than actually occurred.

The first article to recommend to businesses with waiting lines to "entertain, enlighten, and engage" customers is Karen L. Katz, Blaire M. Larson, and Richard C. Larson, "Prescription for the Waiting-in-Line Blues: Entertain, Enlighten, and Engage," *Sloan Management Review* 32, no. 2 (Winter 1991): 44–53. The following is a small sampling of literature that builds on the authors' work: Julie Baker and Michaelle Cameron, "The Effects of the Service Environment on Affect and Consumer Perception of Waiting Time: An Integrative Review and Research Propositions," *Academy of Marketing Science Journal* 24, no. 4 (Fall 1996): 338–49; Mark M. Davis and Janelle Heineke, "How Disconfirmation, Perception and Actual Waiting Times Impact Customer Satisfaction," *International Journal of Service Industry Management* 9, no. 1 (1998): 64–73; Paco Underhill, *Why We Buy: The Science of Shopping: Updated and Revised for the Internet, the Global Consumer and Beyond* (2009), 201–206; Allard C. R. van Riel, Janjeep Semejin, Dina Ribbink, and Yvette Bomert-Peters, "Waiting for Service at the Checkout," *Journal of Service Management* 23, no. 2 (2012): 144–69; Costinel Dobre, Anca Cristina Dragomir, and Anca-Maria Milovan-Ciuta, "A Marketing Perspective on the Influence of Waiting Time and Servicescape on Perceived Value," *Management and Marketing Challenges for the Knowledge Society* 8, no. 4 (2013): 683–98; Phides Warue Mwaniki and Dr. Owino Agaya Okwiri, "Aligning Waiting Management Decisions with Service Demand Context to Improve Perceived Service Quality," *International Journal of Business and Social Science* 6, no. 1 (January 2015): 43–48; Chih-Chin Liang, "Queueing Management and Improving Customer Experience: Empirical Evidence Regarding Enjoyable Queues," *Journal of Consumer*

Marketing 33, no. 4 (2016): 257–68 (for a study in Taiwan); Praba Ramseook-Munhur-run, "A Critical Incident Technique Investigation of Customers' Waiting Experiences in Service Encounters," *Journal of Service Theory and Practice* 26, no. 3 (2016): 246–72, for a study (done on the island of Mauritius) that emphasizes the importance of "social justice"—perceptions of fairness in the movement of a queue—as also key to customer satisfaction in it; and Younghwa Lee, Andrew N. K. Chen, and Traci Hess, "The Online Waiting Experience Using Temporary Information and Distractors to Make Online Waits Feel Shorter," *Journal of the Association for Information Systems* 18, no. 3 (March 2017): 231–63.

Some have proposed, in addition, that ingrained cultural differences or differ-ences among individuals—stemming from a person's life experiences or personal-ity type—are significant factors in our perceptions of waiting. Theorists don't agree on the extent to which management can control these responses. For consideration of cultural differences, see Gabriel R. Bitran, Juan-Carlos Ferrar, and Paulo Rocha e Oliveira, "OM Forum: Managing Customer Experiences: Perspectives on the Tempo-ral Aspects of Service Encounters," *Manufacturing & Service Operations Management* 10, no. 1 (Winter 2008): 61–83. For discussion of individual differences, see Cost-inel Dobre, Anca Cristina Dragomir, and Anca-Maria Milovan-Ciuta, "A Marketing Perspective on the Influence of Waiting Time and Servicescape on Perceived Value," *Management and Marketing Challenges for the Knowledge Society* 8, no. 4 (2013): 683–98. For acknowledgment of both, see Mwaniki and Okwiri, "Aligning Waiting Management Decisions with Service Demand Context to Improve Perceived Service Quality." A further source combines both, acknowledging "subjective" as well as "so-cial," "symbolic," and "natural" stimuli that can influence responses to waiting, and emphasizes their immeasurable and uncontrollable aspects: Mark S. Rosenbaum and Carolyn Massiah, "An Expanded Servicescape Perspective," *Journal of Service Management* 22, no. 4 (2011): 471–90. A recent study of cultural differences in defi-nitions and evaluations of customer waiting is Maria del Mar Pàmies, Gerard Ryan, and Mireia Valverde, "Uncovering the Silent Language of Waiting," *The Journal of Services Marketing* 30, no. 4 (2016): 427–36.

My discussion of the "labor illusion," whereby businesses prominently display employees who assist customers and hide those who don't in order to improve cus-tomer satisfaction with progress while waiting refers to Ryan W. Buell and Michael I. Norton, "The Labor Illusion: How Operational Transparency Increases Perceived Value," *Management Science* 57, no. 9 (September 2011): 1564–79. The following sources, published prior to "The Labor Illusion," deserve credit for making related points: Baker and Cameron, "The Effects of the Service Environment on Affect and Consumer Perception of Waiting Time: An Integrative Review and Research Proposi-tions," 344; and Underhill, *Why We Buy: The Science of Shopping: Updated and Revised for the Internet, the Global Consumer and Beyond*, 201–207.

The 2017 study I refer to that builds on the labor-illusion idea is Lee, Chen, and Hess, "The Online Waiting Experience: Using Temporal Information and Distractors to Make Online Waits Feel Shorter." The authors tested the effects of giving customers temporal information (via progress bar) as well as "distractors." These included not only exaggeration but also hedonic (entertaining or aesthetically pleasing) features, such as motion graphics or views of city nightlife, on 1,386 undergraduate business students (producing 1,025 usable results). The students were recruited by flier from the northeastern United States and asked to use a simulated travel website in eighteen variations of the online e-commerce design.

Industry reports that document the sales effectiveness of tabletop tablets include Sarah Nassauer, "Chili's to Install Tabletop Computer Screens," WSJ.com, September 15, 2013; Vanessa Wong, "How Taco Bell's Ordering App Turns Extra Onions into Real Money," Bloomberg.com, February 4, 2015; and Whitney Filloon, "Why Tablets on Restaurant Tables Are Here to Stay," Eater.com, October 5, 2017. The scholarly study of sales effectiveness that I refer to from 2016 is Alex M. Susskind and Benjamin Curry, "The Influence of Table Top Technology in Full-service Restaurants," *Cornell Hospitality Report* 16, no. 22 (2016): 3–9.

The science of operations management has also recognized the opportunities that queuing systems create for selling more items to customers as a result of the captive-audience effect. An example is Bitran, Ferrar, and Oliveira, "OM Forum: Managing Customer Experiences: Perspectives on the Temporal Aspects of Service Encounters."

The report confirming that Applebee's, Chili's, and BJ's found success with suggestive tipping via tablet is Wong, "The Waiter's Role Changes as Restaurants Encourage Ordering Via App," Bloomberg.com, June 11, 2014.

The news that BJ's starts cooking an order made via mobile app only when the dining party sits down comes also from Wong, "The Waiter's Role Changes as Restaurants Encourage Ordering Via App."

For a thorough exploration of the operational problems and solutions that have recently arisen as restaurants adopt mobile ordering, see Clint Boulton, "Shake Shack's Secret Sauce for Getting Mobile Apps Right," CIO.com, June 20, 2017.

On the topic of anticipatory regret, here are some key studies spanning several decades: Robert B. Cialdini, "Scarcity: The Rule of the Few," in *Influence: The Psychology of Persuasion* (2007), 237–71, previously printed in 1984 and 1994; Itamar Simonson, "The Effect of Purchase Quantity and Timing on Variety-Seeking Behavior" (1990), in Daniel Kahneman and Amos Tversky, eds., *Choices, Values, and Frames* (2000), 735–57; Praveen Aggarwal and Rajiv Vaidyanathan, "Use It or Lose It: Purchase Acceleration Effects of Time-Limited Promotions," *Journal of Consumer Behavior* 2, no. 4 (2003): 393–403; and Aggarwal, Sung Youl Jun, and Jong Ho Huh, "Scarcity Messages: A Consumer Competition Perspective," *Journal of Advertising* 40, no. 3 (Fall 2011): 19–30. The study by Simonson from 1990 is the grocery-store study I refer to in this chapter.

An example of a source suggesting that limited-quantity offers are more persuasive than limited-time is Aggarwal, Jun, and Huh, "Scarcity Messages: A Consumer Competition Perspective."

PART II: SELLING ITEMS

Chapter 4: The Right Amount of Choice

Note that the actual menu for Hanbat Shul-Lung Tang had, on its left side, the same menu in Korean characters. In my transcription of the restaurant's ultrashort menu, I represented only the phonetic and English-translated right side. Otherwise, I represented the totality of the menu as it was at the time of my visit.

Although not always addressing restaurants or menus, research in the psychology of decision-making—at least done within democratic and capitalist societies, where people tend to identify choice with liberty and happiness—supports the notion that the degree of choice on a restaurant menu under similar cultural conditions can attract or repel customers. This body of literature shows that, for us to feel engaged and satisfied by a set of consumer choices, we must have enough of them to not feel restricted, yet not so many that we're overwhelmed. Schwartz, in *The Paradox of Choice*, doesn't just offer a wide-ranging discussion of this literature. He makes an important contribution to it. For a study that also shows that too many consumer choices are stressful, and that they may lead to greater dissatisfaction with the final selection, see Sheena S. Iyengar and Mark R. Lepper, "When Choice Is Demotivating: Can One Desire Too Much of a Good Thing," *Journal of Personality and Social Psychology* 79, no. 6 (2000): 995–1006. In their experiment, some people were offered a limited array of six choices, while others got a more extensive array of twenty-four or thirty choices of gourmet jams or chocolates. Those with fewer choices were consistently more engaged with the process of decision-making and found it less stressful than those with more. They were also more satisfied with the selections they made, ostensibly because they weren't plagued by thoughts of regretting all the possibilities they missed out on. The article also refers to previous research, which showed that a limited choice is preferable to no choice at all.

The study I refer to that tested the "choice overload hypothesis" is Nick Johns, John S. A. Edwards, and Heather J. Hartwell, "Menu Choice: Satisfaction or Overload?" *Journal of Culinary Science & Technology* 11, no. 3 (2013): 275–85.

I examine reasons for gourmets' deference to the chef, since the mid-1970s, in chapter 2 of my book *Smart Casual: The Transformation of Gourmet Restaurant Style in America*.

Details about the 2012 redesign of the Applebee's menu, which included a reduction in contents, are in Megan Garber, "The Engineering of the Chain Restaurant Menu," TheAtlantic.com, March 12, 2014. On IHOP's menu-size reduction, see Horovitz, "Restaurants Shrink Menus, Focus Efforts," USAToday.com, August 24, 2014.

The study showing that perceptions of variety on a tea menu depended on the way the teas were categorized on the menu is Eunjin Kwon and Anna Mattila, "Comparing Benefit and Attribute-Based Menu Assortments: An Exploratory Study," *Journal of Service Theory and Practice* 27, no. 1 (2017): 87–101.

On the relationship between individual OSLs and variety seeking in restaurants, these studies by Jooyeon Ha and SooCheong (Shawn) Jang were most helpful: "Attributes, Consequences, and Consumer Values," *International Journal of Contemporary Hospitality Management* 25, no. 3 (2013): 383–409, for which the authors designed an online questionnaire that yielded 309 usable responses from US subjects; and "Boredom and Moderating Variables for Customers' Novelty Seeking," *Journal of Foodservice Business Research* 18 (2015): 404–422, for which they designed an online survey that yielded 617 usable responses.

Industry journalists have variously documented the ways that chain menus expanded before the trend toward cutting them down began. I learned of the case of McDonald's in an emailed newsletter from the industry reporting source Burger Business.com, entitled "How McDonald's Overloaded Its Menu," sent January 29, 2014. Ruggless documented the addition of healthful items to the T.G.I. Friday's menu in "TGI Friday's Beefs Up Menus with New Atkins Partnership," *Nation's Restaurant News* 37, no. 50, December 15, 2003, 1, 6. Kate Macarthur marked a similar addition to the Applebee's menu in "Applebee's to Roll Out Weight-Watcher's Menu," AdAge.com, July 25, 2003.

Numerous sources have also reported on the trend of chain restaurants cutting the size of their menus in response to flagging sales and rising costs. Reporter Sarah E. Lockyer claimed, in "Casual Dining Shrinks Prices, Unit Counts to Catch Customers"—in *Nation's Restaurant News* 43, no. 24, June 29, 2009—that the difficulties for the casual-dining chain segment—sluggish sales, higher operating costs, and not enough customer traffic—started to affect the segment in 2006. In addition to pointing out their menus' growth in years prior, Leslie Patton's "Casual-Dining Restaurants Seeking Simpler Menus"—on StLToday.com, December 26, 2014—revealed many menu-reduction strategies among full-service casual-dining and quick-service restaurant chains. Further documenting the trend toward menu reductions is Roberto A. Ferdman, "Americans Are Tired of Long Restaurant Menus," WashingtonPost.com, September 18, 2014; and Peter Frost, "Menus Go on a Diet," *Crain's Chicago Business* 37, no. 5 (December 22, 2014).

For the menu-reduction information about BJ's and Tony Roma's in particular, see Horovitz, "Restaurants Shrink Menus, Focus Efforts." About Chili's, Olive Garden, and Red Lobster, see Patton, "Casual-Dining Restaurants Seeking Simpler Menus."

Other sources support the point that simply cutting the number of items on a menu doesn't necessarily help a restaurant simplify operations or save money. The National Restaurant Association (NRA) acknowledges that restaurants can benefit from a long menu if they use the same ingredients in multiple items. See "Don't Fall Victim to Restaurant Profitability Myths," Restaurant.org, undated (accessed April 8, 2018). The restaurant data-analytics firm Upserve supported the NRA's counsel in its survey of millions of sales transactions in a ninety-day period from a cross-section of quick-service and full-service restaurants throughout the United States. Upserve found that, on average, 80 percent of restaurants' sales came from only 16 percent of their menu items. See Vince Dixon, "Why We Might Be Saying Goodbye to Elaborate Restaurant Menus," Eater.com, April 21, 2017.

That restaurants must consider the efficiency of operations and not simply menu size is clear from the example of Starbucks as reported in Julie Jargon, "Why Starbucks Has Bulked Up Its Menu to 255 Items," WSJ.com, December 3, 2014. You can find the example I mention of BJ's simplifying its production of pan pizzas in Thorn, "Restaurant Chains Look to Gain by Streamlining Menus," NRN.com, November 20, 2013.

These sources (in chronological order) discuss the importance of capturing the veto vote or, relatedly, the need for chains to try to be all things to all people: Carol Casper, "Staying Power," *Restaurant Business* 95, no. 13 (September 1, 1996); Anonymous, "Staying Fresh: Rejuvenating Your Brand," *Nation's Restaurant News* 4, no. 2, September 4, 2000; Monica Rogers, "Getting Down," *Chain Leader* 12, no. 6 (June 2007); Molly Gise, "Vanquish the Veto Vote," *Nation's Restaurant News* 45, no. 2 (January 24, 2011); and Gary T. Mills, "Dining Notes: Red Lobster Debuts New Menu for Non-Seafood Lovers," Jacksonville.com, October 18, 2012.

The 2016 study considering the influence of variety perception on menu selection by Hee Jin Kim and Song Oh Yoon is entitled "The Effect of Category Label Specificity on Consumer Choice," *Mark Lett* 27 (2016): 765–77. Also in line with previous consumer studies, the authors discovered that the variety-seeking effects of categorization depended on how familiar subjects were with a particular food category. Familiarity brought entrenched preferences that changes in menu design couldn't surmount.

In my personal menu collection, I have two versions of the 1976 menu from T.G.I. Friday's, which Woody Pirtle designed to look like a school notebook. It has handwritten notes for menu entries, charming doodles in the margins, and red and gold stars pasted in to highlight particular items. I bought it on eBay. I found information about the original chalkboard menu at T.G.I. Friday's, and a reproduction of it as of approximately 1976, in "TGI Friday's Floor Plans," by James Robert Watson, a former server who lead the opening of new Friday's locations in the late seventies (he subsequently became a graphic designer), at JamesRobertWatson.com.

A further point about customizable menus: the added brilliance of this format is that it heightens our sense of agency. As I argue in chapter 3, by being involved in a selection process at each stage of building a dish, we feel we're in control. If the restaurant had put the same components into ready-made combinations, not only would the menu seem smaller; we would feel less empowered.

For documentation of the phenomenal, quick rise of Chipotle, making it a trendsetter in the rise of the fast-casual segment as a whole, see Ferdman, "The Chipotle Effect: Why America Is Obsessed with Fast Casual Food," WashingtonPost.com, February 2, 2015. A sign of Chipotle's trendsetting status is the title of the book by Paul Barron, the founder of FastCasual.com: *The Chipotle Effect: The Changing Landscape of the American Food Consumer and How Fast Casual Is Impacting the Future of Restaurants* (2012). The book isn't specifically about Chipotle, but Chipotle is its chief symbol of fast-casual business success.

My source for The Counter's statement about how many combinations one can derive from its customizable menu was The Counter's website, TheCounterBurger

.com, in 2013, the time of my visit to the restaurant. Since then, the number of combinations the company touts has grown—at this writing, to "over a million possible" from "+85 ingredients."

The extent to which companies such as Sysco and Sygma provide a full menu of services, from supply-chain management to ingredient provision to recipe creation for restaurant chains and independents, is astonishing. A captivating read about this, which features the case of Applebee's, is Tracie McMillan, *The American Way of Eating: Undercover at Walmart, Applebee's, Farm Fields, and the Dinner Table* (2012). See especially chapter 8, "Kitchen Novice," 185–204, and chapter 9, "Kitchen Spy," 205–18. For information about the evolution of the restaurants' relationships with suppliers and distributors, these are good sources spanning time: Bill McConnell, "It's a Food Fight! Gourmet Tastes, Booming Restaurant Growth Feed Takeover in Food Service Industry," *Warfield's Business Record* 10, no. 35 (September 4, 1995): 1; and Scott Chey, "Regional Distributors Give Clients Food for Thought," *Journal of Business* 26, no. 8 (April 7, 2011): A13.

A rating showing the immense popularity of The Cheesecake Factory among consumers for 2014 is in Sonya Chudgar, "Cheesecake Factory Is Consumers' Favorite Casual Spot," FSRMagazine.com, September 1, 2014.

Chapter 5: Secrets

The definitive source on the history of the In-N-Out burger chain is Stacy Perman, *In-N-Out Burger: A Behind-the-Counter Look at the Fast-Food Chain That Breaks All the Rules* (2010). For the historical development of the restaurant's secret menu, see pages 4–5 and 92. I'm not sure when the company put the "Not-So-Secret Menu" on its website, but it must have been after the publication of the following article, which makes no mention of it and indicates that the In-N-Out secret menu is published on other websites: Tom McNichol, "The Secret Behind a Burger Cult," NYTimes.com, August 14, 2002.

Stories of failed attempts to order a cheeseburger with fries inside at In-N-Out include "In-N-Out Secret Menu," DavisWiki.org; and James Kenji López-Alt, "The Ultimate In-N-Out Secret Menu (and Super Secret Menu) Survival Guide," SeriousEats .com, March 2, 2011. I did find a conflicting account in Elie Ayrouth's "Customers Are Lining Up for This Secret-Menu Item at In-N-Out," BusinessInsider.com, June 30, 2013. Under the guise of a Monkey Style burger, some customers allegedly got their burger topped with fries. But even this story proclaims that many operators won't make the item.

When I researched them in October 2015, the menu-hacking websites had social-media accounts and suggested hashtags for extending the conversations about menu hacks. On HackTheMenu.com, one could also subscribe to an email list and contribute to a discussion forum, but most of the dialogue related to the hacking site was on Twitter, Instagram, and the like. Ranker.com, which encouraged users not just to out menu secrets but also to vote for the best, had an active "Comments" section on its secret-menu pages.

On October 11, 2015, I examined the entire feed history related to @HackTheMenu and #HackTheMenu on Twitter, @HACK_THEMENU on Instagram, and the discussion forums—"Community" and "Secret Menu Hacks"—on the HackTheMenu.com website. The bulk of messages began in 2013. On that date, I also examined the Facebook.com page for SecretMenus.com, entitled "Secret Menus." According to the website, the page was established in 2014.

Bedell wasn't the only one to suggest that diners try to get the better of restaurants. At the bottom of the HackTheMenu.com home page, I found a section entitled "Why #HackTheMenu?" with three sets of answers. The third set, entitled "Get Your Food Fresh," gave a justification that shared Bedell's gaming tone, though it came across a little more nobly as the representation of consumer rights to quality food: "Unfortunately, many restaurants premake the items listed on their regular menu. By ordering off of the secret menu, you can force the restaurant to pay a little more attention to your item of choice. Boo-Ya!"

This article conveys an official response by McDonald's when the reporter asked a spokesperson about the secret menu: "This Is the Alleged 'Secret Menu' at McDonald's," Buzzfeed.com, October 23, 2013. A similar statement by a McDonald's spokesperson appears in interview with Laura Vitto, whose article "The McDonald's Secret Menu: Stop Dreaming, Start Ordering," Mashable.com, July 20, 2015, focuses on McDonald's in the United Kingdom.

In *In-N-Out Burger*, Perman discusses the company's less-is-more approach to marketing on pages 92 and 151.

In cases where personalizing restaurants have secret menus that get publicized, by accident or design, the reporting about the off-menu items tends to take the "hacking" tone we find in cases of depersonalizing restaurants. Even "hacking" language is sometimes used in press reports. For an example right in the title, see Heather Platt, "Dish Hack: Spago's Smoked Salmon Pizza," LAMag.com, July 6, 2015.

Customers in the know have been ordering the off-menu "Smoked Salmon Pizza" at Spago "for years" (prior to 2015), says Jenn Harris in "Off-the-Menu Dishes at More than 40 L.A. Restaurants: Breakfast Nachos Anyone?" LATimes.com, August 17, 2015. For other reports about how discontinued items that became well known to customers turned into secret-menu items, see Kristen Cook, "Local Restaurants' Secret Menus Exposed," *The Arizona Daily Star*, November 17, 2011; Katie Little, "Secret's Out: Hidden Restaurant Items for Insiders," CNBC.com, April 8, 2013; and Megan Wyatt, "These Secret Menus Will Blow Your Mind," TheAdvertiser.com, August 11, 2015, updated as "Off-the-Menu Dishes You'll Want to Try" on June 23, 2016.

Since its remarkable increase in restaurant clients between October and December 2015, the Off the Menu app corporate team has continued developing new means of engaging potential diners with tiered benefits for subscribers and offering restaurateur clients an ever-expanding media presence through the creation of online arts-and-culture features of interest to the restaurateurs' target markets.

Chapter 6: Dinner in Pictures

Sixty-three out of the seventy-seven occasions for which I documented menus in my field study—which I subsequently term "sites"—served as a test bench for my investigation of whether or not the visual, material, and linguistic distinctions among menus follow a pattern and why the distinctions exist. (About my use of the word *site*: For restaurants where I dined inside on one occasion and experienced the drive-thru on another, and for visits to more than one location of a chain restaurant, I counted each occasion as a distinct site. I did this because I thought the requirements for menu description might vary with such differences in context.)

From my total sample of seventy-seven sites, I had to exclude some. Because they represented multiple restaurants through a uniform interface, not the full menu style of each place, I omitted aggregators Seamless and Caviar. I limited my consideration of the online ordering systems for Domino's to just one. From the stylistically similar group I tried, the iPad app was descriptively the richest. Finally, I left out liquor lists. Knowing that the often-high number and unfamiliarity of entries on wine lists call for special conventions of identification, and since it's standard to state brand names on liquor lists, but not food, I concluded that menus for wine, cocktails, and spirits would make comparisons between restaurants unnecessarily complicated. Only when the quirks of representing liquor were key to a restaurant's total marketing plan did I make note of them.

Studying sixty-three sites of food menus was challenge enough. In fact, as soon as I started, the task threatened to get out of control.

I needed a classification scheme and a way to view data easily. To these ends, I produced the chart you can view in Appendix B (page 223). I mapped to each site the menu descriptors it had from a list of forty. I derived the relevant ones—pertaining to imagery, materials, language, and the representation of prices—from manuals on menu design, scientific studies of menu features, and direct observation of menus.

For insight into variations in the lighting professional photographers use when shooting for differing types of menus, see Keith Loria, "The Art of Food Photography," QSRMagazine.com, August 2014.

Johnson & Sekin agency designer Shannon Phillips wasn't the only person I interviewed who pointed out how expensive it is to produce high-quality color photos for menus. Douglas Riccardi, owner and lead design strategist at Memo Productions, and Mark Laux, cofounder of menu-engineering firm Hot Operator, also made that point. An example of a restaurant-menu-design manual that warns of the expense of producing high-quality color images is John A. Drysdale and Jennifer Adams Galipeau, *Profitable Menu Planning*, fourth edition (2008). See page 187.

I learned of the yearly planning and seasonal redesigning of Applebee's menus from Dave Eckert, "Applebee's Menu Takes Year in Planning," KansasCity.com, July 16, 2013; and Garber, "The Engineering of the Chain Restaurant Menu."

You might be confused by my reference to a printed menu at NBC Seafood Restaurant, since elsewhere I identified the roaming dim sum carts there as the menu. While I believe we should consider the carts a menu, the same restaurant also has a print menu. I'm considering that a main menu in this context because it comprehensively represents the restaurant's offerings plus a few other dishes, such as noodles.

Since my visits to Din Tai Fung for this book, the menu—at least at the more lavishly designed Glendale location—has changed tack and adopted an approach to photography that is a hybrid of the food-porn aesthetic, with large and seductive images on the introductory page for each menu section, and the grid-like structure of its former taxonomic aesthetic for the majority of menu items in each section. The newer version gains the advantage of both styles: seduction and ease of distinction among many similar items. I visited the location to confirm the changes on July 1, 2017. I thank Fabio Parasecoli for bringing this change to my attention in a conversation on June 15, 2017.

The handholding function I ascribe to some photographs on menus dovetails with a body of theory on expectancy confirmation and disconfirmation. Scholars who study the factors influencing food choice and food satisfaction cite "expectancy disconfirmation theory" to explain the strong impact that confirmation or deviation from expectations have on consumers' degree of satisfaction with a food choice. For a review of foundational literature on this topic, see Nick Johns and Ray Pine, "Consumer Behavior in the Food Service Industry: A Review," *Hospitality Management* 21 (2002): 119–34. Some overview of more recent scholarship on the topic is included in Spence and Piqueras-Fiszman, *The Perfect Meal: The Multisensory Science of Food and Dining*, especially 215–18.

The two studies I discuss that investigate the power of menu imagery to boost sales are Nicolas Guéguen, Céline Jacob, and Renzo Ardiccioni, "Effect of Watermarks as Visual Cues for Guiding Consumer Choice: An Experiment with Restaurant Menus," *International Journal of Hospitality Management* 31 (2012): 617–19; and Yuansi Hou, Wan Yang, and Yixia Sun, "Do Pictures Help? The Effects of Pictures and Food Names on Menu Evaluations," *International Journal of Hospitality Management* 60 (2017): 94–103. The research by Hou, Yang, and Sun revealed that visualizers were much more willing to pay substantially more for items with straightforward names when presented alongside the photo than they were when ambiguous names neighbored the same photo. The negative effect of the ambiguous name and photo combination on visualizers was significantly greater, in fact, than when they were presented with no photo at all. Meanwhile, verbalizers placed far greater value on an item pictured when the verbal description was ambiguous than when the same picture paired with straightforward text or when there was no picture.

Of course, there are caveats to the findings. The researchers themselves admitted that a better method for determining the effects of image-and-text combinations on menus would be to specify to the subjects a restaurant genre. That might establish what biases subjects may have toward the use of certain pictures and textual descriptors vis-à-vis restaurant genre. Better still would be to conduct the study in a real restaurant.

Chapter 7: Defining Mediums

In "The Rapid Rise of Fast Casual," FSRMagazine.com, September 2014, Barney Wolf documents how fast-casual restaurants outperformed sales in all restaurant segments in 2013. He writes, "Market researcher NPD Group reported fast-casual traffic rose 8 percent for the 12 months ending in November 2013, and counterpart Technomic reported that sales at fast-casuals grew 11 percent last year. Both of these data points bested performance in other restaurant segments." Wolf also notes that one way DineEquity (rebranded, in 2018, as Dine Brands Global), the parent company of Applebee's and IHOP, reacted to this competition by setting up quick-service options within its Applebee's and IHOP stores.

Regarding the installation of digital tabletop tablets at Applebee's, DineEquity reported the start of the process in its annual report for 2013. In it, Applebee's announced the rollout of 100,000 tabletop tablet devices in its 1,800 stores. See DineEquity, Inc., *2013 Annual Report*, and *United States Securities and Exchange Commission, Form 10K*, for the fiscal year ended December 31, 2013, filed February 26, 2014, on SEC.gov.

These articles provided me with useful information about the industry of replica foods in Japan: Linda Lombardi and Hashi, "Japanese Food Models, Yesterday and Today," Tofugu.com, May 15, 2014; and Dana Hatic, "Watch: In This Japanese Factory, Fake Food Is an Art," Eater.com, March 8, 2016.

Details of the 2015 Datassential survey about customer satisfaction with menu boards reside in Maeve Webster and Mike Kostyo, "5 Things You Need to Know about Menu Boards," Smartblogs.com for *Food & Beverage*, August 2, 2015.

The National Restaurant Association reported the findings of its 2016 Technology Consumer Survey in "Restaurant Industry 2017 and Beyond," a report compiled by Hudson Riehle, senior vice president, Research & Knowledge Group of the NRA on the occasion of the Fast Casual and Pizza Summit, May 20, 2017, on Restaurant .org. A survey of 6,106 consumers on the topic of tabletop tablets by Market Force Information, Inc., in the same year made a parallel finding. The users who liked the devices most valued them for their speed. For those details, see Ruggless, "Survey: Younger Diners Embrace Tabletop Ordering," NRN.com, August 11, 2014.

A remarkable history of the evolution of the children's menu in the United States from the 1930s through the 1950s is Andrew P. Haley, "Dining in High Chairs: Children and the American Restaurant Industry, 1900-1950," *Food and History* 7, no. 2 (2009): 69–94. It traces the children's menu's transition from merely a diminutive version of adult offerings to a full-fledged sphere of child-centric entertainment.

The specifics regarding the higher cost of laminated, compared with glossy, menu paper come from MustHaveMenus.com. On the access date, the site showed that ten copies of 8.5 × 11-inch menus of "sturdy white 12 pt glossy cardstock with waterproof 3 mil lamination and 1/8″ border" would cost $35.95; whereas the same order with just "sturdy white 12 pt glossy cardstock" and no lamination would cost just $20.95. The higher cost of lamination isn't limited to MustHaveMenus.com. In *Profitable Menu Planning*, fourth edition, on page 170, Drysdale and Galipeau mention that lamination generally costs more.

Menu-design consultants spanning decades have, with good reason, advised that restaurateurs choose menu materials that are durable where permanence is a priority, and flexible where frequent changes to the menu must occur. Here's a sampling: Albin G. Seaberg, *Menu Design: Merchandising and Marketing*, third edition (1983), 234, 308; Judi Radice, *Menu Design 3: Marketing the Restaurant through Graphics* (1988), 122; Jack E. Miller and David V. Pavesic, *Menu Pricing & Strategy*, fourth edition (1996), 43; Drysdale and Galipeau, *Profitable Menu Planning*, fourth edition, 169–86; and Paul J. McVety, Bradley J. Ware, and Claudette Lévesque Ware, *Fundamentals of Menu Planning*, third edition (2009), 136, 153.

Ruggless reported the National Restaurant Association's 2016 research about consumers' receptiveness to variable pricing in "Variable Menu Pricing Could Be Next for Restaurants," NRN.com, March 27, 2014. In its official report on the research—"Restaurant Industry 2017 and Beyond"—the NRA's exact statement was, "3 out of 4 consumers say they would go to a restaurant during off-peak hours if they received a discount."

Chapter 8: Choice Words

The study showing the selling power of "descriptive labels" for dishes on menus is Brian Wansink, James Painter, and Koert van Ittersum, "Descriptive Menu Labels' Effect on Sales," *Cornell Hotel and Restaurant Administration Quarterly* (December 2001): 68–72. In recent years, Wansink has been called to account for suspect research methods, but not, to my knowledge, with respect to this particular work.

You'll find ample documentation of the evolution of truth-in-menu laws I mention in this chapter in Drysdale and Galipeau, *Profitable Menu Planning*, fourth edition, 145–49, 150, and 159; McVety, Susan Desmond Marshall, and Ware, *The Menu and the Cycle of Cost Control*, fourth edition (2009), 33; and McVety, Ware, and Lévesque Ware, *Fundamentals of Menu Planning*, third edition, 151.

A good description of the terms of the FDA menu-labeling law, passed in 2010 as part of the Obama-era Affordable Care Act, is in Tricia Smith, "Menu Labeling 101: What Operators Should Know about New FDA Rules," Smartbrief.com for *Food & Beverage*, December 2, 2014. This article announced the latest delay (as of this writing) in the law's implementation: Samantha Bonkamp, "Calorie Labeling Rule Delayed by FDA until Next Year," ChicagoTribune.com, May 1, 2017.

Warnings by menu-design-manual writers against using too many adjectives or superlatives to describe dishes span decades. See, for example, Annette M. Snapper, "Menus as Sales Allies," *Pacific Coast Record*, October 1939, 18; Nancy Loman Scanlon, *Marketing by Menu* (1985), 130; Miller and Pavesic, *Menu Pricing & Strategy*, fourth edition, 53; and McVety, Marshall, and Ware, *The Menu and the Cycle of Cost Control*, fourth edition, 32.

The sociolinguistic study comparing the Chez Panisse menu to the menu of the so-called Oriental Restaurant nearby is Robin Tolmach Lakoff, "Identity *à la carte*: You Are What You Eat," in Anna de Fina, Deborah Schiffrin, and Michael Bamberg, eds., *Discourse and Identity*, volume 23 of *Studies in Interactional Sociolinguistics* (2006), 151–54.

An outstanding survey of changes in how the ethnically exotic and ethnically assimilated manifested themselves on American menus over the course of the late twentieth century is Naomi Trostler and Liora Gvion, "Trends in Restaurant Menus: 1950–2000," *Nutrition Today* 42, no. 6 (2007): 255–62. The authors examine changes in the form, content, and type of dishes appearing on American restaurant menus from the 1960s through the 1990s. They discuss the relationship of these changes to changing lifestyles, eating habits, lessening home cooking, and assimilation and expression of ethnic identity. In doing so, they pay the most attention to the issue of ethnicity. The authors claim growing interest in ethnically unfamiliar dishes, the country's move toward a multicultural society, changes in health and nutrition consciousness, changes in food quality and diversity, and more dining out as the biggest trends affecting shifts in the representation of ethnicity on menus.

A good example of both exceptions I mentioned to the use of "romancing" menu language is the fast-casual chain Chipotle. It displays real food and tries to serve it quickly. When we were there, the "featured item" was the only one that got the romancing treatment. This exception made sense, however. The featured item was the one dish on the menu that was new, and, since it was also unique to the restaurant, it had to be alluringly described to coax patrons of the chain into trying it. By contrast, the language of the rest of the menu—including the listings "Burrito," "Bowl," "Tacos," and "Salad" in a column on the left signboard panel—couldn't have been more basic.

Some notable exceptions to the tendency of experts to ignore the possibility that what language titillates on a menu depends on the diner type and situation include Tim Lockyer, "Would a Restaurant Menu Item by Any Other Name Taste as Sweet?" *FIU Hospitality and Tourism Review* 24, no. 1, Article 3 (2006): 21–31. He analyzed the responses of forty-eight participants in four randomly solicited and self-selected focus groups in Hamilton, New Zealand. The groups each looked at five made-up menus reflecting five different styles of describing the same set of dishes. These included one "French style menu" ("Consommé Julienne"), one "English with French menu" ("Clear Soup with a Julienne of Vegetables"), a "seasonal menu" ("Spring Vegetables Garnished in a Fresh Clear Soup"), and "elaborate style menu" ("A Delicious, Flavorful Clear Soup Garnished with the Freshest, Most Tasty Vegetables"), and an "organic style menu" ("Naturally Grown Ingredients Made into a Crystal Clear Soup Served with Organic Slivers of Vegetables"). Among other things, Lockyer found that the style that appealed most to the subjects depended in part on which occasion—romantic dinner, family reunion, meal with the mother-in-law, or business meeting—the diners were asked to imagine.

Unfortunately, the study has flaws that make it unreliable. Not only did the study not take place under real restaurant conditions. It's impossible to know if the subjects would have discriminated on the basis of occasion had they not been suggested to do so. A sounder study is Khodr Fakih, Guy Assaker, A. George Assaf, and Rob Hallack, "Does Restaurant Menu Information Affect Customer Attitudes and Behavioral Intentions? A Cross-Segment Empirical Analysis Using PLS-SEM," *International Journal of Hospitality Management* 57 (2016): 71–83. The authors surveyed

293 customers leaving a major dining district in Beirut, Lebanon, regarding the types of restaurants they frequent and what types of information they want to see on restaurant menus for those places. The authors, who also collected demographic information from the subjects, concluded that the types of information (nutrition, product characteristics, or preparation methods and ingredients) differed by diner type and restaurant price point.

The association between the healthful and the not tasty isn't universal. According to a series of studies by Carolina O. C. Werle, Olivier Trendel, and Gauthier Ardito, the French tend to equate good health with good taste: see their article, *"Unhealthy Food Is Not Tastier for Everybody: The 'Healthy = Tasty' French Intuition,"* in *Food Quality & Preference* 28 (2013): 116–21. The following studies corroborate the finding that Americans associate the healthy with the not tasty: Katherine Battle Horgen and Kelly D. Brownell, "Comparison of Price Change and Health Message Interventions in Promoting Healthy Food Choices," *Health Psychology* 21, no. 5 (2002): 505–512; and Rajagopal Raghunathan, Rebecca Walker Naylor, and Wayne D. Hoyer, "The Unhealthy = Tasty Intuition and Its Effects on Taste Inferences, Enjoyment, and Choice of Food Products," *Journal of Marketing* 70, no. 4 (October 2006): 170–84.

The 2016 study that showed the power of "indulgent" labels over other types, including two types of health-oriented labels, is Bradley P. Turnwald, MS; Danielle Z. Boles, BA; and Alia J. Crum, PhD, "Association between Indulgent Descriptions and Vegetable Consumption: Twisted Carrots and Dynamite Beets," *JAMA Internal Medicine* 177, no. 8 (2017): 1216–18.

Chapter 9: Write Prices

This online survey of 106 consumers found that the price sensitivity of consumers varies by attitudes people have toward value, their price consciousness, their knowledge of prices, and their sensitivity specifically to restaurant prices: Michael McCall and Carol L. Bruneau, "Value, Quality, and Price Knowledge as Predictors of Restaurant Price Sensitivity," *Journal of Foodservice Business Research* 13, no. 4 (2010): 304–10.

Regarding the tendency of people to choose items with prices ending in .99 or .95 more often than those ending in .50 or .00, there's some evidence from studies that look specifically at the case of restaurants. For a study based on a simulated menu, see Robert M. Schindler and Lori S. Warren, "Effect of Odd Pricing on Choice of Items from a Menu," *Advances in Consumer Research* 15 (1988): 348–53. For a real restaurant study, see Nicolas Guéguen, Céline Jacob, Patrick Legoherel, and Paul NGobo, "Nine-ending Prices and Consumer's Behavior: A Field Study in a Restaurant," *International Journal of Hospitality Management* 28 (2009): 170–72.

Sybil S. Yang, Sheryl E. Kimes, and Mauro M. Sessarego provide evidence that people spend less when there are monetary cues such as the $ symbol or the word *dollar* in "Menu Price Presentation Influences on Consumer Purchase Behavior in Restaurants," *International Journal of Hospitality Management* 28 (2009): 157–60; and the same authors' "$ or Dollars: Effects of Menu-Price Formats on Restaurant Checks," *Cornell Hospitality Report* 9, no. 8 (May 2009): 4–11.

I refer to various studies that show that diners and restaurateurs associate certain price endings with particular restaurant genres as well as value-versus-quality categories. For the consumer perspective, see Sandra Naipaul and H.G. Parsa, "Menu Price Endings That Communicate Value and Quality," *Cornell Hotel and Restaurant Administration Quarterly* (February 2001): 26–37; and Naipaul, "Psychological Pricing Strategies and Consumer Response Behavior: An Empirical Investigation in the Restaurant Industry," dissertation, Ohio State University, 2002, UMI microform 3039507. For the views of restaurateurs, see Schindler, Parsa, and Naipaul, "Hospitality Managers' Price-ending Beliefs: A Survey and Applications," *Cornell Hospitality Quarterly* 52, no. 4 (2011): 421–28.

The studies that show that price writing, at least in the United States, has been strongly segmented by restaurant genre are Parsa and David Njite, "Psychobiology of Price Presentation: An Experimental Analysis of Restaurant Menus," *Journal of Hospitality and Tourism Research* 28 (2004): 263–80; and Parsa and Naipaul, "Price-ending Strategies and Managerial Perspectives: A Reciprocal Phenomenon, Part I," *Journal of Services Research* 7, no. 2 (October 2007–March 2008): 7–26. Page 12 has an informative discussion of previous literature on this subject.

Some research has demonstrated that conventions of price writing vary across cultures. In the following study, data collected from menus of three European countries and compared to menus in the United States and Taiwan showed that the price-ending strategies on European menus differed from US strategies and had more in common with Taiwan's: Hsin-Hui "Sunny" Hu, Parsa, and Jin Lin Zhao, "The Magic of Price-ending Choices in European Restaurants: A Comparative Study," *International Journal of Contemporary Hospitality Management* 18, no. 2 (2006): 110–22.

The piece of advice I quoted—stating that menu designers should focus on conveying value, not price—comes from Miller and Pavesic, *Menu Pricing & Strategy*, fourth edition, 153. An important precursor to this text, which covers many aspects of menu pricing with considerable nuance, is Pavesic, "Psychological Aspects of Menu Pricing," *International Journal of Hospitality Management* 8, no. 1 (1989): 43–49.

The field known as "menu engineering" was christened by Michael L. Kasavana and Donald I. Smith in their book *Menu Engineering: A Practical Guide to Menu Analysis* (1982). Menu engineers, including these authors, address more than pricing alone, such as whether or not to keep items on a menu, how to change the composition of menu items, and where to position items on a menu.

The 2014 review of previous market research that showed that prices themselves can influence perceptions of value is included in David R. Just, Özge Siğirci, and Wansink, "Lower Buffet Prices Lead to Less Taste Satisfaction," *Journal of Sensory Studies* 29 (2014): 362–70. The article reports as well on a study by the authors that confirms that body of literature, but I didn't discuss it due to retractions Brian Wansink has made of his own findings from experiments he conducted during this period. It isn't clear whether or not this particular study was tainted, but I omit reference to it out of caution.

To follow the evolution, since the 1950s, of theorists' break from the rationalist "demand theory" of price perception, start with André Gabor and C.W.J. Granger, "Price as an Indicator of Quality," *Economica* 33, no. 129 (February 1966): 43–70. Studies of the hospitality industry have since elaborated upon Gabor and Granger's questionnaire. For example, they've asked not just what prices for dishes are too much or too little but also at what point a price is too high to be considered regardless of quality, and at what point a price is so low that quality becomes suspect. See, for example, Robert C. Lewis and Stowe Shoemaker, "Price-Sensitivity Measurement: A Tool for the Hospitality Industry," *Cornell Hotel and Restaurant Administration Quarterly* (April 1997): 44–54; and Carola Raab, Karl Mayer, Yen-Soon Kim, and Shoemaker, "Price-Sensitivity Measurement: A Tool for Restaurant Menu Pricing," *Journal of Hospitality and Tourism Research* 33, no. 1 (February 2009): 93–105.

Lewis and Shoemaker recount and discuss the implications of the 1988 Taco Bell experiment in "Price-Sensitivity Measurement: A Tool for the Hospitality Industry" on page 46.

Some justification for the belief that a restaurant's environmental cues affect diners' perceptions of value and therefore price is in Joost W. M. Verhoeven, Thomas J. L. van Rompay, and Ad T. H. Pruyn, "The Price Façade: Symbolic and Behavioral Price Cues in Service Environments," *International Journal of Hospitality Management* 28 (2009): 604–611.

Marta Pedraja Iglesias and M. Jesús Yagüe Guillén study how people factor nonmonetary "sacrifices" of a restaurant transaction into their assessments of value in "The Components of Total Perceived Price: An Empirical Analysis in Restaurant Services," *Journal of Foodservice Business Research* 5, no. 1 (2002): 1–22.

These sources explore various ways that the price mix on a menu can affect diners' perceptions of the value of individual items: JoAnn Carmin and Gregory X. Norkus, "Pricing Strategies for Menus: Magic or Myth?" *Cornell Hotel and Restaurant Administration Quarterly* 31, no. 3 (November 1990): 44–50; and Dostal, "Redefining Value," *Nation's Restaurant News* 47, no. 10, May 2013, 1. For my understanding of the related concept of price elasticity, Lisa Timouk was tremendously helpful in an email correspondence on May 12, 2014. I met Lisa while she was an intern at Patina restaurant in partial fulfillment of her MBA in Hospitality and Food and Beverage Properties Management at the Vatel Business School.

A good summary of the field of behavioral decision theory, prospect theory, and behavioral economics and their underpinnings, going back to psychological studies of the nineteenth century, as well as a discussion of the fundamentals of anchoring, is in William Poundstone, *Priceless: The Myth of Fair Value (and How to Take Advantage of It)* (2010). See especially pages 6, 10, 17, 31–32, 40, 53–61, 74, 79, 143–48, and 159–60. Discussions of anchoring appear on pages 40 and 143–44. An excellent anthology of key texts in the development of behavioral economics, compiled by significant pioneers in the field, is in Kahneman and Tversky, eds., *Choices, Values, and Frames*.

The source of the specific concept of "coherent arbitrariness" is Dan Ariely,

George Loewenstein, and Drazen Prelec, "'Coherent Arbitrariness': Stable Demand Curves without Stable Preferences," *The Quarterly Journal of Economics* 118, no. 1 (February 2003): 73–105.

The literature on the "compromise effect" suggests that it was first discussed by Simonson in "Choice Based on Reasons: The Case of Attraction and Compromise Effects," *Journal of Consumer Research* 16, no. 2 (1989): 158–74. The first study to test and confirm the compromise effect in a real restaurant context is Pia Pinger, Isabel Ruhmer-Krell, and Heiner Schumacher, "The Compromise Effect in Action: Lessons from a Restaurant's Menu," *Journal of Economic Behavior and Organization* 128 (2016): 14–34. This last also points out common restaurant scenarios that previous studies have shown may inhibit the compromise effect. These include the presence of a large choice set, the option of no choice, and the likelihood that, if customers arrive in groups, they may make decisions through discussion with others.

A foundational study of the "polarization effect" is Simonson and Tversky, "Choice in Context: Tradeoff Contrast and Extremeness Aversion," *Journal of Marketing Research* 29, no. 3 (August 1992): 281–95.

For details of Qdoba's rollout of its all-inclusive pricing scheme, see "Qdoba's Gamble on All-Inclusive Pricing," BurgerBusiness.com, November 20, 2014. Jennings reported on the scheme's success in "Qdoba Sales Propelled by Simplified Pricing," NRN.com, February 18, 2015.

Sources that compare complex and minimal menu-item descriptions on purchase intentions and diner perceptions of quality and price include Shoemaker, Mary Dawson, and Wade Johnson, "How to Increase Menu Prices without Alienating Your Customers," *International Journal of Contemporary Hospitality Management* 17, no. 7 (2005): 553–68; and McCall and Ann Lynn, "Effects of Restaurant Menu Item Descriptions on Perceptions of Quality, Price and Purchase Intention," *Journal of Foodservice Business Research* 11, no. 4 (2008): 439–45.

Instances of menu-design consultants advising restaurateurs to bargain with suppliers, subtly reduce portion sizes, substitute a component of a dish for one that costs less, or boost sales in other areas of the business before resorting to raising menu prices occur in Ann Hoke, *Restaurant Menu Planning*, revised edition (1964); and Miller, *Menu Pricing: A Cahners Special Report* (1976), 23–24.

Other sources I encountered make recommendations about the timing of price hikes. In *On the Menu: The Art & Science of Profit* (2014), 70, Ronald F. Bryant recommends not raising all prices at the same time. In "5 Factors That Affect Restaurant Pricing Strategies," NRN.com, June 20, 2014, Brandau reports on the technique of avoiding price hikes at times of the year when families are most financially strapped and, therefore, price sensitive.

I found two sources that recommended pricing items just under the dollar amount when pricing in cents. One is Emily Arnoult, "Designing Menus That Sell," *Restaurants USA*, May 1998. The other is McVety, Marshall, and Ware, *The Menu and the Cycle of Cost Control*, fourth edition, 110.

The recommendation that prices that change often be advertised on menus of less permanent, and thus less expensive, materials comes from Seaberg, *Menu Design: Merchandising and Marketing*, third edition, 305–6.

The following sources suggest distracting diners from price hikes by changing the commodities themselves. Miller, in *Menu Pricing: A Cahners Special Report*, 23–24; Seaberg, in *Menu Design: Merchandising and Marketing*, third edition, 305–6; and Brandau, in "Raising Value," NRN.com, July 11, 2011, propose formulating new ways to bundle items. Meanwhile, Miller and Pavesic, in *Menu Pricing & Strategy*, fourth edition, 153–54, and Liz Barrett, in "How to Formulate a Strong Menu Pricing Strategy," Restaurant-Hospitality.com, February 8, 2016, say it's a good idea to alter the composition or the names of items.

Chapter 10: Selective Selling

Kevin Welby, general manager of Patina, wasn't the only representative of the restaurant I interviewed to express the goal of achieving a balance in the sales mix. Charles Olalia, then-executive chef, did as well.

A notable exception to the menu-design experts I read who gave advice on menu design that assumed menus in the style of Applebee's, as opposed to Patina, is Anonymous, "Menu Design: For Effective Merchandising," *Cornell Hotel and Restaurant Administration Quarterly* (November 1978): 38–46. On page 39 of this text, which has served as an official vehicle of the ideas of influential restaurant consultant William Doerfler, Anonymous recognizes that so-called "exclusive continental restaurants" (dated language from 1978 that today might refer to fine-dining restaurants) are exceptions to Doerfler's advice about selective selling on menus. The article says that menus at these places "need not be designed to draw the reader's attention to any one part of the menu because patrons need no extra encouragement to buy, say, appetizers, because they enter such establishments already intending to enjoy several courses and they expect the courses to be listed in a sequence."

My references to studies that examined the effect of drawing boxes around menu items were to Charles Feldman, Haiyan Su, Meeva Mahadevan, Joseph Brusca, and Hartwell, "Menu Psychology to Encourage Healthy Menu Selections at a New Jersey University," *Journal of Culinary Science & Technology* 12 (2014): 1–21; and Dennis Reynolds, Edward A. Merritt, and Sarah Pinckney, "Understanding Menu Psychology," *International Journal of Hospitality and Tourism Administration* 6, no. 1 (2005): 1–9.

The overwhelming majority of experts on menu design discuss how people focus on parts of a restaurant menu in terms of "prime spaces" or "sweet spots." I did, however, find one author, Steve Bareham, who brought up a completely different line of inquiry. Briefly, he discussed how our cognitive *schema*—our preexisting knowledge and biases—affects the extent to which we process particular information on a menu in his book *How to Write Great Restaurant Menu Descriptions*, e-book (2013). The following passages refer to the possible applicability of "schema theory" to menu design: section 14, pages 1–4. There, he gives a brief overview of potentially relevant dynamics: selective perception, selective comprehension and distortion, selective retention, selective exposure. But, alas, while Bareham mentions these mental processes, he doesn't discuss any instances of schema affecting attention on menus, and I've yet to encounter scientific studies on the subject.

In my discussion of ideal selling positions for menu items on a list, I refer to various menu experts who specify ideal positions. Representatives of the view that the first position on a list is best are Hoke, *Restaurant Menu Planning* (1940), 9–10; and Seaberg, *Menu Design: Merchandising and Marketing,* third edition, 122.

Those who think the first and last are the best positions include J. O. Dahl, *Menu Making for Professionals in Quantity Cookery,* second revised edition (1941), 27; Paul J. McVety and Bradley J. Ware, *Fundamentals of Menu Planning* (1989), 158; Miller and Pavesic, *Menu Pricing Strategy,* fourth edition, 32; McVety, Marshall, and Ware, *The Menu and the Cycle of Cost Control,* fourth edition, 59; McVety, Ware, and Lévesque, *Fundamentals of Menu Planning,* second edition (2001), 143–44; National Restaurant Association Educational Foundation, *Menu Marketing and Management: Competency Guide* (2007), 43; McVety, Ware, and Lévesque Ware, *Fundamentals of Menu Planning,* third edition, 152; and McVety, Marshall, and Ware, *The Menu and the Cycle of Cost Control,* fourth edition, 37.

The view that first, middle, and last positions are optimal appears in Bryant, *On the Menu: The Art & Science of Profit.* More specifically, he argues on page 54, that, upon first inspection of the menu, we read the first item on a list first, then we jump to the middle and then to the last item. If we don't find what we're looking for, we'll start reading from the bottom up; however, we'll miss the second and second-to-last items or read them last. High-margin items, he says, should go in the areas we attend to first.

I found the claim that the first and last two positions on a list have the best chance to sell items in Miller, *Menu Pricing: A Cahners Special Report,* 21; and Julian Stafford, *How to Design a Profitable Menu, Basics for Beginners,* e-book (2016).

The following menu-design manuals and articles by experts represent the full spectrum of propositions about "sweet spots" on printed menus in all of the page configurations that I cite in this chapter: Hoke, *Restaurant Menu Planning,* revised edition, 62–63; Anonymous, "Menu Design: For Effective Merchandising," the source of record for the views of reputed restaurant consultant William Doerfler; Seaberg, *Menu Design: Merchandising and Marketing,* third edition, 17 and 122; Lothar A. Kreck, *Menus: Analysis and Planning,* second edition (1984), 180; the interview with Michael Bradshaw, a restaurant management consultant and educator at New York Restaurant School, New York School for Research, in Radice, ed., *Menu Design: Marketing the Menu through Graphics* (1985), 39; McVety and Ware, *Fundamentals of Menu Planning* (1989), 158; Seaberg, *Menu Design: Merchandising and Marketing,* fourth edition (1991), 23; Miller, *Menu Pricing: A Cahners Special Report,* 21; Lendal H. Kotschevar and Marcel R. Escoffier, *Management by Menu,* third edition (1994), 177; Jack Bernstein, *The Menu and How It Can Help Increase Your Sales* (1994), 64 and 68; Miller and Pavesic, *Menu Pricing Strategy,* fourth edition, 32 and 34; Scanlon, *Marketing by Menu,* third edition (1999), 140–41; National Restaurant Association Educational Foundation, *Menu Marketing and Management: Competency Guide,* 43; Bryant, *On the Menu:*

The Art & Science of Profit, 52–53; McVety, Marshall, and Ware, *The Menu and the Cycle of Cost Control*, fourth edition, 37; McVety, Ware, and Lévesque, *Fundamentals of Menu Planning*, second edition, 143–44; Drysdale and Galipeau, *Profitable Menu Planning*, fourth edition, 175; McVety, Ware, and Lévesque Ware, *Fundamentals of Menu Planning*, third edition, 152; Aaron Allen, "How to Design a Menu: The Art and Science of Menu Engineering and Design," blog post for AaronAllen.com, December 7, 2012; Joshua R. Embry, *Menu Planning: A Guide for Cafés, Coffee Shops, and Quick Serve Food Service*, Quick Pocket Guide Edition, self-published digital title (September 10, 2015); Stafford, *How to Design a Profitable Menu, Basics for Beginners*, e-book; and Aditaya Nova Putra, Pudyotomo A. Saroso, and Samuel P. D. Anantadjaya, *Physical Menu Design: One Important Marketing Tool* (2015), 20.

Of the sources that proposed best zones for selling items on signboard menus (above interior counters or along drive-thru lanes), Bernstein, in *The Menu and How It Can Help Increase Your Sales*, says the middle of the signboard is optimal. Michele Vig, vice president of marketing for Caribou Coffee, reportedly states—in Kathy Hayden, "The Writing on the Wall," QSRMagazine.com, July 2014—that the right side of the board is best. From their controlled experiment, Marion Gross Sobol and Thomas E. Barry—in "Item Positioning for Profits: Menu Boards at Bonanza International," *Interfaces* 10, no. 1 (February 1980): 55–60—conclude that the upper-right zone of the board is the sweet spot in stores with right-side entry aisles. Based on his company's extensive field research, Underhill—in *Why We Buy: The Science of Shopping: Updated and Revised for the Internet, the Global Consumer and Beyond*—opines that we scan a menu board quickly and superficially till we find what we're looking for.

The work that established the "serial position curve" of list memorization is Francis Eugene Nipher, "On the Distribution of Errors in Numbers Written from Memory," *Transactions of the Academy of Science* 3 (1878): CCX–CCXI. You'll find it more easily in Stephen M. Stigler, "Some Forgotten Work on Memory," *Journal of Experimental Psychology: Human Learning and Memory* 4, no. 1 (January 1978): 1–4, where it was reprinted.

The Taiwanese restaurant study that tested the impact of prior exposure on the likelihood a diner would choose a menu item is Ming Hsu Chang and Hsiao-I Hou, "Effects of Prior Exposure in Restaurant Menu Product Choice," *Journal of Foodservice Business Research* 18, no. 1 (2015): 58–72. The authors present multiple studies in this publication. The one I refer to (because I believe it is most relevant to a real restaurant situation) relates to their test of "Hypothesis 5."

Expositions of the Tel Aviv lab and real-restaurant experiments, which tested the effect of menu-item placement on diner selections, are in Eran Dayan and Maya Bar-Hillel, "Nudge to Nobesity II: Menu Positions Influence Food Orders," *Judgment and Decision Making* 6, no. 4 (June 2011): 333–42.

The experiments I claim examined the relationship between the graphic layout of menu items and item selection under unrealistic conditions are as follows: Gallup Organization, "Through the Eyes of the Consumer," *The Gallup Monthly Report on Eating Out* 7, no. 3 (October 1987): 1–9; Yang, "Eye Movements on Restaurant Menus:

A Revisitation on Gaze Motion and Consumer Scanpaths," *International Journal of Hospitality Management* 31, no. 3 (September 2012): 1021–1029; Feldman, Su, Mahadevan, Brusca, and Hartwell, "Menu Psychology to Encourage Healthy Menu Selection at a New Jersey University," *Journal of Culinary Science & Technology* 12 (2014): 1–21 (which also tested the effects of menu-item description, boxing, and nutrition information on choice); and Jeong-Gil Choi, Byung-Woo Lee, and Jin-won Mok, "An Experiment on Psychological Gaze Motion: A Re-examination of Item Selection Behavior of Restaurant Customers," *Journal of Global Business and Technology* 6, no. 1 (Spring 2010): 68–79.

The studies of sweet spots I cite that took place under realistic, real restaurant conditions are John T. Bowen and Anne J. Morris, "Menu Design: Can Menus Sell?" *International Journal of Contemporary Hospitality Management* 7, no. 4 (1995): 4–9; Clark S. Kincaid and David L. Corsun, "Are Consultants Blowing Smoke? An Empirical Test of the Impact of Menu Layout on Item Sales," *International Journal of Contemporary Hospitality Management* 15, no. 4 (2003): 226–31; and Sarah Daniels, "Understanding Menu Psychology: An Empirical Investigation of Menu Design and Customer Response," *Working Paper Series* no. 02-21-04 of The Center for Hospitality Research at Cornell University (February 21, 2004): 2–10.

The potential for social suggestion or pressure to direct how diners pay attention to and choose items from menus is also noted by Bryant in *On the Menu: The Art & Science of Profit*, albeit in a different way from my discussion of the social factor. On pages 54–55, Bryant reports on an experiment he conducted, which showed that, for "most larger groups (in a study of 6 to 20 adults), the highest traffic area and first traffic area is usually the top left (appetizers). The focus and scanning patterns are longer and they tend to spend more time on items [than smaller parties] that are easily sharable." But the only details he gives about the research are as follows: "The majority of my research and conclusion comes from a test group of parties of 24 people dining out at both lunch and dinner." While the suggestion that people in variant social situations might scan menus differently is compelling, it's hard to take the suggestion seriously without more information about the study. Also, Bryant didn't address the question of whether or not the scanning patterns were related to selection patterns.

The menu consultants deserve some credit for recognizing the selling power of servers. The same body of literature that advocates prime spaces also tends to note various ways that servers can augment a menu's persuasiveness. But I have yet to read a menu-design manual that prioritizes or attempts to come up with an integrated understanding of the relative strengths or relationships between server selling efforts (or any other contextual factors) and the graphic design of the menu.

In this chapter, I discuss several scientific studies of suggestive selling by servers. The earliest is C. Merle Johnson and Roseann M. Masotti, "Suggestive Selling by Waitstaff in Family-Style Restaurants: An Experiment and Multisetting Observations," *Journal of Organizational Behavior Management* 11, no. 1 (1990): 35–54. Underhill reports on a study his company did in *Why We Buy: The Science of Shopping*

(2000), 235, but this mention didn't make it into the book's 2009 edition. Further research is by Ellen van Kleef, Oriana van den Broek, and Hans C. M. van Trijp in "Exploiting the Spur of the Moment to Enhance Healthy Consumption: Verbal Prompting to Increase Fruit Choices in a Self-Service Restaurant," *Applied Psychology: Health and Well Being* 7, no. 2 (2015): 149–66. In addition to using cash-register data, during the testing period, Kleef et al. gauged customer response through a survey of 393 customers. From that, they learned that the customers felt little obligation or pressure to buy the additional items. The final study of server-suggestive selling I cite in the chapter is J.S.A. Edwards, H. L. Meiselman, "The Influence of Positive and Negative Cues on Restaurant Food Choice and Food Acceptance, *International Journal of Contemporary Hospitality Management* 17, no. 4 (2005): 332–44.

Some cross-cultural research on what people of various countries want from restaurant service and how they react to it suggests that there could be cultural differences in the sales effectiveness of suggestive selling by servers. See, for example, Cherylynn Becker, Suzanne K. Murrman, Kent F. Murrman, and Gordon W. Cheung, "A Pancultural Study of Restaurant Service Expectations in the United States and Hong Kong," *Journal of Hospitality & Tourism Research* 23, no. 3 (August 1999): 235–55; and Mikyoung Kong and Giri Jogaratnam, "The Influence of Culture on Perceptions of Service Employee Behavior," *Managing Service Quarterly* 17, no. 3 (2007): 275–97.

I don't consider wine sales in my discussion of suggestive selling by servers because dependence on the server or sommelier for wine advice is unusually high and therefore not comparable to other menu conditions. There has, however, been research on the subject. For one example, see Ben Dewald, "The Role of Sommeliers and Their Influence on U.S. Restaurant Wine Sales," *International Journal of Wine Business Research* 20, no. 2 (2008): 111–23.

On the sales impact of food-and-wine-pairing suggestions printed on a menu, see Lohyd Terrier and Anne-Laure Jaquinet, "Food-Wine Pairing Suggestions as a Risk Reduction Strategy: Reducing Risk and Increasing Wine by the Glass Sales in the Context of a Swiss Restaurant," *Psychological Reports* 119, no. 1 (2016): 174–80.

The industry sources I refer to that discuss the power of suggestive selling via digital technologies, ones that predict what individual customers might want to order in the future based on past orders, are Noah Glass, "Big and Little Data: A Gold Mine," FastCasual.com, June 19, 2013; National Restaurant Association, "3 Steps to Implement Predictive Ordering Technology," Restaurant.org, January 13, 2016; and Restaurant Hospitality Editors, "Takeout Trends: Big Data for Small Restaurants," Restaurant-Hospitality.com, October 7, 2014.

The mobile-targeting experiment I cite is Xueming Luo, Michelle Andrews, Zheng Fang, and Chee Wei Phang, "Mobile Targeting," *Management Science* 60, no. 7 (2014): 1738–56.

INDEX

ABOUT THE AUTHOR

ALISON PEARLMAN is an LA-based art historian and cultural critic who looks at the design and marketing of restaurants to tell our social story. She is a professor of art history at California State Polytechnic University, Pomona, and the author of *Smart Casual: The Transformation of Gourmet Restaurant Style in America*. Pearlman blogs as *The Eye in Dining*. After decades of being collected, her mounting stacks of restaurant menus demand (persuasively, of course) that she house them in properly capacious furniture, finally giving them the dignity they deserve.